SELF-PORTRAIT

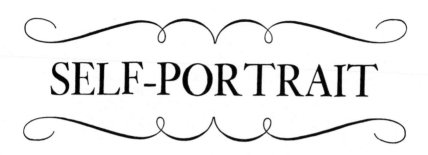

SELF-PORTRAIT

Gene Tierney

with Mickey Herskowitz

Wyden Books

Copyright © 1979 by Gene Tierney and Mickey Herskowitz

All rights reserved. No part of this book may be reproduced, stored in a retrieval system or transmitted in any form by an electronic, mechanical, photocopying, recording means or otherwise, without prior written permission of the author.

Manufactured in the United States of America.

FIRST EDITION

Trade distribution by Simon and Schuster
A Division of Gulf + Western Corporation
New York, New York 10020

Designed by Tere LoPrete

Library of Congress Cataloging in Publication Data

Tierney, Gene.
      Self-portrait.

      1. Tierney, Gene. 2. Moving-picture actors and actresses—United States—Biography. I. Herskowitz, Mickey, joint author. II. Title.
PN2287.T48A37   791.43'028'0924 [B]   78-26161
ISBN 0-88326-152-9

To my husband, Howard Lee

. . . But if the while I think on thee,
dear friend,
　All losses are restor'd and
sorrows end.

　　　　—WILLIAM SHAKESPEARE,
　　　　Sonnet 30

Contents

SELF-PORTRAIT

CHAPTER
I

The View Below

It is a terrible thing to feel no fear, no alarm, when you are standing on a window ledge fourteen stories above the street. I felt tired, lost, and numb—but unafraid.

I wasn't at all certain I wanted to take my own life. I cat-walked a few steps away from the open window and steadied myself, to think about it. The fact that I could no longer make decisions was why I had gone to the ledge in the first place. What to wear, when to get out of bed, which can of soup to buy, how to go on living, the most automatic task confused and depressed me.

I felt everything but fear. The fear comes to me now, twenty years later, knowing that at any moment I might have lost my balance. Then the decision would not have been mine. On that day, if I jumped or fell, either way would have been all right. There is a point where the brain is so deadened, the spirit so weary, you don't want any more of what life is dishing out. I thought I was there.

By then I had been in two mental hospitals in three years, and sensed that I was going back. I did not understand what had happened to me, or why a future that seemed so perfectly aimed had gone wrong. My career as an actress was in limbo and probably finished. I had been forced to give up one daughter, born retarded, and had lately neglected another. A failed marriage was behind me. I had fallen in love twice with the wrong men. I could not work or function. Some days I could hardly wake up. This day had been one of them. Trying to make order out of my life was like trying to pick up a jellyfish.

A half hour before noon the street below me was nearly empty. A taxicab stopped and a passenger climbed in. A bored doorman held the leash and glanced away while someone's dog stained the curb. A couple passed below me on the sidewalk. No one looked up. No crowd collected. I had no audience and that was fine.

Minutes passed. The day was clear and pleasant, as spring days in New York are supposed to be. The sun, caught in the shaft between the tall buildings, was bright but not warm, almost fluorescent. I wore a housecoat and bedroom slippers. The wind tugged at my hem.

I was living with my daughter, Tina, in my mother's apartment at East 57th Street. Our windows faced Sutton Place, a quiet, elegant neighborhood. To avoid looking down, I fixed my eye on the building across from us. Marilyn Monroe lived there with her husband, the playwright Arthur Miller. Sutton Place was so exclusive that for a long time some of the landlords wouldn't rent to actors. I had not seen Marilyn. For weeks I had rarely left my mother's apartment.

That morning, when my mother tried to wake me, I begged her to let me sleep. I was in one of my spells when I could literally sleep around the clock and wake up groggy and exhausted and limp. I was not on medication, but I felt and acted as though I had been drugged. My mind, like a dead car battery, would not turn over.

Mother asked me to go to the grocery for her, just around the corner. I said I couldn't.

"You mean you won't."

"Please, Mother. I mean I can't."

"Well, you ought to get up. At least you can be dressed when Tina gets home from school."

I rolled over and closed my eyes.

"All right," she said, "I'll do the shopping myself." She waited for my reaction. There was none.

At the door she hesitated, and when she spoke, her voice was tense and worn. "What are you, Gene? Are you sick or just lazy? You know, you're not being a good mother."

Her words cut through the fog that seemed to enclose me. After she had gone, those questions echoed in my ear. Was I sick? Was I a bad mother? Yes, yes, it must be so. I began to toss and turn. My mind grew frantic, consumed with the idea that I was useless. What chance would Tina have with a mother who was in and out of mental hospitals?

Slowly, I swung myself out of bed, walked into the living room and raised the window. The next thing I knew I was on the ledge. It was hardly more than two feet wide. I kept my arms and back pressed against the building, my fingers digging into the rough surface. But I felt almost serene, calmer than I had in months. My mind was detached, as hard and dull as the amber brick behind me. It was as if I was waiting to see what I would do next.

Then, standing there, I remembered what I had been told once by a friend, the actress Constance Collier. Sometimes, she said, when you get up in a plane and look down, your troubles seem so insignificant compared to the vastness of the world. I looked down for one sweeping moment. The thought struck me, "I don't want to end up on the pavement like so much scrambled eggs, my face and body broken." If I was going to die, I wanted to be in one piece, a whole person, and look pretty in my coffin.

Vanity saved me. I had stood on the ledge for twenty

minutes. Still, nobody seemed to have spotted me. Now I backed myself through the window into the security of the living room. I lighted a cigarette and noticed that my hands trembled only slightly. I had taken a risk and gotten away with it. I felt refreshed.

Then I heard the wail of a siren in the next block, growing louder until it seemed to wind down just outside our building. A woman across the street had seen me from her window, I learned later, and had phoned the police.

When my mother returned from the grocery store the police car was still parked at the curb. The doorman met her and said nervously, "Now don't be frightened, Mrs. Tierney. Everything is all right. But there are policemen in your apartment. There has been a problem with your daughter."

The blood drained from her face. "A problem?" she repeated. "What kind of problem?"

The doorman did not know a tactful way to tell her. "Well," he stammered, "the police . . . she . . . uh, they say someone reported that a woman tried to jump out of your window."

When my mother flung open the door of the apartment, I was calmly sitting on the couch, a policeman on either side of me, chatting away. "Don't get excited, Mother," I called out. "I'm perfectly all right."

I had been convincing the officers, I thought, that their report was absurd. "Where could anyone get such an idea?" I said, with a laugh. "It was only me, cleaning the windows."

People who are ill often turn cunning when they feel cornered. The police were startled and, in a vague way, pleased to discover that their attempted suicide was Gene Tierney, the actress. I poured them coffee, answered their questions, told them I had been busy with family matters but would probably make another picture soon. I might have convinced them it was all a mistake if my mother had not walked in when she did.

She blurted out, "Oh, Gene, how could you?" She began to cry. I went to her quickly and slipped an arm around her waist.

"I was never going to do it, Mother," I said softly. "I was only looking to see how far down it was."

I realize now I could not have made much sense to the police. They soon left. I never knew whether they filed a report of the incident, but nothing ever appeared in the press.

Mother walked to the phone and called our doctor. I went back to bed. I had come down from whatever high I had gotten from my adventure on the window ledge and my acting job for the cops. The doctor arrived and gave me a shot. I didn't resist. When I woke up the next day I was on my way to another mental hospital, my third. This time—in the early spring of 1958—I had been accepted by the Menninger Clinic in Topeka, Kansas.

For months I had lived in dread of returning to a sanitarium. I had been locked in rooms no larger than a cell, with bars on the window. I had tried to escape and was chased and pounced upon like a loose dog. I had been subjected to electric shock treatments that deadened my brain, stole chunks of time from my memory, and left me feeling brutalized.

But I resigned myself to going back. I would either give myself up to the doctors, I thought, or I would find out at last the nature of my problem, what had caused it, how it could be controlled. I still had no answers for the well-meaning friends who kept asking my mother, "What's wrong with Gene? What does she have?"

It gave me great satisfaction once, just once, to answer

a lady at a party who put the question to me and tell her directly: "Haven't you heard, my dear? I'm crazy."

I didn't really care what others thought, although I understood their curiosity. We did not know then about the link between certain kinds of mental illness and an imbalance in the body chemistry—a flaw, literally, in the blood. I only knew that my periods of aimless depression had become more frequent, had lasted longer and dug deeper into my will. I wondered whether my mind had been tipped by the conflict between the private me and the public life I led, all the pressures of a career and obligations of the heart—and how one grew up.

When I became ill, my mind often returned to my childhood years, for those were the pure and uncomplicated times. Yet at a certain point even those years were not as blissful as I later wanted to remember them.

There were those who would hear about my illness, shake their heads and say, simply, "She was a Hollywood star." Sometimes the tone suggested that this status explained my problem. Weren't most Hollywood people neurotic? At other times this description was offered almost accusingly, as though any actress who lost her mind had abused a privilege.

Until I was simply too ill to carry on, I thrived on my work. Hollywood can be hard on women, but it did not cause my problems. I was harmed more by feelings I hid, the troubles I locked inside me. I need to coax myself even now, but I am getting better at it. I do not like to think that in 1958 I had a grim impulse to attempt suicide, but there is no nicer way to describe it. I survived. Some don't. When Marilyn Monroe took her life a few years later, the scene on the window ledge came flooding back to me. I recalled with chilling clarity that morning, the wind plucking at me, staring at the building where Marilyn lived. Now Marilyn was gone, and I endured.

Though I wasn't frightened, not then, the incident left an imprint. I have suffered ever since from acrophobia, a fear of heights. Today I can't look out the window of a plane or a tall building without feeling dizziness or panic. It was a long while before I realized that my reaction to a crisis often came later, days or months after the event.

For the flight to Kansas I had to be sedated. I remember little about the trip, and only a blurred impression of my brother leading me into the admitting office at Menninger's. In fact, it should be said that I have no recollection of some of the incidents described in this book, other than a face half-seen, a voice half-heard. I have had to recover the details from sources outside myself, from my family and friends, scrapbooks and letters.

I had been invited in 1956 to the inauguration of President Eisenhower. That memory was just about the last I had until I woke up one day and wondered how it happened to be 1959. The years seemed to have telescoped. I didn't know who was running the government. I didn't know that Russia and the United States had fired rockets into space. I didn't know who Elvis Presley was, or the names of any new books or songs or movies. I did not try to read a newspaper for three years.

But I do recall clearly that I did not go to the Menninger Clinic hoping, or expecting, to be released quickly. If I was to get well I had to understand how I got there. I knew I could not cope with the future unless I was able to rediscover the past.

CHAPTER
2

The Screen Test

"Young woman, you ought to be in pictures."

That line was not even new in 1938. But I listened. The speaker was a Hollywood director named Anatole Litvak. My older brother, Howard Tierney, Jr., known as Butch, nearly spoiled the moment by laughing out loud. I could have kicked him. But Mr. Litvak did not seem to notice, so intently was he staring at my face.

What made the scene even more improbable was that, at the time, we were standing in the wings of a movie set. We—my brother, mother, and younger sister, Pat—were on a guided tour of the Warner Brothers Studio.

It turned out not to be a line. I was given a screen test the next day, was offered a contract, and shed a few tears when my father refused to let me accept it. I was not yet eighteen. But whether my father knew it or not, my career as an actress had begun.

Among Hollywood discovery stories, mine might not rank with Lana Turner's, sipping a soda at the counter of Schwab's drugstore. But as far as I am aware, no other actress was discovered right in the studio, in the middle of a sight-seeing tour.

We had not exactly wandered in off the street. My father, Howard Tierney, Sr., was a New York insurance broker whose clients did business with several of the studios, including Warner's. We had landed in Hollywood halfway through a cross-country vacation trip, armed with the name of a contact at each studio.

Each visit was the same. At the main gate we would drop our name, and in a few moments someone would arrive from the front office to show us around the lot. At MGM we had lunch in the commissary at a table opposite Spencer Tracy and Clark Gable. I would co-star with both of them in the years ahead. That day we could not take our eyes off them. Mother always insisted that they stared back, probably impressed, she said, with our wholesome American family look.

At Warner's our host was Gordon Hollingshead, greeted by my mother as a "long-lost cousin." How long lost he was I could not be sure. But he *was* a cousin, and had won five Academy Awards. With Brian Foy—one of the Foys of vaudeville—Gordon headed the short features department at Warner's. He led us to the set of *Elizabeth and Essex*, where Anatole Litvak was directing Bette Davis and Errol Flynn.

We met them both. I found Miss Davis radiant, though not as pretty as Flynn. To a teenage girl—as well as many considerably older—he was a knight in armor. We watched, spellbound, as they played their scene.

A few years passed before I would learn—never firsthand—of Flynn's reputation as a Casanova. According to one story, he had once confided to his co-star: "I'd love to proposition you, Bette, but I'm afraid you'd laugh at me."

Sweetly, she replied: "You're so right, Errol."

Litvak was stocky, white-haired, distinguished. A Russian immigrant, he was part of that wave of European directors and actors who had fled to America in the 1930s to escape the growing repression of their own homelands.

Our reactions were mixed when Litvak said I should be in movies. My brother thought it was a joke. My mother, I could tell, wanted to encourage my interest but feared what my father would say. I was flattered and curious. Hollywood was a world beyond my horizon. In my circle you finished school, married a Yale boy, and lived in Connecticut. It was a quiet road, and a safer one.

All around me I had seen young actresses. All beautiful. All ambitious. The studios swarmed with them. At that moment I saw Hollywood as a sort of beauty contest. If you enter one, even if you don't believe in it, you want to be voted pretty. I wondered how you entered.

I suddenly felt very grown-up. I was wearing a red silk print dress and a large, straw-colored Milan hat festooned with wildflowers. Veils, feathers, and flowers were high fashion then. Some hats looked like the centerpiece at a Junior League garden show. I thought I must look older than seventeen.

The next step was up to cousin Gordon, who did not take Litvak's opinions lightly. He swept us off to the casting director; a decision was made to test me. A screen test! Those were magic words in 1938. Movies were in their golden age. I had never given acting a serious thought. I did now.

Mother and I huddled quickly. "Can I do it?" I asked, my eyes pleading.

"Your father won't allow it," she said.

"It's only a test," I said. "It'd be fun to tell my friends when we get back home."

She turned to my brother, who was twenty and a student at Yale. "What do you think, Howard?"

Butch was bored. "I think it's a waste of time," he said. "She ought to go to college."

I said nothing more and let my mother convince herself. "I don't see how it can do any harm," she said, finally. I hugged her.

Irving Wrapper, Bette Davis's dialogue coach, prepared me for the test and John Farrow directed. I was to stand alone onstage, in front of the camera, and read the lines from "A Telephone Call," the monologue by Dorothy Parker. A personality test, they called it.

One would have been hard-pressed to tell which of us was more excited, my mother or me. And I am not sure which of us he was teasing when John Farrow said, "Maybe we ought to test the mother instead."

By anyone's standard, Belle Lavinia Taylor Tierney was a beautiful woman. She had soft brown hair, dark eyes, a sculptured face, and perfect white teeth, not crooked ones like mine. I could tell Farrow was taken with her. He was even then a famous director, but not yet a famous father. His daughter Mia would have an acting career of her own, and marriages to two musicians, Frank Sinatra and André Previn.

I don't know which Warner executives watched my test, or exactly what they saw in me. I was told only that I photographed well. On the strength of that, I was offered the standard studio contract at $150 a week. With me leaning over my mother's shoulder, we called home to tell Father the news. He did not let me entertain the idea long. He reminded us that I was, in his eyes, still a child. I had not yet had my coming-out party!

"If she wants to act," he said, "we can discuss it when she gets home. But Hollywood is not the place to start." Father considered Hollywood to be the moral equivalent of purgatory. He was also shrewd enough to know that for $150 a week, you would most likely be given a part where you wore a uniform and walked into a room and announced dinner.

From Los Angeles we headed north toward San Francisco and the long journey home. The wheels of the car were turning no faster than my mind. I was disappointed but not crushed. We had been taught not to question my father's judgment. We were not a very demonstrative family. I would always be put off by the hugging and touching and kissing that was the Hollywood party custom.

I was more serious than many girls my age, more eager to take responsibility than perhaps I should have been. I had returned after two years of school in Switzerland to find changes at home that puzzled and disturbed me. Father was in debt. We had lost our house to the bank while I was gone and had moved into a smaller one, a fact their letters never mentioned. Father cut back on his style of living—reluctantly. My parents argued more than I remembered, about money and all the little things that disguise the truth that you are still arguing about money.

The screen test had started out as a lark. But I saw the movies now as a way I could contribute and repay part of what my family had given me. When I thought about my childhood I remembered love and gaiety. I wanted it to be that way again.

I would become an actress. And I would begin by practicing on my father. I thought I could convince him to let me try. Far from being angry or upset, I felt secure and calm as the countryside sped past.

That was the summer I had finished my senior year at Miss Porter's School, in Farmington, Connecticut. The trip west was Father's idea. I had been to Europe twice and he felt it was time the family saw America. He had to stay behind to run his business. He was like a general who snaps a chart into place, extols the glory and excitement of combat, and then tells his troops, "I only regret I can't make the landing with you."

Not for another two years would I learn that our vacation was something else. He had wanted to spend the summer with the woman who would take him away from my mother. That was the beginning of a bitter time in my life. I had loved and admired my father. I never could square his actions with the lectures he gave his children about honesty and morality and doing what was right. Those were my values. I believed in them, and in him.

By the time we returned from California to Connecticut we had traveled nearly 8,000 miles. Butch did most of the driving, with Pat, then eleven, and me asleep in the back seat, and my mother in front telling Butch to slow down. We had packed so many clothes for the trip we had to hitch a small trailer onto the back of our station wagon.

As we neared home, my feelings soared. Everyone should see Hollywood once, I think, through the eyes of a teenage girl who has just passed a screen test. What may have struck others as tacky, I saw as fresh and charming. Where there were cheap shops and billboards and clutter, I saw action and life.

The emotion inside me was so strong that it seemed to have been there always, like a pulsebeat. Yet I had no acting experience outside of my own imagination. In school I had even chosen the glee club over drama.

I was an avid moviegoer, had collected photographs and kept scrapbooks and entertained the family with my impressions of Katharine Hepburn. At St. Margaret's School, in Waterbury, Connecticut, I was the class romantic. As a freshman editor of the school paper, I revealed an endless capacity for turning out poetry. Later on, every romance or crush I had invariably inspired a poem.

At thirteen, at another of my schools—I attended several as our fortunes rose and fell—I was expelled from class one day and ordered to the principal's office for mimicking a math teacher who always tapped the radiator and the windows with a pointer as he talked. I was amusing my classmates with my impersonation when the teacher walked in. Poor timing on my part.

Mr. Churchill, the principal, fixed me with a frosty look and said severely: "Gene, do you wish to be a clown or a lady?"

"A lady, I guess, sir."

"Then I suggest you cease this foolishness," he said, "and start behaving like one."

As I closed the door to his office behind me, the thought lingered and tantalized me. I wondered what it would be like to be a clown. I did not then know the word "comedienne," but I had in mind a role somewhat above doing pratfalls at the circus between the animal acts.

Of course, the thoughts of a young girl are made of spun sugar.

After our return from Hollywood, my father and I struck a bargain. I would forget the movies for the time being and would make my debut, as planned. After three months, if my feelings had not changed, he would help me find a job on the Broadway stage.

I plunged into what was known as the debutante social whirl. To see their daughters in chiffon, slow-dancing to an orchestra, with their names now and then on the society page, was one of the ways fathers justified their own hard work and sacrifices. At least, in a certain circle, at a certain time, they did. War and riots and grim moral issues have cured some of us of such frills.

The Tierneys had been through the lean-and-green-years cycle, and back again, as had many families wiped out during the Depression. My father's business had still not recovered, but he fought to protect his social position. I was presented to society on September 24, 1938, at the Fairfield Country Club. For the party Father had hired the orchestra of Rudy Newman, then playing at the Rainbow Room in New York's Rockefeller Center.

The parties continued. I knew there had to be something more than country club dances and long dresses and dates with boys whose chief virtue was that they looked well in tails. One night, as I returned to our table between dances, my father just beamed and, taking in the room with one sweep of his hand, said, "Don't you love it?"

I made a pouting teenager's face. "I am so bored I think I will die," I said, much to his surprise. "The fellows cut in on me so often I never get a chance to talk with anyone. I'm just bored stiff."

That very night Father gave in. He agreed to set aside every Wednesday, instead of going to his insurance office, and devote the day to helping me look for a job in the theater. I don't think he ever gave me a more precious gift. If I was to become an actress, he insisted, I had to prove myself on the stage before he would allow me to leave home and try my luck in Hollywood.

Now my sights and heart were set on Broadway. Father cautioned me not to get my hopes too high. I knew he was hoping that I would grow quickly discouraged and give up this whim. My theatrical training, if one could call it that, had consisted of a class once a week the year I was thirteen. I studied with a retired actress named Ann Hastings Richards. The local mothers had considered the course a sort of charm school; the point was to teach us the proper way to enter a drawing room as well as graceful carriage and good diction. We read out loud from the script of *The School for Scandal*, by the English playwright Sheridan. As a result, I began to enunciate, instead of mumbling my words as kids will do. But the idea of my someday becoming a professional had occurred to no one, including me.

Whatever else I had going for me, I knew I had been

offered a Hollywood contract before my eighteenth birthday. I would learn soon enough that Broadway producers
were not so easily impressed. But it gave me the spark I
needed not to let loose of my goal. I wanted to be an
actress. Nothing else mattered.

I suppose that thousands of girls of my generation
talked that way, and some of them meant it, but most
wound up as carhops or returned home to marry their boy-
friends. I could not be sure then what drove me. Not ego.
I was more interested in the money than the fame. I
suppose I kept going because of my father, and in spite of
him. He had encouraged us to compete and to achieve. He
had groomed his son for a career in business almost from
the moment Butch was tall enough to rake leaves. But
what he wanted for his daughters was what most fathers of
his day wanted. He wanted us to marry well. If he was
skeptical about my acting, I didn't know enough to be
skeptical. I needed to be accepted, not humored. I intended
to act.

Through a family friend, a playwright, we contacted a
list of agents and producers. When the first Wednesday
arrived I was up at sunrise so we could catch the eight-
fifteen train to New York. I would like to say that I met
the day with excitement. But I have never in my life leaped
out of bed. I have always been a restless sleeper, given to
nightmares. I am grouchy and uncivilized until I have had
my first cup of coffee or a glass of orange juice.

That morning I put on a gray fox coat my father had
given me, a red hat with a purple bow, and red lipstick to
match. I intended to show Broadway no mercy. Father
laughed out loud when he saw me.

The train ride into the city was nice. But then came
the part I learned to dread: knocking on doors, sitting
through long, empty minutes in sterile reception rooms.

Everywhere we went I was asked what plays I had been in and where I had studied. These interviews tended to be polite but brief.

One was with the eminent Arthur Hopkins, who years before had produced a play written by my aunt, Lelia Taylor, Mother's younger sister, when she was twenty-two. Her play, *Voltaire*, starred Carlotta Monterey and Arnold Daley. At the final curtain on opening night the audience yelled, "Author, author," and Aunt Lelia stood bowing in front of the footlights, one of the purest and most exciting moments of the theater. She had studied under Professor George Pierce Baker at Harvard, as a classmate of Moss Hart and George Abbott, in a remarkable group of writing talents. When her play opened, Baker sent Arthur Hopkins a telegram which said: "You have my most brilliant pupil making her debut tonight."

Hopkins remembered my aunt well. She had died at thirty-five, tragically, as a result of a bungled minor operation. Hopkins was polite but told me I needed experience before he could offer me a job on the stage.

It soon became obvious that no one wanted an actress who had not yet acted. Herman Shumlin, who was casting a tense and biting drama by Lillian Hellman, *The Little Foxes*, was next on our list. His eyes glazed over when I told him I had never appeared on a stage but had been offered a film contract by Warner's. I left my name and number. A year later, after I had received favorable reviews in two Broadway roles, Shumlin hired me for a play he was producing. He did not remember our first meeting at all.

At night, after our rounds, we returned home to the same ritual. Mother would ask how the day had gone. Father would wink and say heavily, "Well, we didn't have any luck at all. This must be the saddest business in the world."

But only three weeks had passed and I had no thought

of giving up. My break came even sooner than I had a right to expect. On the next Wednesday, we walked into the offices of Louis Shurr, an actor's agent.

My father was the best salesman in the world and what he had to sell was me. But when we called on a producer he sent me in alone to do my own talking. That was the creative part of our mission. However, with an agent, he stayed right by me; he was there to protect me.

We chatted awhile and Father asked Shurr, "Do you think you can get this girl a job?"

Louie Shurr was stocky and bald and homely. But he had an instinctive warmth for actors, even unproven ones. "Yes, yes," he said. "We'll sign her up for a picture."

"She's not ready for pictures," my father said. "I want her to learn to act."

I broke in. "What I need, Mr. Shurr, is a job on the stage."

Shurr looked me up and down. Then he said, "George Abbott is casting a play about Irish immigrants. He sometimes gives a chance to uknowns." He walked over to his coffee table, opened a copy of *The Saturday Evening Post*, handed it to me, and said, "Read this in an Irish brogue."

I had a quick ear and often walked around the house imitating whatever actress I had seen in a movie that day. But even now I have no idea where I had heard, or acquired, the thick Irish brogue that rolled off my tongue as I read from the article in the magazine. My father seemed flabbergasted when I finished, and so did the agent.

But, after all, I *was* a Tierney. I had a touch of the shamrock in me.

Quickly, Shurr said, "My dear, you sign with us for the movies, and I think we can get Mr. Abbott to hear you read for the part of the ingenue in his new play."

I said quietly, nicely, "You get me the audition and I'll sign with you. The audition comes first."

I had learned a few things from my father about closing a deal. He had demanded obedience from his children; now I was tasting my first sip of a new tonic: how to think for myself. I may have over-tried in later years, and my efforts would lead me down hard roads. But for those few exciting weeks, I was my father's partner.

After a few more words, still friendly, Shurr walked us to his door. As we left, I winked at my father, knowing our next call would be at George Abbott's office.

C H A P T E R

3

Broadway Lady

It was the winter of 1938. On Broadway, Mary Martin was emerging as a star at the Shubert Theater, singing "My Heart Belongs to Daddy." Robert Morley was packing them in as Oscar Wilde, and Tallulah Bankhead opened to great critical acclaim in *The Little Foxes*. Raymond Massey had the title role in Robert Sherwood's *Abe Lincoln in Illinois*. And George Abbott had another hit, *The Boys from Syracuse*, with Eddie Albert.

The only play I cared about existed only on paper. It was called *Mrs. O'Brien Entertains*.

"I understand you're casting an Irish play," I heard myself telling George Abbott's assistant, a young man named Bob Faulk. "I'd like to read for it."

Routinely, he took my name and address and said I would be notified when to appear for a reading. I had no real faith that I would hear from them. Within a week I received a notice in the mail, telling me to return to New York for the tryouts. My feet did not touch the ground again until I walked into the theater with my father and realized there were sixty girls onstage, all waiting to be auditioned, all looking very professional, very sure of themselves.

I had a moment of wanting to flee. Whatever confidence I had brought with me all but vanished. I *knew* I would not get the part. There are times when no pleasure is sweeter than proving yourself wrong.

The field was reduced to six. I was one of them. A week later we returned for a final reading. A day or so later I was called to report to Mr. Abbott's office. I had won the part.

Long after I made my first successful films in Hollywood, someone asked Abbott what he had seen in me. "She read very well," he said. "Some people have a gift for it even without training—and I thought she was personally very attractive." Father? "I don't remember the father at all." I had begun to be my own person.

I had seen George Abbott only through the glow of the footlights as he sat in the first row of the theater while one girl and then another read her lines. He listened attentively, sometimes talking to the people around him without moving his head.

I can't recall all that was said in our first conversation, except that he gave me the best reassurance a producer can give a new actress. He said to report for rehearsals on time and my salary would be sixty dollars a week. I would have a coach to help me with my Irish brogue.

Eagerly, I told him I had just begun to work with a drama group in the Village. He gave me a slow, bemused look and said, "Well, don't overstudy. I don't want you to become mechanical."

Mother and I busied ourselves getting me settled in New York. I moved into the American Women's Club, a suitable place for a young working girl. My father approved of the fact that men were not allowed above the first floor. I was going to live on my salary or go down swinging. I rode the subways, ate in drugstores and at the Automats, and bought my clothes at a bargain store on 14th Street called Klein's. No one would have mistaken it for Bloomingdale's.

To improve my stage presence, Abbott gave me a walk-on part in *What a Life*, a comedy starring Ezra Stone. I carried a dipper of water. At the same time, I was an understudy for *The Primrose Path*. When Abbott asked about my progress, Stone reported: "She's very beautiful and quite shy and I think the language [in *Primrose*] shocks her." Indeed, I had a great deal to learn, about acting, about reality.

When *Mrs. O'Brien Entertains* went into rehearsal, I soon discovered the playwright had little faith in my ability to play the part. In the first five days of rehearsals—when, according to Equity, you can be replaced without notice or compensation—I was literally terrified I would be dropped from the cast.

George Abbott was a very perceptive man. On the fifth day he came backstage, patted me on the shoulder, and said, "You can stop worrying, Gene. Today you're an actress." The deadline for firing anyone had passed. I was a permanent member of the cast.

The play opened on the road in Baltimore. While we were there, Abbott startled me by offering a raise. "When I hired you," he said, "I hired you as an amateur at sixty dollars a week. Now I consider you a professional and I'm going to pay you seventy-five."

You had to understand the mystique of the theater, at least in the 1930s. Except for the stars, salaries went up in pennies. Yet few complained. This was art. This was soul work, not to be confused with Hollywood, where coins poured forth as if from some giant slot machine.

I was flustered, uncertain how to react. I said, "Oh,

that's all right, Mr. Abbott. I'll work for sixty. You don't have to pay me more."

"Can you use the money, Gene?" he asked.

"Oh, yes. I really can!"

"Then I suggest you take it."

I did as he suggested. I did almost everything George Abbott suggested. By the time the play reached Broadway, I realized I was developing a whale of a crush on him. I had turned eighteen in November. He was fifty-three, but brilliant, tall, with a marvelous way of walking, like a panther.

I was just six months out of school and impressed with men of intellect. I went to an assistant director for advice. "Mr. Abbott has asked me to go out with him," I said. "Do you think I should?"

He looked at me as if I had asked him if I should run for public office. "Gene, that's up to you," he said with a shrug.

I considered that an endorsement and said, "Yes, I think I will." I was still living at the American Women's Club. On our first date George was more nervous than I was. He didn't know quite what to say or how to act. So he just brought me a paper bag filled with hard candy.

One night I confided to my mother that I was so charmed by him I was afraid I might *slip*. He was never anything other than a gentleman, but I knew several stage-struck young girls who were being taken advantage of. Mother, who sometimes spoke in Confucian riddles, smiled and said, "A romance that doesn't blossom is like a leaf falling and blowing in the wind in autumn. It just disappears."

I think she was telling me that there was no danger. She was right. Certainly, the family felt that Abbott's interest in me was fatherly. He sensed I had a crush on him and tried to tease me out of it. "Gene," he said one night, "I could never marry you. In years to come you'll want to dance. And I won't feel like dancing." He was, and would remain, one of the true friends of my life. I ran into him in a nightclub in Palm Beach, Florida, when he was eighty. He still played tennis every day. And I still thought him an attractive man.

Regrettably, *Mrs. O'Brien Entertains* was not to entertain very long. The critics panned it and the show closed after thirty-seven performances.

Luckily, acting is a team game only in the sense that any number can play. My own notices were glowing and I considered myself the luckiest girl alive. Several critics said it was worth going just to see the young ingenue, Gene Tierney. In *The New York Times*, Brooks Atkinson, the most important of the critics, wrote: "As an Irish maiden fresh from the old country, Gene Tierney in her first stage performance is very pretty and refreshingly modest."

I am not one of those who believes that early success brings later trouble. Nor could a few sympathetic lines in the paper turn my head. Besides, not every judgment was favorable. I received a letter from one theater patron, saying I belonged on the stage about as much as a hot dog belonged on a Thanksgiving dinner table. I saved that one.

But the reviews were strong enough to attract new offers, including another from Warner Brothers. When their Hollywood publicity chief, Robert Taplinger, came east he invited the Tierney family to lunch to discuss my signing a contract. Taplinger later said he found the experience "unnerving and physically wearing."

My parents did most of the talking and considerable kicking. Whenever one of them thought the other was saying the wrong thing, someone got kicked under the table. Once or twice it was Taplinger.

Father rejected Warner's offer, which amounted to not much more than their standard contract. He had accepted that acting was to be my career. The life of a New York debutante held no allure for me: the same places, the same faces, the same conversations about people you have always known. Debs did their acting in society. I wanted to get paid for mine.

Father thought a better offer would come along; he was right. Columbia Studio mailed us a contract that would pay me $350 a week for the first six months, increasing to $500 if my option was exercised. I didn't want to accept this one, either. I was ready to go into stock and learn my trade. My father said, "No, this is important money. You can't afford to turn it down."

So it was done. I signed with Columbia and within six weeks, still chaperoned by my mother, I was off to Hollywood. As a going-away gift, one of the New York critics, George Jean Nathan, sent me a copy of his latest book. Inscribed inside were the words "To Gene Tierney, with a prayer and the whole faith of George Jean Nathan."

I welcomed both the prayer and the faith, but what I really needed was a part. I had a lovely summer. I bought a beaver coat. I went to the beach with various Yale boys, friends of my brother's, who lived in California. I also had an appendectomy, for which I paid, and I helped my parents by sending a little money home. I did everything but make a movie.

Under the circumstances, the salary I received—for amusing myself, if no one else—was lavish. Day after day, I waited to be told to come to work. I spent long afternoons in the talent pool, being told how to walk, how to talk, how to sit. No one quite knew what to do with me. In the new tests that I made I felt awkward and unsure.

Someone at Columbia had pegged me as a Penny Singleton type. She was an adorable actress who played

Blondie in the Dagwood Bumstead movies. I was no Penny Singleton. But they tested me for a comedy part in a movie with Joe E. Brown. I failed, in spite of the best efforts of Joe E. Brown.

In one scene I was to enter a room and break into a squawl of tears. I couldn't do it. Joe took me aside between takes and tried to teach me how to do a comic cry. He squeezed his face as if he had been sucking lemons; suddenly tears streamed down his cheeks. He had been a circus clown at one time, and his face was a truly remarkable instrument. I could not shed a tear. Words can make me cry. But not laughter.

Finally, I was cast in a picture with Ralph Bellamy and Randolph Scott, called *Coast Guard*. I put the other actors through hell. I kept forgetting my lines. Worse, I looked more like the daughter of the two leading men than their romantic interest. After the first day of shooting, Harry Cohn, the head of the studio, saw the rushes and replaced me on the spot.

The word spread quickly around the lot that I was out. I was hurt and began to have doubts. But I was liked, and people went out of their way to encourage me. There was talk of a script that might be perfect for me. Charles Vidor was working on the screenplay, but it was still being developed. Ten years would pass before *National Velvet* finally reached the screen, making an instant star of a thirteen-year-old actress named Elizabeth Taylor.

I heard that my name was discussed in staff meetings, but no one could find the right slot. In a business always crying for talent that was "fresh," they wanted you to look like someone else. They couldn't deal with you until they decided what type you were.

"She's another Deanna Durbin," Cohn said, "except that she can't sing." I thought he was paying me a compliment. Deanna was gorgeous. What he meant was that I had a sweet, innocent, untouched look. More was needed. At least, Durbin had a voice.

I became all the more determined to work hard, and study, and develop as an actress. I felt idle and frustrated. Those were boom times in Hollywood and I wasn't a part of them.

That year, 1939, was the kind that can happen only once. It was a vintage year, not for me unfortunately, but for the motion picture industry. It was the year they released *Gone with the Wind*, *Ninotchka*, *Stagecoach*, *The Wizard of Oz*, and *Goodbye, Mr. Chips*.

The search at every studio was for glamour. It was always for something: innocence, sex, hair. Sometimes talent. I had attended boarding schools, traveled abroad, made my debut. By Hollywood's definition, I was high society. I realized I wasn't ready for the movies, or the tough, often erratic men who made them. My background, I think, had made me more interesting to them than I really was.

I had heard in New York that the casting couch was a way of life in Hollywood: it posed no threat to me. For one thing, my mother was a constant chaperone, hovering over me like a Secret Service agent. For another, I had been brought up to believe that you only went to bed with the man you married. In my day girls married younger.

I heard Bette Davis say once, and I agree, that the casting couch existed only at a certain level. It tempted the fringe people, the women—and men—who lacked talent or confidence. At best, they might have picked up a bit part. They were not smart enough to know that it wouldn't last. Once they came across, the bosses didn't want them around.

When Miss Davis was appearing in one of her first movies, a secret door slid open in the wall of her dressing room and in walked a studio big-shot. She was sitting at her vanity table, brushing her hair. She looked up and said hello. And kept on brushing her hair. He stood there, waiting. After a while, he said, "Nice to have seen you, Miss Davis," and left by the same hidden door. She had not known why he was there, and he was smart enough to make a discreet exit. She didn't recognize it as a pass. Innocence can be a very effective defense.

More common were the stories of studio heads who promoted the careers of their sweethearts. That was different. Relationships were involved, and often these unions were not cheap or insincere.

I knew little of such things in 1939, and paid attention mostly to what was happening in the talent pool. At Columbia they were grooming a starlet named Rita Hayworth. Her photographs were hanging in all the halls of the studio. Her face, looking at you straight-on, one shoulder turned, was on nearly every magazine cover. I used to run into her in the makeup department. Rita was the one I envied. I envied Rita her sophistication, although she was no more than a year or two older than I. That look made a difference in how the studio perceived you—as a sub-adult or a glamour girl. Not until years later would anyone refer to an actress in public as a "sex bomb."

I remember how offended my mother was when a director at Warner's said, "Your daughter is a real cutie." He meant it nicely, but she snapped, "If that's all she is, she'll never be an actress."

I was sure I would. Either way, I intended to remain Gene Tierney. Then, much more than now, the studios loved to tinker with names. Gene was a boy's name (it was, in fact, my late uncle's). George Abbott had warned me to refuse any such liberties. "Helen Hayes isn't a very fancy name," he said, "but I notice people have no trouble remembering it."

Rita Hayworth's name had been changed from Marguerita Carmen Cansino. Hayworth was her Irish mother's maiden name. She had never gone beyond the first year of high school, but no one had trained harder for stardom. Rita took lessons in voice and drama, dyed her hair, peeled off pounds. She had appeared in fourteen cheap B pictures at Columbia when she made her move. She squandered five hundred dollars on an evening gown and, with her husband, reserved a table in a nightclub in full view of Harry Cohn, and then let nature take its course.

Our careers spanned the same era. I had a difficult romance with a man who had been her husband, Prince Aly Khan. When I read, in mid-1977, of Rita's financial and emotional problems I felt more than just a twinge of sympathy for her. I understood some of what she had been through.

It is not a new Hollywood story, of course. Wealth, beauty, and fame are transient. When those are gone, little is left except the need still to be useful, even though the parts get fewer.

I would like to think I am not the kind of woman who, with constant references to the curse of beauty, excuses her mistakes while at the same time reminding us of what used to be. I do not recall spending long hours in front of a mirror loving my reflection. Only once in my life did I ever openly, honestly, gladly thank God for the looks I had, and that was during a period when I was trying to retrieve that half of my mind that kept slipping away. One day, wrapped in restraints, unable to move my arms or legs, I hoped a young doctor would feel pity for a pretty and helpless woman and release me.

Except for that dismal memory, I have always needed to believe that my career survived on more than how I looked. I have no deeper meaning to plumb, no point to make about beauty and craziness. A friend once asked a doctor if he thought my life might have been easier, if I might not have needed confining, if I had been less pretty. "No," he said bluntly. "They have ugly people in there, too."

I simply did not want my face to be my talent. As a young girl, I would be embarrassed if people turned and stared at me. I would drop my head and avoid their eyes.

In a funny way, I learned quickly at Columbia that the only eye that mattered was the one on the camera. I had a more cherubic look then, full cheeks that hinted at baby fat. A cameraman warned me that I needed to lose weight to photograph well. A certain thinness would add attractive contours to my face, he said.

I mailed off a dollar to *Harper's Bazaar* for a popular diet the magazine featured. You were supposed to lose a pound a day without sacrificing any nutrition. I followed the diet religiously for the next twenty years, eliminating starches, living on salads and lean meats and small portions. I held my weight at 117, about right for my 5-foot-7 frame, and I developed contours and tested my discipline.

I loved to eat. For all of Hollywood's considerable rewards, I was hungry for most of those twenty years. I can't say that people turn on themselves when they become ill, or if there is even a connection. But in later years, during what might be called my gray-outs—when I was conscious but not myself—I craved foods that were almost always fattening.

CHAPTER
4

The Elusive Mr. Hughes

Although I wasn't working, I was far from bored in Hollywood. My salary financed voice lessons and modern dance classes. I was befriended by a very gracious older woman, Rhea Gable, the first wife of Clark Gable. And through my agent, Leland Hayward, I met a young and handsome Texan, who eventually owned the RKO Studios.

Hayward was then married to Margaret Sullivan. They were both great snobs. Leland made a fortune as an agent and later became a producer. I found him cold and rather above-it-all. He collected his ten percent but seemed to have little interest in his clients until one broke out of the pack. The moment I was nominated for an Academy Award in *Leave Her to Heaven*, he began to treat me with deference.

But, in 1939, agents and other Hollywood point men were only too willing to introduce Howard Hughes to young starlets. The supply was nearly unlimited, but Mr. Hughes had a short attention span.

Howard was then planning his flight around the world, one that would set new speed records and establish him as an international figure. The three subjects Howard most loved to talk about were airplanes, movies, and ham radio. He did not talk about women. He collected them.

When he spoke of flying his eyes glowed and his language was almost sensual. I could sense the excitement in him one night as he talked about his flight. He went on at length about what a superb machine his plane was, how it responded when he did this or that, all the while quoting weights and measures and ratios that were just so much confetti to me. Then he hesitated, looked at me, and I could tell he was trying to think of a way to bring me into the conversation.

Finally, he said, "Gene, I wish I could put you in a cookie jar and take you with me."

Howard used his planes as an ultimate weapon in his courtship of the women who caught his eye. I think he felt it was very impressive, which it was, and it gave him a chance to fly, which gave him pleasure even if the date didn't work out. Once he flew my mother and me to lunch in Mexico, reserving an entire restaurant and a band in Tijuana just for the three of us. He always took the controls himself, usually without a co-pilot.

Another time he flew us to Santa Barbara, so I could visit an old friend from boarding school for an hour. I had mentioned casually that I had not seen her in two years. The next thing I knew we were in a car heading for the airport, and when we arrived, the plane's engines were warming up.

Why he did such things I can't really say, except that he was generous with people who asked little of him. He liked my mother and put a car at her disposal whenever she came to Hollywood. He never carried much cash and was quite absent-minded about money. But once, when he left town for a week and knew that Mother and I were living on a budget, he left word at a restaurant we liked to charge all our meals to him.

He never pushed, never came on too strong in a physical way. He was like a singer who lies back and lets the audience come to him, instead of leaning into your soup. He was sweet and quiet and almost aesthetic-looking before his accident.

He did not make conversation easily, and his endearments often sounded as though they had seen frequent use. But you tended to believe him. He was gentle and well-bred and reminded me of the young college men I had dated at home, although he was close to forty when we first met.

Before our first date he sent me flowers. Not just flowers, but a roomful of gardenias. My mother looked around the small, modest apartment we had rented in Westwood and said it smelled like a funeral home. I had gardenias floating in every available container.

Howard was not my ideal man. His reputation was against him. But I was young and anxious to be happily married, as girls are when they get to be nineteen or twenty, and I daydreamed about him. In a notebook I kept, I wrote a poem to him. I still have it, dated July 6, 1939:

> The dark street sleeps under a new moon,
> Through the garden shadows weave
>   strange patterns on the grass,
> And with every rustle of a falling leaf
>   I think I hear you pass;
> Rushing to the window I sigh to find
>   I'm wrong,
> And mockingly the jasmine sends up a
>   lover's song.

The poem was partly just pillow thoughts, but I was trying to put on paper how elusive I knew Howard was, what a wisp of cotton he would be in my life.

My mother was excited that we were seeing each other. Like any mother, she saw him as a "great catch." I soon realized he wasn't very serious about me. On one of our dates, he said to me, "Gene, would you like to be a star?"

I thought I detected a come-on, and not a very subtle one. I said, "Yes, and I'm going to be one, too. Just watch me."

Later that night he asked if I minded if he took a little time to swing by a hilltop home he was building and check on the construction. He cautioned me that it wasn't complete and apologized for any rubble we might find. When we arrived, I asked if the plumbing was in and excused myself to use one of the bathrooms. It was equipped with guest towels, toiletries, and cosmetics. The house didn't look all that unfinished to me, either. I got the hint. When Howard saw how nervous I was, we left.

When I walked into the apartment after telling Howard good-night, my mother asked how things were going. She was practically dry-washing her hands.

"Not very well," I said, a little let down. She didn't understand, and I made no effort to explain. That night I stopped daydreaming about Howard Hughes and the idea that he might play any continuing role in my life.

He did become my friend, though he popped in and out at unexpected times. It was Howard to whom my mother turned when she was trying to prevent me from eloping with Oleg Cassini. Even after I married Oleg, and no one in my family was speaking to me, Howard kept a promise he made and gave a job to my brother, Butch.

It was done with typical Hughes casualness. I mentioned one night that Butch was finishing his first year at Harvard Business School. I was hoping he would spend the summer in California. Howard said, "Why doesn't he? Tell him to come out and he can go to work for me."

Butch discussed it with Father, who thought it was a splendid idea. Father was a great one for names, and Howard Hughes was a heavy name.

My brother was opposed to Hollywood, the theatrical life, and most of what went with it. But he was not opposed to learning something, and went to work for Howard Hughes with enthusiasm.

In the three months that he worked at Hughes Aircraft, he saw his boss exactly once. Butch had a literary, classical background and planned to teach, but he quickly picked up a few of the finer points of engineering and was working one evening on the prototype of a fighter plane. It was the one Hughes would later crack up, almost losing his life and disfiguring his face.

Butch was working in a small office right off the hangar when a lanky fellow walked in, his pants unpressed, wearing sneakers, unshaven and looking as though he needed a shower. At first Butch thought a young boy was with him. Then he realized it was a skinny girl with very stringy hair.

The man said, "You're Howard Tierney, aren't you?"

Butch said, "Yes." Then he looked up from his blueprints, did a double-take, and said, "Yes, Mr. Hughes. I'm Tierney. Pleased to meet you."

Hughes turned and said, "I want you to meet Katharine Hepburn."

There were a few strained moments of silence; then Hughes asked, "Well, how do you like your work here?"

"Fine," said Butch. "I like it fine."

"Well, we're glad to have you. Always glad to have you bright young men around." And with that Howard Hughes and Katharine Hepburn walked away.

The Howard Hughes I knew began to change after his plane crash in 1941. How much the change had to do with the loss of his looks I can't say. But there had been a soft, boyish, clear-eyed quality about him. Now the eyes had turned beady, the face had tightened. Rather than adding character, the scars only aged him.

He had crashed his plane in a street in Beverly Hills, avoiding any homes. His face was burned and cut, and he had more broken bones than the doctors could count. He grew a mustache to cover some of the scars and began to retreat from people.

When he was released from the hospital after months of surgery and treatment, he gave the doctor who had operated on him a blank check.

He was a strange and impulsive man, but at heart a kind one. When I complained of stomach pains that summer, he sent his own physician, Dr. Vernon Mason, to examine me. Dr. Mason brought in a surgeon who recommended that I have my appendix removed. There were days when I was literally rolling on the floor from pain, the sweat pouring from me, my hair wet and tangled. I had the operation. Two weeks later the pain returned. It developed that I was suffering from a chronic nervous stomach, a problem I would endure for many more years.

Not until I was out of the public eye and happily married did the attacks finally cease. I can no more explain what caused them than I can what cured them. It was as if an ulcer had healed itself. Certainly I felt the strain of wanting to do so well in a world that was new to me. There were people who depended on me, and many who had encouraged me. I *had* to deliver.

Those who become mentally ill often have a history of chronic pains. Perhaps I should have read my symptoms as a yellow light, an early warning signal of trouble to come. But my throttle was wide open. I approached everything, my job, my family, my romances, with intensity.

Howard Hughes reentered my life some years later, under circumstances quite different from our first encounter. He would perform a great kindness when I was seeking help for my baby girl, born deaf and retarded. I was separated from my husband at the time we began to see each other again socially.

In some ways, Howard had not changed at all. One evening he came to my home carrying a briefcase. Inside was a jeweler's tray filled with diamonds and pearls. He said, "Is there anything in here you'd like?"

Needless to point out, I got the pitch right away. I had little jewelry of my own. I spent money freely on clothes, furniture, and antique silver. Cars, furs, and gems were not my weaknesses.

I picked up an exquisite pair of diamond earrings and said, "I'm going to a party tomorrow night and I'd like to wear these. I'll return them to you."

He said quickly, "You don't have to return them."

The night after the party, Howard stopped by. I put the earrings in his hand and thanked him. I don't know if the jewelry tray was one of his standard techniques. He did understand that I was not returning the favor. He took them back with no strings and no speeches. I found that attractive.

The last time I saw him, he asked if I would fly with him to a lodge atop Big Bear Mountain. I said, "What would we do when we got there?"

He didn't answer. For a moment our eyes locked.

I said, "No, Howard. I'm not going to Big Bear."

My mother always worried about him. She fussed over the fact that he had lost both of his parents by the time he was in college. She saw him as a gangly fellow who sometimes showed up at the house with his cuffs two inches above his ankles and his socks showing. For all his millions, she was touched by some emptiness in him. She kept insisting he needed to be loved. The problem was, I don't think Howard could have loved anything that did not have a motor in it.

I was glad I knew him. I did not recognize the description of the man who died in April of 1976, the withered, eccentric, drug-addicted recluse, who had not touched a woman during the last eighteen years of his life. I could only wonder what really happened to the Howard Hughes so many of us had known in the Hollywood years.

CHAPTER 5

Twice Around

There was nothing, and no one, to keep me in California. At the end of six months, Columbia offered to renew my option—at the same salary. Under my contract, I was entitled to a raise. If they were going to pay me *not* to work, I wanted to be paid what I had been promised.

I wrote George Abbott for advice. He shot back a telegram, saying I should tell the studio to go to hell and return at once to New York. He had a part for me.

I packed my bags. Once more, I could hear the lullaby of Broadway.

Perhaps this is the place to make a distinction. For most of us who wanted to act, especially in those years, there existed an eternal conflict between New York and Hollywood: stage and screen, big money versus tradition. The conflict continues to a lesser extent today, complicated by the convenience, for some, of television.

For many actors who felt their work could only be taken seriously if performed on a stage, the choice was a painful one. Katharine Hepburn once told Constance Collier—her companion of many years, and at one time my voice coach—that her mother was never impressed by any picture she made. "If you ever play Shakespeare," the dear lady told her, "I'll be sitting in the front row." Long after her mother passed on, Katharine played Shakespeare and told Constance: "Now she'd be proud of me."

I returned to New York and a small part in *Ring Two*, which opened in November with Betty Field and Paul McGrath playing the leads. Unhappily, this was another disaster for George Abbott, a whetstone for the critics' blades. I had never known a despair more real than to rehearse a play for two months and have it fold after two nights.

A flop on the stage is totally different from one in Hollywood, where the verdict may be months in coming, by which time you can be miles and another movie away. The death of a Broadway show is like a flood, ravaging a family and leaving it homeless. I did what others in the cast did. I trod the streets, looking for a job.

Within a few weeks I was the beneficiary of one of those famous show business breaks. I heard that the actress signed to play the ingenue in *The Male Animal* was pregnant and unable to continue. She was Mary Lou Daves, the wife of a fine writer, later a director whose credits included *Never Let Me Go*, my picture with Clark Gable. We became close friends. Mary Lou went on to have a large and handsome family and I don't believe she ever regretted that turn of the wheel.

I was hired for *The Male Animal* by Herman Shumlin, who directed it, and who the year before had turned me out of his office. The cast, which included Elliott Nugent and Don DeFore, was first-rate. My part, as a coed with ultramodern ideas, seemed made for me.

Now an exciting new universe opened up to me. I became, in my mother's words, "the darling of the critics." In *The Times*, Brooks Atkinson wrote: "[She] blazes with animation in the best performance she has yet given." Richard Watts, of the *Herald Tribune*, predicted: "I don't see why Miss Tierney shouldn't have an interesting career if the cinema doesn't kidnap her."

My career was really made by the critics. One night Jean Dalrymple, an agent for many concert musicians and a friend of all the critics, came to my dressing room. "They want to meet you," she said. "The whole bunch. They're expecting you at Twenty-One after the show."

A New York favorite since the days of Prohibition, "21" was then, and maybe still is, a place where celebrities went to be noticed but not disturbed. I had never been there. "I'll go," I said to Jean, "if you'll come with me and make the introductions."

Critics have always been feared on Broadway; they do hold the power of life or death. That group was special, with talents that went beyond the criticism of someone else's talent. They would write their own books and plays and scripts.

Jean Dalrymple waltzed me right in, right up to a table that had become known as the Critics' Circle. Richard Watts, Robert Benchley and George Jean Nathan rose to meet me. I was soon a regular, if not an insider. As a quiet observer, I learned who was in love with whom —Julie Hayden with George Jean Nathan, for example. I learned that writers, unlike actors, prefer the company of their own kind. I met John Gunther, the author of *Inside USA* and *Inside Europe*, and Louis Bromfield, the novelist in whose home Bogart and Bacall were married. Some nights Lucille Ball sat with us. Every night there was someone new and brilliant.

I had casual dates with Robert Morley, soon to turn writer as well as actor in *Edward, My Son*. I acquired a taste for caviar and he teased me about it. Once, at the Maisonette Russe, he ordered a salad bowl filled with caviar, chilled on a platter of ice, all for me to dig into. A normal portion of caviar would be enough to cover a cracker, like chopped liver. Morley beamed and said, "Now, my dear girl, you may have all your heart desires." I made a meal of it and could do the same today.

When he asked me out for the first time, Morley did not recall that we had met before. He had stopped me one day on Broadway, as I was walking to work. Out of the blue he just blocked my path, removed his hat, and said, "You're like a red, red rose." The line was from Shakespeare and it brought a blush to my cheeks. I thanked him for brightening my day and we had gone our separate ways. I knew who he was—Robert Morley's name was in lights—but there was no reason for him to know me.

The Male Animal was a hit. I was featured in *Life* magazine and photographed by *Harper's Bazaar* and *Vogue*. The movie offers began to come in again.

The play had been running two weeks when an MGM talent scout appeared backstage to offer me a contract. By this time I was wiser. I had given my only appendix to Hollywood. I didn't have another six months to lose.

The scout had a sleek narrow head and thin, pale hair, and he thought I would jump when he introduced himself. I shrugged and said, "Come to me with a contract saying I will be put in a picture right away, and I may consider it."

"You're a nervy one," he said, amused.

"No, I'm just happy with what I'm doing. I don't want to go back to Hollywood. So why bother to talk to me? I'm busy." And I closed the door.

Nothing intrigued Hollywood scouts more than to learn an actor or actress was happy on Broadway.

There was excited whispering one night before the

show. Darryl F. Zanuck, head of Twentieth Century-Fox, had flown in from the coast and was in the audience. During the performance, he told an assistant to make a note of my name.

Later, Zanuck dropped by the Stork Club, where his eye fell on a young woman on the dance floor. He nudged his assistant: "Forget the girl from the play. See if you can sign that one." I was the girl, of course. Zanuck wasn't easily convinced. I always had several different "looks," a quality that proved useful all during my career.

There would come a time when I would have to grope for my identity, but I can't connect that search with what was basically a model's trick. Whatever look a scene needed I could create, whether it was a fresh-air kid in shorts or a sophisticated lady, all silk and sulfur. I had, in fact, modeled between Broadway jobs for John Powers.

There were more meetings with Zanuck or his agents; I still played hard to get. At one point I received a wire from the studio which said, in effect: "If Miss Tierney hasn't enough faith in Mr. Zanuck to believe he will give her a picture, she can consider our offer withdrawn."

Finally the terms were settled. My father helped negotiate the contract, and for those times it was unique. I started at $750 a week, with a raise every six months. I was to be given half a year off—with written notice to the studio—to appear on Broadway. I had to be working three weeks from the day of my arrival or the contract was void.

I had learned from my last experience. I would not be kept idle between films, would not have to change my hair color or length, or have my teeth straightened. As curious as the last condition may seem, my dentist had warned me that any such attempt might change my smile. In a time of glossy, look-alike glamour, my imperfect teeth became an asset.

Darryl Zanuck appeared to be serious about launching my movie career. This time we formed a family corporation, called Belle-Tier, into which my income would be channeled. I had no way of knowing that the company would become the center of a terrible family dispute and would fan my insecurities.

I had mixed feelings about leaving a hit play. Before my last performance, I was taken aside by a member of the cast, a wonderful old actor named Ivan Simpson. Ivan was a character, in his eighties, but alert and whimsical. The theater had been his life. He said to me, "Child, I think you should see the great John Barrymore. He won't be with us long at the rate he's drinking."

Barrymore's antics in *My Dear Children* were the talk of Broadway that season. He was sometimes ill, more often drunk. Some evenings he was unsure of his lines. He always went on. "Yep," the doorman told us, "he arrives every night, dead or alive."

Once, unable to stand with any degree of security, Barrymore commanded a stagehand to fetch a wheelchair. "I'll play Lionel," he said, a reference to his brother, crippled by hip injuries and arthritis.

Ivan took me to an actors' matinee. The play was to be John Barrymore's last. He did it, I think, only because his wife, Elaine Barrie, was given a part as one of his daughters. She was an absurd woman, the love of his old age. In his sober moments he adored her. Ivan took me backstage to meet Barrymore. Even then I thought him one of the handsomest men I had ever seen. He wore a white silk shirt and gray flannel slacks and black patent leather pumps.

He was very sweet. Ivan told him I had signed with Fox. He said that while I was in Hollywood he might be able to find a part for me in his next picture. I heard that he did ask for me, but the part went to Anne Baxter. The picture, *The Great Profile*, turned out to be a bomb. I was fortunate to miss it.

Gordon Hollingshead, my mother's cousin at Warner's, had known Barrymore in his prime. They sailed together, the great actor often rising abruptly and reciting long passages from Shakespeare. He must have been an unforgettable sight, braced on the deck, shouting into the wind. He had a photographic memory then. At the end—he died in 1942 at the age of sixty—there was not much left of it.

For my second attempt at the movies, I took with me another thoughtful gift from George Jean Nathan. He guessed I would enjoy the company of a German shepherd pup, one raised by Madge Evans, the actress, and her playwright husband, Sidney Kingsley. I had met them both at the Critics' Circle at "21." With such a pedigree there was no reason why the pup should not have been stage-smart. Nathan had named him Butch—unrelated to my brother's nickname—and he came to be well known by everyone I worked with at Fox. He was so well trained that he never stirred after the commands: "Quiet! Camera! Action!" He seemed to understand the word "cut" and moved only after he had heard it.

Four months after my opening night in *The Male Animal*, I caught a flight to California. Mother stayed home with my sister, Pat, then thirteen, and planned to join me later. When I alighted from the plane I was presented with a plaque inscribed, "You are a pioneer on the maiden transcontinental flight—1939."

I felt like giving it back to them. I did not consider that kind of courage one of my stronger qualities. I did not want to be a pioneer. I thought people traveled to the coast by plane all the time.

I had now made my way to Hollywood by car, train, and plane. The only thing left was by boat. I reflected on my last trip, when my mother and I spent three nights on the Santa Fe Chief, almost too excited to sleep. A passenger on the train was Henry Ginsberg, one of the powers at Paramount Studios. He kept calling us "you girls," and inviting us to the club car for cocktails. Each time we declined he would tell us, "You two girls handle yourselves very well."

He assured me I would have a wonderful career in motion pictures. There had been no sign of one during my last stay. Now I was ready for round two.

CHAPTER
6

The Dream Factory

All my life I have been reminded by the people closest to me that I am an incurable romantic. I was never quite certain what they meant. Their tone suggested that it was a good-natured warning. A romantic, I think, picks the rose and is careless with the thorn.

Without question, my sense of Hollywood was a romantic one. Soon after my mother arrived, we started hunting for an apartment. I was charmed with one on Canyon Drive, although it offended my mother's Connecticut taste. Furnished with French reproductions and upholstered in satins and brocades, the apartment was just what a girl of nineteen would think a movie star's home should be. It had two bedrooms, a kitchen, a small dinette, and a living room. I thought it looked like Marie Antoinette's Petit Trianon. I begged my mother to let us move in. Finally, laughingly, she agreed.

Even now, when I think of those weeks that were the real beginning of my film career, I remember a scrap of dialogue from *A Streetcar Named Desire*, Blanche du Bois saying: "I don't want reality. I want magic! Yes, yes, magic . . ."

I reported to the studio and was told I would start work within days on *The Return of Frank James*, starring Henry Fonda. I now learned that Darryl Zanuck had been in New York scouting me as a replacement for Andrea Leeds, whose slow recovery from surgery had forced her to withdraw from the female lead. In show business the saying seems too often true: it isn't enough to succeed; someone else must fail.

I was sent to the wardrobe department for fittings and the makeup department for appraisal. I was painted, powdered, and coiffed. I met Henry Fonda, who was gentle and thoughtful and went to some lengths to put me at ease. I knew what a fine actor he was and regarded him with awe. He had begun his career on the stage and was always letter perfect in his lines. The crew called him "One-Take Fonda." I vowed to follow his example, memorize my lines, and become "One-Take Tierney."

If I didn't quite achieve that distinction, at least I came to the set prepared to give my best effort on the first take. Not all actors do. They prefer to hold back until they feel more comfortable. With some, it is like an athlete warming up.

I had never thought of myself as a perfectionist. Now I knew that good enough would never do. Sometimes, after dinner, I would return to the studio, sit in a projection room, and study one picture after another, four or five in a night, until the projectionist begged me to let him go home. This was my classroom.

I drove myself, knowing I lacked the training of so many actresses, with their years of drama classes and their summers in stock. The stomach cramps would come and go. I ignored the pain when I could, doubled over when I could not. I would swallow whatever pills the doctor had given me and go back to work. Tierneys did not cry. Or run to psychiatrists.

Henry Fonda approved of me. He was delighted that I knew my lines so well. At one point, he went to the front office and told them he was glad they had assigned me to the picture; I had talent, he told them, and something Henry called gumption. It was an unselfish gesture, prompted in part, I think, by an incident that took place during the early shooting.

I tended to keep my lower lip open when I wasn't talking, the kind of habit that can look so unattractive on the big screen (unless you were Marilyn Monroe). The director, Fritz Lang, stopped one scene and barked at me, "You little bitch! When you have no lines, keep your mouth shut."

I suppose he thought I was mugging for the camera. Fonda reacted instantly. He rushed up to Lang and said sharply, "Don't you dare speak to that girl in that way!" I was a surprised but flattered observer of this exchange. Actually, the tip was a useful one. As the work went along, everyone, including Fritz Lang, tried to be helpful and I began to feel that I belonged.

I always had a need not just to be in love, but to think I was. And, of course, I soon had a crush on Henry Fonda. The crush ended when a friend of Henry's, John Swope, who later married Dorothy Maguire, took me along one day to visit the Fonda household. I saw him, a happily married man, playing with his two small children, Jane and Peter.

For my performance in *The Return of Frank James*, I was honored by the *Harvard Lampoon* as "The Worst Female Discovery of 1940." My brother, Butch, was attending Harvard graduate school at the time and I told the press that I suspected his influence had helped me win. The worst male discovery was Robert Preston, who would enjoy a fine career and a memorable success in *The*

Music Man. The *Lampoon* also named Mickey Rooney and Jane Withers as "the screen's most objectionable children."

I did not feel undeserving of the award. When I saw myself for the first time on the screen, at a preview in Westwood, I sank down in my seat from embarrassment. Mother warned me that if I didn't sit up she would stand and tell everyone where I was sitting. I could not believe how high and strident my voice came across. I sounded like an angry Minnie Mouse. "My God," I thought, "if that's really how I sound, I'll never make it."

In a not very commendable way, the problem solved itself. When I was nervous, which was often, I smoked. The smoking helped lower the register of my voice.

Within three months, I had completed my first film and begun a second, *Hudson's Bay*, opposite Paul Muni. Muni, twice an Academy Award winner, had not renewed his contract at Warner's. Now, as a free agent, he had been free to accept the script shown him by Fox, where he had begun his career in 1928. "Every actor," he said, "wants to be independent enough to turn down those parts he does not care to play." In time I would know exactly what he meant.

One of the minor characters in *Hudson's Bay* was played by Nigel Bruce, the Dr. Watson of Sherlock Holmes fame. One day, when the scenes had not gone well, Nigel crooked his finger and said to me, "Come here, my little darling, and let me press you to me." A lovable old fellow, I think he sensed I was frightened and so wanted to succeed.

That film was the occasion of my first professional kiss, supposedly a *big moment* in the life of any young actress. I can assure you I have no special memory of it, even though the scene—with John Sutton—had to be shot three times. I don't believe the kiss made much of an impres-

sion on John, either. Several weeks later I was made up
as Ellie May for the filming of *Tobacco Road*, and John
walked right past me in the commissary without recog-
nizing me.

Tobacco Road was described as "the most daring movie
of all time" by the *Hollywood Reporter*, at least in part
because of a seduction scene between myself and Ward
Bond. The crew referred to it as a "horsing" scene—kind
of lowdown, grubbing, wrestling around in the dirt. If
you are wondering how far candor has come since 1940,
you should know that I asked the director, John Ford, to
clear the set first. I played a frustrated girl of low mental-
ity making love to a simpleton. I was embarrassed at the
kind of passion the scene required, and I didn't want
strangers gawking.

For the role of Ellie May, I was sprayed each morning
with a thin coat of oil—over my arms, legs, and face—
after which dirt was rubbed on. My hair was caked and
stringy. John Ford told me, half joking, that if I washed
it while the picture was being shot he would fire me. I
wore a dismal calico dress which looked as if it had been
fried in grease and then rolled in a dustpan.

I spent an hour or two every night scrubbing my face
and soaking in a hot tub. My scalp itched constantly. But
an important thing was happening to me. I began to feel
like an actress, to get at least a sense of the rhythms of
making a film.

I was so young and so impulsive and so filled with
questions. Once, while the cast was having lunch, I asked
John Ford how he happened to pick Jane Darwell, a
plump and ponderous woman, for the role of Ma Joad in
The Grapes of Wrath, a movie about people who were
starving. I said it struck me as odd. Ford put down his
fork, stared at me and said, "You know, some people
wonder how I happened to pick *you* to play Ellie May!"

The putdown was a friendly one, but I got the point, and asked no more questions that day. Ford had given me a chance to break away from the image I had, as a Blue Book graduate of the Waldorf Astoria stag line.

I was to be fortunate throughout my career to work under directors who were, most of them, brilliant, emotional men. Preminger, Lang, Lubitsch, Von Sternberg, Ford. All the clichés you may have heard happen to be true. A cast is only as good as the director. He is father, mother, priest, and ship's captain.

I had completed three films in twelve months, the most important of which was *Tobacco Road*. Now I was to be groomed and given the Treatment, the new starlet build-up.

I was turned over to the studio's top publicity woman, Peggy McNaught, and a photographer named Frank Polony. Soon Peggy had me posing for Frank's camera at the beach, at poolside, in nightclubs, on the set, and in the studio gallery. She lined up interviews and pushed me for fashion layouts in magazines and newspapers. Peggy was one of those souls who enjoyed helping people and found a way to make a career of it. She was a wonderful friend to all of us who were starting out at Fox.

We were the Fox Girls, a label I would wear proudly for the next thirteen years. I don't know that any studio ever assembled a more interesting collection at one time. There was Linda Darnell, a natural beauty who looked, I thought, like the Sistine Madonna. Brenda Joyce had just been discovered at UCLA and was filming *The Rains Came*. Anne Baxter, a fine young actress, was the granddaughter of Frank Lloyd Wright, the architect. The amusing Kay Aldrich had been a top New York model. Maureen O'Hara, a great titian beauty, was an import from the Irish Abbey Players. Betty Grable, with her sunny blond looks and million-dollar legs, would become a pinup favorite of American doughboys. And then there was the classic Cobina Wright, Jr., another fugitive from Café Society, who would become my lifelong friend.

We were a happy, unthreatened, lighthearted bunch. We felt blessed. If the world was our oyster, we could pry it open with a fingernail file.

About my career I was serious and earnest, sometimes impatient. I would get so caught up in a conversation that the words would come out slightly off center. The family teased and called me "Miss Malaprop." One night, at the dinner table, I had blurted out, "Don't any of you understand? I'm *infested* with my career."

I dated dozens of young men, had fun with all, made commitments to none. I didn't have the time. Mostly I moved in a circle of friends who had been discovered, as I had, by George Abbott, and then struck out for Hollywood and a crack at motion pictures.

June Allyson and Van Johnson had signed with MGM. Desi Arnaz came west, with Abbott, to repeat for the cameras his performance in *Too Many Girls*. Eddie Albert was under contract at Warner's.

Both Desi and Eddie looked me up and we dated. I listened to Desi, over dinner, tell me how much he loved Lucille Ball. It wasn't long before they were married. Eddie was watching his weight, as I was, and we sometimes wound up our evenings at a spot not usually frequented by nightclubbing Hollywood couples. We would drop by Terry Hunt's health club, Eddie trotting off to the men's steam room and me to the ladies'. We roared with laughter through the brick-walled sauna at our separate but equal suffering.

Eddie Albert never quite made it to the leading man roles, but he had a rewarding career as the perpetual nice guy and best buddy. He was splendid company, even-tempered and considerate. He spent the better part of one

morning persuading my mother to let me go sailing with
him on his schooner. We left San Pedro harbor for Catalina and Eddie seemed quite reliable as a skipper. Alas,
as we neared Catalina he ran aground. We had to get to
shore in the boat's dinghy to find help and telephone my
mother, letting her know we'd be late. Once on our way
again, Eddie regained his confidence and we sailed home
peacefully under a beautiful California moon.

There were many long days, not so many romantic
nights. If I did not have a terminal case of star fever, I
had taken to heart my description by one columnist as
"Hollywood's summer girl, Broadway's winter girl." I
still intended to continue working on the stage. On a trip
to New York to see my family, I was invited by John Golden to read for a new play he was doing.

The play was *Claudia* and I read for Mr. Golden and
the author, Rose Franken. They offered me the lead and
I needed only the approval of my studio to close the deal,
or so I thought. According to my contract I had the right
to do a play every six months. I did not realize that, as a
minor, the matter was out of my hands. My father had
already advised Fox I would waive my option for that
year. I had to turn down an attractive role or risk having
a lawsuit slapped on me by the producer of the play. This
was the beginning of the larger differences yet to come
between my father and me.

Instead, Dorothy Maguire was given her first leading
role in *Claudia* and went on to score a tremendous hit. I
could not help but recall that my own career had taken off
when I replaced another actress in *The Male Animal*.
Fair is fair.

Back in Hollywood, with my contract at Fox renewed for another year, my mother and I went house-

hunting. I was tired of apartment living and had passed through my Marie Antoinette stage. We bought a small but contemporary home in Beverly Hills, and there we entertained the freshest and brightest of the young Hollywood crowd.

I was linked in the gossip columns with Robert Sterling, whose most enduring fame would come years later in a television series called *Topper*. I developed a sisterly affection for Mickey Rooney, who did not exactly endear himself to my mother on their first meeting.

I met her at the door after one of her trips back east. "Oh, Mother, Mickey is here," I chirped. "You'll just love him. He's darling."

With that Mickey bounded toward us and called out, "Hello, Duchess. Come on in and take a load off your tomato."

Later, I asked her how she liked him. "Well," she said, "I thought he was going to slap me on the back. He seems rather an *au naturel* type and I suppose you have to appreciate that."

Mickey Rooney could make me laugh simply by ordering a meal. Mother was more pleased, even thrilled, when Harry Brand, the head of publicity at Fox, arranged for me to be seen with Rudy Vallee. I have no idea why. Vallee was years older and I had no more interest in him than I would have in a wax dummy. But my mother remembered him as the "Vagabond Lover," a song he made famous, and she always came along on our dates.

Mother was my best source of Hollywood gossip. She missed very little, and often startled me with her information. "That's odd," she said after one party. "Charlie Chaplin and Howard Hughes are always getting girls for one another, but I can't tell which one is the procurer."

How it came about I can't recall, but Mother accepted an invitation to dinner at Ciro's one night from Mr. Chaplin. She brought along Pat and a girlfriend of Pat's. Their escorts were the two Chaplin sons, Sidney and Charles, Jr.

The boys had a need to feel that their father was liked and respectable. At one point young Charlie whispered to my mother, "Do you like my father, Mrs. Tierney?"

"Yes, I think he is charming," she said.

He nodded. "Do you know, Mrs. Tierney, there are countries where they don't know Jesus Christ and they know my father?"

"He's very popular," she agreed.

The evening wound up with my mother and Charlie Chaplin jitterbugging on the Ciro's dance floor. The floor cleared and the audience clapped. Mother said it would have been a big moment for her, except she kept worrying what Pat would think, and whether I would speak to her the next day. Pat was one of those clapping, and as for me, I was sorry I missed it.

Chaplin was notoriously strict with his sons and rarely gave them spending money. It was his way of teaching them self-reliance. Pat used to ask Mother for her loose stamps, so young Charles and Sidney could take them to the post office and cash them in, a practice the government later stopped. Pat became a friend of both the boys.

Meanwhile, I lived and dated quietly and was occasionally seen with a volume of Nietzsche under my arm. My attitude toward romance was best reflected by a breezy, offhand statement I gave to one interviewer:

"Men are wonderful. I adore them. They always give you the benefit of the doubt."

CHAPTER
7

Runaway Bride

By the end of 1940, I thought I had my life well structured and under control. Of course, just when we think that, fate tugs at our sleeve, a thread pulls loose, and all the yarn unravels.

My career was speeding ahead. I had time to date several men, but not just one. Then, at a dinner party at the home of the actress Constance Moore and her agent-husband, Johnny Maschio, I met Oleg Cassini.

Oleg was then a $200-a-week designer at Paramount. He had created the wardrobes for Constance and Veronica Lake in *I Wanted Wings*. A bachelor, twenty-eight, he had come alone to the party, as had I.

I thought he was the most dangerous-looking character I had ever seen. Not handsome, but dangerous in a seductive way. Thin-lipped, languid, with wavy hair and a mustache. Perhaps if I had never gone to school in Switzerland I would not have found Oleg as interesting as I did.

He represented all the things that were different and glamorous and continental. We spoke French to each other. He had a beautiful speaking voice. My ear always has been sensitive to how people sounded. As a child, I was so attuned to other voices that my mother could tell where I had been the moment I walked in the house. "You've been with Celine Shut," she would say. "You're talking just like Celine Shut."

A few days after the party, Oleg called and asked me for a date New Year's Eve. I had made other plans, but I let him talk me into breaking them.

Before the night had ended we ran into my other date, who was surprised to find me not so deathly ill after all. My embarrassment was only temporary. I was intrigued with Oleg and had a hunch we were ringing in more than just the new year, 1941.

He was suave and his polished attentions were battering to a woman. He had inherited a title through his mother, a Russian countess, whose name he kept. His father, born in Poland, was Alexander Loiewski, a White Russian diplomat. Oleg had gone through a hard adjustment to the strange ways of a new country, but there was no melancholy in him, only gaiety and a wit that often had the touch of a hot match.

When Louella Parsons once wondered in print why women found him attractive and concluded, "it must be the mustache," Oleg promptly sent her a telegram: "OKAY LOUELLA. YOU WIN. I'LL SHAVE OFF MINE IF YOU SHAVE OFF YOURS."

One of our early dates was to a costume ball at Ciro's, given by Rex St. Cyre, an admirer of Cobina Wright, Sr. Costume parties seem to have gone the way of scavenger hunts, but they were a popular entertainment then. Elsa Maxwell, the gossip columnist and society hostess, used to give one every year, for which the guests came dressed as their "pet hates." Elsa had to limit the number of couples who wanted to come as the Roosevelts, Franklin and Eleanor. The President and his wife were not, in those New Deal years, generally popular among the people who could afford to attend costume balls.

At Oleg's insistence, we went to the party at Ciro's in Russian costume. He was a Cossack; I wore a peasant dancer's dress. The party was delightful and, from then on Oleg Cassini had an ever-growing place in my heart, and in my closet.

In my early days in Hollywood I tried to be economical. I worked with a dressmaker and designed my own clothes, much to my mother's distress. I had a good deal of fun whipping up what I now realize were atrocities. One night when Oleg came to call I was wearing one of my own creations. I shudder to think of it: a navy blue and pink striped dress, with a navy wool cape lined in the same print. I had on a straw hat, floppy and pink, decorated with a pink rose. I wore pink suede gloves and matching bag, and navy shoes.

Oleg strode in the door, took one look at this ice cream confection, and almost passed out. "I won't take you out dressed like that!" he bellowed. "First, take off the hat and cape and then go and get a navy bag. Forget the gloves, if you don't have any navy ones." Oleg winked at my mother, which made me furious, but I began to suspect that my clothes were getting to be a bit much.

At least on one occasion I know I caused him to lose a promising assignment. I went to dinner decked out in gray—a jersey evening dress, wool cape, and a muff of the same material. I was crazy about capes and thought them dramatic and sophisticated. I must have looked like a West Point cadet. A producer who was considering hiring Oleg saw me that night and assumed he was designing my wardrobe. End of job opportunity.

On the other hand, he was making great headway in my affections, despite a growing opposition to him at home and at work. There was then, as there could never be today, a tendency on the part of the studio to dominate your private life. I was only twenty. Oleg was twenty-eight, once married, considered something of a playboy.

He was also the exact opposite of everything my parents had drilled into me. He wasn't a Yale man. He hadn't even gone to Harvard. On top of it, he was a foreigner. All of which made him all the more attractive to me. Nothing strengthens a woman's determination to be in love quite so much as being told that she cannot.

If there was any doubt in my mind that Oleg loved me, it disappeared during the filming of *Belle Starr*, my fourth picture, opposite Randolph Scott and Dana Andrews. The part had been intended for Barbara Stanwyck, who at the last minute was unavailable.

I was suffering great distress from an eye problem, a rare one that nobody seemed to know how to cure. My eyes were swollen and red and watery. Makeup made them itch. I could not appear before the cameras, and the cycle grew vicious. The more nervous I became, the worse the problem.

There were creams to relieve the itching—it was like hives—but no treatment for the cause. The allergy lasted a week, sometimes more. The skin would finally dry and crack and peel and itch unbearably. My memory of that time is so unpleasant that I still have a fear of recreating the symptoms if I think or talk about them.

No one suggested psychiatric help. No one saw it then as a clue to the mental breakdown still ahead of me, or the kind of trick the mind plays on the body. My mother suffered at times from the same condition; whether this was a sympathetic reaction to mine or the result of worries of her own, I don't know.

One allergist told Darryl F. Zanuck I would have to contend with this condition the rest of my life. Another doctor treated me with a shot of adrenaline and my heart nearly stopped beating.

I felt like the object of a voodoo curse. The condition came and went, as had the stomach pains. I filmed on those days that my eyes were clear, stayed home and worried and cried on days that they were not. I was miserable and helpless. Not until I had saved enough money to consider myself a financial success did the eye problem vanish.

I was earning $1,250 a week, most of it being funneled into the Belle-Tier Corporation. Once I worried about not having money. Now I worried that it wouldn't last. I asked myself many times why I felt so insecure, what it was that made me suffer, why I so often found it hard to enjoy the good things that were happening.

Through years of therapy I would eventually, slowly, get in touch with my own feelings. Some of the answers seem so obvious now. But memories do not move like a stream. They tumble out in a way that is kaleidoscopic, until the picture we finally see is the answer we get.

I was a Depression child. My family had lived well, with at least the trappings of wealth—servants, memberships in the best clubs, a boat, and horses. One by one they were gone. We did not eat shredded wheat for dinner, but my mother did her own cooking, and I saw my father erect a wall of false pride against his losses.

People recall the bread lines of the early 1930s, but they seem to forget that the Depression lasted until the start of World War II. Some of the traces are with us still. I had seen my Grandfather Taylor, who had done well in textiles, wiped out in the stock market. He spent his last days in a one-room walk-up apartment, cooking his food on a hot plate. He was a man who had retired in his forties to travel and read.

At some point during those years I had vowed never

to be poor. I felt like Scarlett O'Hara in *Gone with the Wind*. When I finally had enough money of my own to invest some, I told a stockbroker I did not expect him to make me rich. I just did not want him to make me poor.

At a time when most Hollywood stars bought palatial homes and drove big cars, I lived so frugally that Otto Preminger teasingly called me "Hetty Green," who was then famous as the miser of Wall Street, a little old lady who had made a fortune and was determined to keep it.

Once I put off a trip to Europe I had wanted to take with Oleg, figuring that sooner or later the studio would pay our way. Over time, I bought three or four small houses, which I lived in briefly, repaired, and restored, and then sold at a nice profit. One year I made more money in real estate than from the movies.

I developed a fear of failing. But there are many ways to fail. Some reject success. And others do not recognize it when success comes.

In time, whatever flaw I was born with would turn my life into a powder keg. My problems would sputter and burn out, but the fuse was getting shorter. The immediate problem was real and threatening. My career could have been over before it had begun. Months passed before my eyes were normal. As was often to be the case, the kindness and understanding of others carried me through it.

My eyes would puff up so much that I could see only through the slits that were left, giving me a distinctly Oriental look. On my worst days, Oleg would kiss me and say, "It doesn't matter, Gene. You always look beautiful to me."

I could never repay the patience of Randolph Scott. He was on loan to Fox for a limited number of weeks. His contract entitled him to additional salary for every day that the film ran over schedule. There were days when

I simply could not work unless the studio wanted Belle Starr portrayed as a Chinese.

By holding Fox to the contract, Scott could have put them in the position of either having to replace me or lose a substantial sum of money. Instead, he waived his rights under the contract and said, "We need Gene in this picture. I'll wait. Until she's well, you'll find me on the golf course." Not every actor, I can assure you, would have shown that much compassion or faith.

My condition, I learned later, was called angioneurotic edema. Science is only now unraveling all of the complicated links between the mind and the body. But I remember what a coincidence I thought it was when the people I met in the sanitarium would tell me of their itches and twitches. I never met one who did not at one time have an allergy of some kind, an allergy to life.

I was not, needless to say, at the top of my form for *Belle Starr*, and the reviews reflected it. In addition to the anxiety I felt over my allergy, the role of a female outlaw was not exactly custom-made for someone recently out of a finishing school. I loved to ride, but I was no stunt lady. Still, my director, Irving Cummings, was determined that I do as much riding as possible.

In one scene I had to gallop my horse around a dangerous curve, with a precipice just a few feet away. I could have been thrown off. I was terrified. Finally, Cummings lost his patience and said, "If you don't want to do it we can always get another actress!"

I knew he would. I had been a burden on this production too long.

"It's an important shot," he went on, "and we need to show that you're doing some of the riding."

I took a deep breath, gave the horse a jab with my spurs, held on for dear life—and made it.

Even bumpier than that ride was my romance with Cassini. The efforts to break us up continued. He had been fired at Paramount, partly, I heard, because Henry Ginsberg saw him too often in nightclubs—usually with me—and didn't think he took his work seriously. My family had helped foster the idea that Oleg was taking advantage of me and my career. My studio, Fox, refused to hire him.

At one point, Oleg decided to leave Hollywood. "Your family is so against us," he said, "I might as well go back to Washington."

His parents lived there and he had been thinking about joining his mother in the fashion business. His younger brother, Igor, was doing well as a Washington society columnist. He would shortly go on to a wider audience with the Hearst syndicate, under the by-line of Cholly Knickerbocker.

Oleg had a sense of chivalry and was willing to get out of my life. He knew how difficult all the opposition was for me. He suffered at the time from that strange conflict in the American character: we pride ourselves on being the melting pot of the world but we insist on regarding most immigrants with suspicion.

Oleg's was a distinguished family. His line could be traced back to the Teutonic knights on his father's side. He was the son of a diplomat under Czar Nicholas II, the grandson—on his mother's side—of the Count of Cassini, the Russian ambassador to the United States, in the administration of Teddy Roosevelt.

Oleg renounced his title when he became an American citizen. The Cassinis had left Moscow and fled to Italy when the Bolsheviks overran the White Army. After the revolution, the family lived in Rome and Florence, until the Fascists rose to power and the Countess feared her sons would be drawn into the coming European war. In school they had to join the Black Shirts and march for hours every day. Mama Cassini knew they had to leave again, and so they sailed for America.

Even in their teens, Oleg and Igor were quite grown-up. Oli—his nickname—studied for the law. But he had talent as an artist and his mother encouraged him to design fashions, in Europe an esteemed career for young men of such gifts. He worked with her in a couturier shop she opened in Rome. Rosalind Russell once told me that she had been to Italy in the 1930s, and bought a lovely dress from Marguerite Cassini.

Theirs was a colorful and flamboyant family. Appropriately, Mama Cassini wrote about their flights and escapades in a book called *Never a Dull Moment.*

My parents did not object to Oleg until we began to talk about marriage. Then they saw him as an adventurer, saw me as young and inexperienced, and viewed the whole affair as a threat to my career and future.

Father wrote me a long, anguished, and hurtful letter. "Gene," he warned me, "if you marry that man I will have you declared mentally unstable. I do believe you have taken leave of your senses."

It was the sort of threat authoritarian fathers flung at rebellious daughters in those gentle, conformist times. I ignored it.

"What ever do you see in him?" my mother asked. "I can't see him for dust. And you . . . you have the handsomest men falling for you, right and left."

"That's very unfair," I said. "You don't know him and you won't give him a chance. Oleg *is* attractive. He's a gentleman. And he makes me laugh." I rather liked the fact that he did not have the glossy-picture looks of so many actors.

Although we had known each other only a few months,

I was completely infatuated. And I was saying to my parents, as all children eventually do, "I am my own person."

Father sent me a telegram, asking me to wait at least until fall before I made any decisions. I guessed what he had in mind. My brother planned to spend the summer in Hollywood and Butch, my father hoped, would "straighten me out."

I was not much different than any other girl of twenty. I wanted a church wedding, to wear white, to have my family beside me, celebrating with and for me. There is a special torment reserved for those who are forced to choose between people they love.

Oleg and I decided to elope. I gloried in the arrangements, the keeping and exercising of a secret so close to my heart. But our first attempt was literally grounded. We had chartered a plane and hired Paul Mantz, the pilot for several stars, to fly us to Las Vegas. An unseasonal California rainstorm stopped us.

That night my mother and I had another shouting match over my romance with Oleg. "He's a phony," she hissed. "Can't you see that? He isn't even working. Why doesn't he go to the ten-cent store and sell ribbon by the yard?"

Hurt and confused, I stumbled to my room and slammed the door. I fell on the bed and cried myself into a restless sleep. When Oleg phoned the next morning, I was no longer certain of our plans. He was no man with whom to trifle. He began to stay away. I dated others, tried to get interested, but could not. Oleg later claimed that I would call him in the middle of the night to describe my evening, trying to make him jealous. If so, the effort failed. He listened but he did not come back.

In late April I traveled east by train to see my father. He met me at the station with Helen Burdick, a divorcee, a friend of my mother. I sensed immediately that they were having an affair. Children have an intuition about such things. Mother suspected nothing, although her absences had put an additional strain on the marriage.

Howard Tierney was bound to be attractive to women. Even as he aged, the blue eyes stayed intense and the hair dark, and he had what people then liked to call good bones. He was a fastidious man, always combed and pressed. Yet he shopped infrequently and would wear the same suit for years.

When I could not reach my father in his office the next day, I called the home of Mrs. Burdick in Fairfield. "Let me speak to my father," I said coldly.

"He isn't here," she said.

"I know he is," I snapped. "But never mind. I'll speak to you. I just want to tell you to leave my father alone. Just leave him alone! And I hope you fall down the next manhole you come to." With that I slammed the receiver.

I no longer had any reason to consult with my father about my future. I was shocked and disgusted and heartsick for my mother. I flew back to California, unsure what to do or how much to say. But I had made up my mind about one thing. I was going to marry Oleg Cassini.

I told my mother nothing of what I had discovered in New York. But she was frantic over my latest declaration of love for Oleg. She began to seek advice everywhere.

She went to the office of my agent, Leland Hayward, told him she was afraid I would marry Cassini and would he use his influence to stop me?

Leland laughed it off. "Oh, Belle," he said. "You just hop on that train back home. Get rid of that couple you have working in the house for you. Leave Gene alone in the house and let Oleg live with her for a while."

Mother was stunned. "I have never heard of such a thing," she said. "I couldn't face her father if I did that."

Hayward shrugged and said, "I'm telling you, it would be a sure cure. Let him live with her for about six weeks."

Mother left Leland Hayward's office wondering if Western civilization, as we knew it, had come to an end. On a Friday morning she called on Howard Hughes. We no longer dated but were still friendly. He tried to re-assure her.

"Now, don't you worry about a thing, Mrs. Tierney," he said. "I have to go to Canada tonight on business, but I'll be back Monday morning. And I know I can persuade Gene not to marry him. So don't worry."

I never found out what Hughes thought he could say or do to dissuade me. By the time he returned from Canada it was too late. Oleg and I had bought tickets for that Sunday on a commercial flight to Las Vegas. So as not to arouse my mother's suspicions, I left the house dressed casually in a blouse and skirt, and told her I was going on a picnic. I bought my ticket under the name of "Belle Starr," a clever move that would throw her off the track, I thought, if she decided to check the airlines.

For his disguise, Oleg dressed like an American busi-nessman, or rather, his idea of one. He looked about as much like a businessman as I did, dressed in a polo coat and a felt hat and carrying a briefcase. We sat several rows apart. From time to time I would take out my com-pact and wink at him in the mirror. A heady feeling, to be a conspirator. If my parents would not relent, I would simply present them with a fait accompli.

When we arrived in Las Vegas, looking around fur-tively, a chauffeur and limousine were waiting for us.

The man said, "Where to, Miss Tierney? My name happens to be the same as yours, so I keep tabs on you." I thought that very odd, if not astonishing. But we had him drive us to the home of a certain Judge Brown, a justice of the peace. We had to wait until Judge Brown, in his home, wrestled with his domestic problems. Then, in his living room, amid the squawling of his infant child and the persistent ringing of the telephone, he performed the ceremony.

When the judge got to the part about "With this ring I thee wed," Oleg turned and looked at me blankly. He had given me a diamond engagement ring, but in the excitement had forgotten that he needed to buy a wedding band. I slipped off a gold earring and handed it to him, and that was what he slipped on my finger. I saved the earring for years.

I had begged Judge Brown not to answer the telephone until the wedding was completed. When he finally did, he put down the receiver, turned to me and said, "It's a Mr. Harry Brand. Says he's with the Twentieth Century-Fox publicity department. He's here and he needs to talk to you."

Harry's first words were: "Gene, you can't do this!"

I said, "Harry, I've already done it."

"In that case," he said, "drop by the hotel and have a wedding toast with Sybil and me."

The date was June 1, 1941, and I was now Mrs. Oleg Cassini. Harry and his wife hastily ordered a wedding cake and champagne and were very sweet to us. I called my mother from their room and we had a very brief, hurtful exchange over the phone.

When she answered, my voice sang with excitement: "Mother, dear, you've got the most wonderful son-in-law . . ."

"Where are you?" she asked.

"I'm in Las Vegas, and Oleg and I have just been married."

"You can keep him," she said. Before I could get out another word I heard the phone click.

A friend from New York, Richard Watts, the drama critic for the *Herald Tribune*, had stopped by the house, I learned later. He was on his way to a party at the home of Douglas Fairbanks, Jr., and wanted me to go. Mother told Dick I was on an outing and should be home at any moment. She asked him to wait.

After my call, Mother fell into Dick's arms and cried uncontrollably.

I wasn't doing too well at my end, either. I fought back a few tears and told the Brands we had to leave. I wanted to catch the next flight back to Los Angeles. I had to pacify my mother before I could even think about tackling my father.

On the flight home I worked out a strategy. I told Oleg it would be best if he dropped me off at my place and he returned to his, and I would call him later. He shook his head slowly and said, "This is certainly a strange way to spend one's wedding night." He laughed, but I knew he was as anxious as I was to patch things up.

My house was dark. The cook was gone, along with her husband, our butler. The door to my mother's room was closed. I kept knocking and pleading with her to let me in and talk to her. My words were met with silence. I spent most of the night outside her room.

The next morning I decided to just barge in, something I had been conditioned from childhood never to do. I discovered I had been pounding on the door of an empty room. Mother had fired the servants and flown back to New York. The news of my marriage had been reported on the radio when she made up her mind to pack her bags.

The next day my mother issued a statement to the

press: "Gene is a misguided child who has been carried away . . . by this suave man of the world." Father accused me of "going Hollywood" and said he would attempt to have the marriage annulled. For a time, at least, my parents were united again.

Reporters soon sought out my reaction. I replied that I was sorry, "but I have my own life to lead. I am his wife. I hope it will be this way always." Declarations of eternal fidelity do have a way of haunting us.

If my public words were mild and formal, I was coming apart inside. At what should have been the happiest of times, I had been rejected by both of my parents.

I tried to call them. "We have nothing to talk about," my father said. "When you leave him, we can talk."

My feelings toward my father had been hardening, and I could justify, in my own mind, the break that was coming. But what had I done to deserve my mother's denial? How could she not understand? Hadn't she told me herself, many times, that she and my father had eloped? My mother would not talk to me for weeks, would not stay under my roof for as long as I was married to Oleg.

Such was the beginning of our marriage. In retrospect, it might not have lasted six weeks if either of my parents had held out a hand to me. They waited until the first signs of trouble between my husband and me. Then they were available, eagerly so. Once, my father told me quite seriously, "Gene, you come home. All you need is some hot soup." He sounded as if I had the flu.

My father and I would never be close again. Mother and I needed each other in the years ahead, and our need helped us overcome the mutual hurts we had inflicted. But she never accepted Oleg and avoided him when she could. In the face of that hostility, he could not be a very loving son-in-law, and I was caught on a barbed-wire fence.

The wonder was that our marriage lasted as long as

it did, given the early strain and hard bumps. Oleg was out of a job. I was working constantly, at one point finishing a movie in the morning and starting another in the afternoon.

Oleg's parents came to Hollywood to give us their blessing, which underscored the fact that mine had not. For the most part we were alone, except for what Oleg jokingly referred to as "our crowd . . . you and me and Butch," my German shepherd.

For the next six months we were not invited to anyone's home, except to play tennis. I still received party invitations addressed to "Miss Gene Tierney." It's difficult to picture this now, I know, but then the studios were so powerful you simply did not defy them. When Oleg and I did, by getting married, we found ourselves cut off socially. Again, it may sound grotesque today, but we had no circle of friends. We were not accepted as a couple. I took his sketches to Darryl Zanuck, who returned them to me without comment.

A former school chum of mine wrote a catty letter, belittling Oleg's claim to a title and comparing him to Mike Romanoff, a self-styled Russian "preenz" who became a restaurateur and Hollywood character. The letter upset me and I asked Oli about it in a silly and defensive mood.

"It doesn't matter," I said. "I love you anyway. But you're not like Romanoff, are you?"

Oleg was indignant. "I happen to be Count Cassini," he snapped. "My grandfather was Count Cassini, the ambassador from Russia to the United States during the time of Theodore Roosevelt. All of that is behind me now. It has nothing to do with us or how we live. And, Gene, don't ever bring it up again."

Nothing offended Oleg more than to be thought a phony or a treasure hunter. Although few knew it at the time, he insisted on signing an agreement when we married, relinquishing any rights he had to our community property.

We moved into Oleg's cottage, which he rented for fifty dollars a month. For any woman with a domestic urge, there is no greater challenge than to take over a bachelor's quarters. My bridegroom did not even have a lock on the front door! On our second night together we repainted the bathroom. I was, in a very real sense, an actress in a new role. It was fun being a newlywed. And we were in tune.

I might have been able to shut out the outside world, except for a sad and unexpected irony. After twenty-five years, the marriage of my parents was about to break up.

CHAPTER
8

Rich Girl, Poor Girl

When Belle Tierney left our home in Connecticut to attend to my career in California, she asked her best friend to "look after Howard," her husband, my father. He was so well cared for that he divorced my mother and married the friend.

Even now, writing this, I remember the bitter heartache I carried for so long over the parting of my parents. We had been a happy family, I thought. I did not want to believe otherwise, and there were bad signs I refused to recognize.

When I was away at school, in Switzerland, my roommate would wake me and tell me I had been talking in my sleep. I would mumble, "They're fighting again," referring to my mother and father. It isn't hard to figure out what the nightmares meant. I cannot stand scenes or arguments. Never could. I walk away from them. The things we try to ignore often come back to us in our sleep.

For nearly a year after my marriage, I spoke to my father only through our lawyers. He had taken me to court. My marital status allowed me, though still a minor, to be responsible for my own career. A new contract was drawn, in which the studio no longer assigned twenty-five percent of my salary to the Belle-Tier Corporation, our family company.

Until I married, I lived on an allowance and never saw my paychecks. I couldn't buy a dress or order steaks for the household without running the bills through the company. Once, when my mother was in the East, I walked into a store and charged an alligator handbag for $85, an extravagant and frivolous thing to do. My parents hit the ceiling. But I still own that purse today, which proves that quality lasts.

Father sued me for $50,000, contending that Belle-Tier should still be recognized as my agents. I won the suit, but at a cost far too dear. I had not been given an accounting of my savings during the two years I had worked in Hollywood. Whenever I asked for one, my father smiled and said, "Don't worry your pretty little head about that. Everything is fine."

When the case went into litigation, the figures became available to my business manager. I sat in his office and heard him say, "Guess how much your share of the company is worth, Gene?"

"How much?" I asked.

"It comes to zero-zero-zero," he said. "There is no money in it. Not a cent."

My father's insurance business had foundered during a long dispute with his partner. Father had gotten heavily into debt, had used my money but was pressed for more. My mother told me years later that he carried a gun for a long time, thinking of killing himself so we could collect on his insurance.

His business problems had been building for years. They actually began during the time I was in school abroad. He had started his own firm and saw it prosper, with the help of a bright young man he hired out of Princeton, Jimmy James. My father owned sixty percent of the company and James, who was married to Gladys Underwood, of the typewriter family, held the other forty percent.

In 1935, Jimmy sued my father to reverse the percentages. He had brought in a lot of accounts and, in spite of his closeness to our family, was egged on by his wife. She was popular and wealthy and could afford to support him in the courts for a long time, which she did. During those years, my father was restrained from drawing any money out of the company beyond his salary.

One day he went to his partner, his young friend, and pleaded with him. "Jimmy," he said, "don't do this to me. My daughter is in school in Europe and I can no longer afford to keep her there."

James said, "Why should she be there anyway? Bring her home and put her in public school."

I was unaware then of any of these matters. I returned to Connecticut, but it was my father's pride, not mine, that led to my enrollment at Miss Porter's School. His financial problems did not ease until his divorce from my mother was final and his new wife paid off his debts.

She was the daughter of a wealthy railroad man, and ten years younger than my mother, who had stood by her through a messy local scandal. Her husband had shot and wounded her father.

Although I think my mother enjoyed the anger and sympathy of her children, she often tried to defend Father. "He wanted only one thing from that woman," she said, "her money. He wouldn't have left me for anything in the world. But he needed the money."

Even after he filed for divorce, my mother acted as though she was not really losing him. The papers were served. She never read them. She received no alimony and no settlement. She could have sued her wealthy rival— under the old alienation-of-affections law—but she refused. Her emotions were such that she could not reduce her marriage, in her mind, to a business proposition.

"I didn't want to give him up," she said. "To me it was too much like blackmail, trying to get money out of him."

For months after he had walked out of our home, and even years later, Mother would suddenly burst into a song from the musical *Carousel*, and march through the house belting out the words to "When you walk through a storm." My sister, Pat, thought she was going mad. But it was her way of chasing off the memories that would not stay buried.

Soon my mother went to work as a bridal consultant at what was then the largest store in Washington, D.C., Woodward and Lothrop. She always maintained that she went to work instead of having a nervous breakdown. That approach, I can surely testify, does not succeed for everyone.

The unbelievable sequence of my father's actions, the dishonesty and the infidelity, one on top of the other, had a destructive effect on me. In my own mind, the two were connected. The amount of money he stole from me was around $30,000, over a period of two to three years. It was not a huge sum, but large enough to a desperate man. And he *was* desperate. Had he come to me, I would have given him that much and more, out of my earnings. But I would have attached a condition: that he stay with my mother.

The idea may have been unrealistic. But I would have done anything to keep her from being mistreated. She never remarried, nor loved another man, nor saw one she thought as handsome. A few weeks before she died in the spring of 1978, she said one day: "I hope there is a next incarnation, so when I die it will all be explained. I believed everything he told me."

He said he loved her almost to the day he asked for a divorce. Whatever he did, he always said he did for her and his children. I think she wondered which words were meant not to hurt, and which ones simply hid the truth.

I am not sure she wanted to know. We were so alike in many ways, including our slowness to see things as they were and to accept what could not be changed.

Oleg and I had just moved into a new house, in November of 1942, when my father stopped off in Hollywood, hoping to visit me. He had been in Reno, Nevada, where he had gotten his divorce and then remarried a day or so later. I told him I would see him, but not with his new wife. I would not be a hypocrite. I considered her, and still do, the woman who broke my mother's heart.

Father came alone and stayed an hour. The meeting was strange and tense. I suppose he wanted to know he was forgiven, or at least not despised. I could not accommodate him. I could not give him the release he must have wanted. He had taught us by example to guard our emotions, and not to fall all over anyone. As I showed him through my home, I was polite but reserved.

He brought us a gift, three or four young apricot trees. And he said flattering things about the house. Oleg, who had never met him, and expected an ogre, was pleasantly surprised. Of course, Oleg would not have been one to frown on a married man getting involved with another woman.

I was relieved when my father looked at his watch and said he had to leave. At the door he hesitated and said, not unkindly, "Well, Gene, you got what you wanted and I got what I wanted." I think he felt I was on my way as an actress and had my own life to lead now. And he hoped I would understand his need to do the same.

I would not see my father again for sixteen years—once while I was ill, and then only before his death.

In many ways, his desertion—for that was how I saw it—hit my brother harder than me. Butch was still in college and had loved his father in such a way that to question him was unthinkable.

Father wanted him to go to Hotchkiss and be an athlete; he played football and captained the track team. Father wanted him to go to Yale, and he did. His effect on Butch was nearly that of a Svengali.

Unknown to me, their estrangement began when Father told Butch he was using my money. The bank had called in a loan. He wasn't asking for permission. He just wanted his son to reassure him there was no harm. But Butch was outraged.

"No," he said. "You don't touch Gene's account. You go into bankruptcy if you have to, but leave her money alone."

He had been loyal enough to his father to keep quiet, even after he came home one night, found the door to my mother's bedroom closed and the other woman's car parked in front of our house. The car was still there the next morning.

With Butch, the break with Father was not just the result of a moral hurt but a feeling of having been absolutely used and disillusioned. If Father had not preached such a good game, none of us would have expected him to be a Christlike figure. But he had, we did, and the effects were excruciating and lasting.

In later years, when Howard Tierney, Jr., was established in business, he left word with his secretary in case

Father called: "Just say I don't have a father." It was an awful vengeance, but I knew precisely how Butch felt.

How do I explain my own conflicts—a daughter rejected, or so she thinks, by an adored father who had his own demons to quell and questions to answer. My gratitude, my awareness of what he had sacrificed and what I owed him, did not change. For twenty years he had been a doting father, and this was how my mother wanted me to think of him. I try.

Father had deep blue eyes, with coal-black hair and a ruddy complexion. He favored Grandfather Tierney and was a typical, charming Irishman. My mother was a gymnastics teacher when they began to court in 1916, in Brooklyn, where their families had known one another. That same year, they eloped to Greenwich, Connecticut, and were married.

Her father was so furious that he insisted they have a "proper" wedding. So the next day, Grandmother Taylor hauled her daughter off to Bergdorf Goodman to buy a gown, and the family minister was asked to preside at a second ceremony.

Rumbles of war in Europe touched this country when a German U-boat sank the *Lusitania*, with many Americans aboard. Months later, the United States declared war on Germany and my father enlisted as a buck private in the infantry. By then Mother was pregnant, expecting my brother.

Father was later transferred to the Army Air Corps, looked gallant in his leather coat and flying cap, rose to the rank of lieutenant, and served in France and Italy. Howard, Jr., "Butch," was a year old when the shooting stopped in November, 1918. Mother was so overjoyed at the prospect of her husband coming home, she wheeled her son out into the sunlight, placed a newspaper whose headline read "ARMISTICE DAY" on his pillow, and took his picture. The whole family cherished that snapshot, and the many emotions it reflected.

My childhood seemed happy and secure to me. The story of the Taylors and the Tierneys was something else: checkered with bad luck, early deaths, divorce, and a mental breakdown.

I was born Gene Eliza Tierney on November 20, 1920, in a lovely brownstone house in old Brooklyn. Mother thought the initials were prophetic. "It may take her a while," she often said, "but Gene will usually get whatever she wants."

She named me after her only brother, who died of diabetes at seventeen, years before the discovery of insulin. His death was considered a family tragedy and my grandparents never talked about it.

My uncle had fallen into disfavor by running away from military school. The military life was an admired one among the Taylors. My great-grandfather had been a captain of the New York Seventh Regiment and was honored for valor at the Battle of Chapultepec, in 1847. When my uncle returned home, Grandfather punished him for running away. He gave him a whaling. A week later the boy fell ill with diabetes and never again left his bed.

As a child, I can remember sitting on my grandfather's knee and playing with a locket on his pocket watch. He slapped my hand, snapped shut the watch, and said gruffly, "Leave that alone!" I was too startled to cry. Inside the locket was a picture of the boy, Gene. I began to know something that day about the privacy of grief.

I was given my uncle's cape from military school—blue velvet lined in red—and I wore it to my dancing classes. Late in her own life, my poor grandmother developed diabetes, but the illness was controlled by shots of insulin. She could never really accept the fact that her only son had lost his life for want of a medicine that now prolonged hers.

Gene was a handsome boy. All of my mother's family were strikingly attractive people. Aunt Claire had auburn hair and brown eyes. She was the eldest sister and, at sixteen, had an encounter with mental illness. According to my mother, many of her symptoms were the same as mine, many years later. She grew withdrawn. If she saw someone she knew walking toward her, she would cross the street to avoid them. From quite a nice character, she turned nervous and vindictive.

By the time I was a young girl, old enough to notice how adults behaved, Aunt Claire seemed quite normal. She was gentle and cheerful and I liked to be around her. No one in the family talked about her illness. It was well after my own became fact that any comparisons were made.

In a way, I found it comforting to believe I had inherited a weakness from my aunt, as opposed to believing that I had just gone mad. My mother encouraged that theory, although I do not recall any of my doctors being very impressed. I did ask questions about her case, and came to know it as well as my own.

No one knew what ailed Claire, including the doctors. But in those days families that had any choice at all did not consider sending a child to an asylum. They were for crazy people. The social stigma was to be avoided, if at all possible.

Someone suggested she be sent to a girls' camp, and

away from the family. In a short time, the director of the camp called the Taylors and said they could no longer keep her. She would not take part in the activities they had scheduled. She would just wander off, alone, into the fields.

Her father wanted Claire to stay. He persuaded the camp director to give her another chance, after agreeing to let my mother, two years younger, move into a cabin with her. Mother was soon writing alarmed reports back to her parents. Claire hardly touched her food.

"I hope you didn't eat much of that stuff," she would complain back in the cabin. "It was poisoned." She thought everything had a peculiar smell and contained poison.

For the next year, the Taylors kept Claire at home, in an upstairs bedroom. They hired a nurse to walk the floor with her. She was never institutionalized. I don't know if Aunt Claire and I actually had the same disorder. A diagnosis thirty years after the fact may not be very reliable. But I would often wonder if my own weakness was in some way related to hers, and why my treatment, unlike hers, had to involve years of hospitals and anguish and endless therapies.

I have gone back and forth in my feelings about my case. I am convinced that much of my early treatment was a waste, and some of it harmful. I tended at times to put too much faith in my doctors and too little in what I could do for myself. I have mostly positive thoughts about the staff at Menninger's and the care I received there. Yet I am still in therapy, seventeen years after I left a hospital for what I hope was the last time.

There are no magical cures, I know. But I ask myself: would I have been any worse off if I had stayed home or lived on a farm, and instead of shock treatments received rest and quiet and the good medication that finally came along? There is no way of knowing, and so I wonder. What was it, was it just love, that worked for Aunt Claire?

My other aunt, Lelia, was a brunette who wore her hair in bangs, Joan of Arc style. She was the brilliant one, the writer, who died in the early bloom of her talents. She had worked at one time as a secretary for the polar explorer Admiral Richard Byrd. Though both were married at the time, and he was a Catholic, there were whisperings of a romance between them.

My grandfathers were very important to me when I was young, in a way that was true with most of my generation. They took us on long strolls, sat us upon their knees and told stories, and taught us history. Has television done away with that relationship? Or do children simply grow up too fast today?

On my strolls with Grandfather Taylor, I discovered buttermilk and Jewish egg bread, and all the delights of the delicatessens that were so much a part of the West Side of New York. We had doughnuts and ice cream sodas at the drugstore—treats unavailable at home, where my mother urged us to drink our orange juice and eat our boiled eggs.

Those were pleasant moments spent with a dear and unhurried old gentleman who knew how to entertain a little girl. He lived well, retiring at forty-five to travel with his wife, Carrie, all over the world. The income from their investments supported them until the stock market crashed. To save his stocks he reinvested. He finally had to sell my grandmother's diamonds, and everything was lost. He died poor.

I remember being surprised when Grandfather Tierney, and my grandmother, Nellie, were divorced. Children don't understand about people loving each other and then suddenly not. But I sensed the distress that swept through the family. Grandfather Tierney had to retire from J. P. Morgan's bank because of it. An unsophisticated man, he fell for a woman who had been married to a musician, who had traveled and knew music. She must have seemed worldly to him. But she was a very homely woman and we grandchildren always laughed at the name by which grandfather called his new wife, Bob.

By contrast, our grandmother was quite pretty, with eloquent ways. She had been born into the old Dutch society and was a member of the Daughters of the American Revolution. She went back to a schoolgirl romance, remarried, and moved to Kinterhook, New York.

As they say, like father, like son. My own father had remarried a woman who had been divorced and was very plain. When men grow older they often seem to marry younger women whose looks would not have attracted them in their prime.

I can't honestly say I ever forgave my father for what I considered his "mistakes." He hurt us terribly. But time has a way of tempering bitterness. My brother owes his drive and success to him and I know I do. He gave us the best kind of education and encouraged each of us to be resourceful.

We belonged to the country club and the yacht club, and we rented a stall at the hunt club for a horse given to my brother by a family friend. We were given the earth as children. Sometimes we had to give it back. Those were hard lessons, perhaps much too hard, but we learned from them. At least I like to think so.

Butch was at Hotchkiss three months when he was
called into the office and told his father had been unable
to pay his tuition. They could have sent him home. The
alternative was to allow him to stay as a scholarship student. They kept him. For the next four years he waited
on tables and cleaned up classrooms to pay for his schooling. At Yale, he ran the college laundry.

I don't remember that Butch ever complained. All he
wanted was his father's approval. As a boy, he learned
to make applejack and Father would pay him a quarter
for his product. He would come home from school in the
afternoon and head for the cellar, where he distilled it
seven times on an old kerosene stove. The formula was
not difficult. The liquid ran through a coil and dripped
off, you threw the gunk away, put the rest back on the
stove and repeated the process seven times.

Butch also made the cocktails for Sunday lunch. He
would take a pint of ice cream and a pint of applejack,
shake it vigorously in a shaker, then put in some ice and
serve them as pseudo Alexanders.

Those were happy times, a period of grace and luxury
between 1928 and 1931. After that, Father took his
buffeting. It came gradually. Inside he must have felt
the pressure, but on the surface he was stronger than
ever. At least for a while, on an income of around $15,000
a year—extremely comfortable at the time—he had the
servants, the boat, the horse, and three—yes, three—cars.

I don't know that I was even aware at the time that my
father had experienced money problems. But I went to
school one year in hand-me-down dresses left to me by
my Aunt Lelia. They were originally nice clothes, but
much too grown-up, and my classmates giggled at the
sight of me. I tried not to be bothered.

The best times were those before and between school,

when we lived in the Connecticut countryside and spent our summers on Long Island, in neat rented bungalows. Every now and then, when my parents were on a trip, we children also had a chance to stay with our great-aunts in the big house at 119 Brooklyn Avenue.

My great-aunts, Helen and Annie, were often at each other, but they remained loyal and devoted to their brother, my Grandfather Tierney. And they were splendid hostesses. We loved going there. They would drive us to the sea and let us run and stroll along the boardwalk, hungrily inhaling the fresh breezes off the Atlantic. They gave us ice cream cones and pennies for the weight machines. There were shopping jaunts to Abraham and Straus, more of a country store than anything else back then.

Their home fascinated me. I picture it now as a near replica of the dainty clutter in *Arsenic and Old Lace*. The kitchen was located where cellars are today, under the street level with steps leading down to the kitchen door. The front stoop was long and high above the street. Inside the front door was a parlor, and the dining room was off to the left. A butler served us on pretty blue-and-white onion-patterned china on those nights when Aunt Helen or Aunt Annie didn't bring us our dinners on a tray.

I grew up during those years when well-to-do children in the Northeast had European governesses, the way Southern girls, in another time and place, had mammies. Mine was a sixteen-year-old German girl named Louise, who taught me the Palmer method of handwriting and sang pretty German songs to me, sitting in the park overlooking the Hudson River.

If there were any bad or jarring moments, I must have blocked them out long ago. We lived, after I was five, in a lovely farmhouse on a hill at Greens Farms, Connecticut, with Indian sumac and milkweed everywhere. We owned thirty-five acres, with a view of Long Island Sound.

The Tierneys were among the first New Yorkers to settle Fairfield County for the purpose of living there year round. In the late 1920s, when my father left for his office, his was one of only three cars parked at the railroad terminal. Commuting had not become a way of life. My mother was one of the women who lobbied to keep the roads from being paved. When they paved the roads, she fought the thruways. We Tierneys were not much on "progress." We treasured peace and other old virtues.

You could wake up in the morning and peek out your window and see deer loping in the woods. I never have known a place more serene.

In 1928 my father sold off the farmhouse and most of the land and built a new house on a meadow across the road, four hundred yards away. We moved in before the house was completed, and my father, over my mother's protests, insisted on giving a weekend party. The bathroom tiles were not even laid, and the guests had to step on planks to cross the floor. But there had not been much entertaining in the farmhouse, and my mother loved the excitement. She got the hired man to help her haul two oaks out of the woods in our station wagon; with great effort they planted the trees in the front yard.

The house was two stories, with two fireplaces downstairs, and bedrooms for the children upstairs. The master bedroom overlooked a garden. There was a guest room, a study with a half-bath for my father, and up the back stairs were the servants' quarters. The house cost over $60,000. In those years that sum bought you a mansion. It was beyond our means, but that was the theme song of the 1920s. Father was making money on Wall Street. You bought a stock and just tried to relax while you waited for it to go straight up. It usually did, seemingly without limit.

Houses are to this day one of my passions. I probably should have been an interior decorator. I had, and still have, a strong sense of those homes that *feel* happy and those that do not. Often I could describe every detail of a room, but little of the people who moved around it.

An armchair psychologist might see in this a tendency to trust things, not people. I settle for simpler answers, such as the instinct of an actress to fix in her mind the arrangement of a set. But, then, chairs and tables seldom let us down.

Long before I had any notion of what my calling would be, or where my life would lead, I sensed inside me a touch of good fortune I thought I could never lose. I used to annoy my father by telling him how much I felt luck was with me.

He was superstitious. At such moments his face would darken. He warned me I was "tempting" fate by making such statements. Was I? I wonder still.

CHAPTER
9

On Location

The strains on my marriage to Cassini would not be long in coming. Two weeks after the wedding I left for New Mexico, alone, to begin the filming of *Sundown*, a desert story set in East Africa. I played the daughter of an Arab trader.

I could hardly bear the stifling heat and the stench of the camels. One of them tried to take a nip out of my derriere as I walked along in a dusty caravan.

Fox had sent me on loan to United Artists to appear opposite Bruce Cabot and George Sanders. Oleg stayed in Los Angeles at the request of Walter Wanger, the movie's producer. Wanger had served in the First World War with my father, and I suspected that he was trying to accommodate both my family and the studio by keeping us apart.

The film was shot at a place called Ship Rock Hill, a New Mexico landmark. Twice a day we had to climb a steep slope to reach the set, an Arab village the crew had constructed. I thought it remarkable what a motion picture company can do with a patch of desert. They had hundreds of people to feed and house. We were almost like a little city sprung up overnight, living at the foot of the hill in barracks that were temporary.

Donkeys were used for loading and hauling equipment. And the presence of the camels, along with our isolation, encouraged the feeling that we could just as well have been in North Africa.

Our costumes were designed by Kalock, for Joe Snitzer, whose company my father once insured. Mine were veiled and scanty but not quite daring enough to suit Walter Wanger. At the fittings one day he asked for a pair of scissors. Then he proceeded to cut out an opening in front, at the waist, and another in the back. I ended up having a low-slung skirt with my navel exposed and a bra with black and gold threads, a kind of harem girl costume. Walter stepped back, admired his handiwork and said, "There. Now you look right for the part."

So attired, and with long hair flowing down my back, I appeared on the cover of *Life* magazine in the summer of 1941.

Wanger was a distinguished-looking man, married to Joan Bennett; many years later, he was charged with shooting her agent in a jealous rage. But I knew him only as the playful older man who one day flipped a dime that dived right down my blouse, between my bosoms.

It was the first time anyone had made me furious in Hollywood. "I don't think that's funny," I said, "but I'll show you something that is." With that I jumped on his back and just held on, sort of piggyback, while he staggered around trying to shake me off. He was visibly embarrassed in front of the crew, this famous producer, nattily dressed, carrying a twenty-year-old girl on his back with both legs locked around his middle.

Wanger did not like to be seen in an undignified pose. When I climbed down, I said, "Well, we're even now. You embarrassed me, too."

I was on location three weeks, lonely and miserable most of the time. I spent my few free moments writing letters to Oleg or reading his. Once or twice a week Bruce Cabot drove me into the nearest town so I could telephone my husband.

Those trips were an adventure. Bruce kept a gun between us on the seat. The first night, after a few miles of nervous silence, I confessed that the gun frightened me. "Good Lord, Bruce," I said. "Isn't it dangerous? Who, or what, do you expect to shoot?"

"Oh," he said, "I like to pop off a few coyotes on the way. I'm a huntsman."

When we reached the nearest pay phone, Bruce would get Oleg on the line, assure him I was fine and then hand me the receiver. Those few minutes of conversation would make the ride back to the camp almost bearable.

I returned from location to find that the knuckles were raw on Oleg's right hand from pounding his fist against the wall. "It was just so frustrating," he told me, "not having you with me on our honeymoon."

I don't know that I ever went into a movie more excited, with what turned out to be less cause, than I did for *The Shanghai Gesture*. The picture was to be a comeback for the German director Josef Von Sternberg, who had launched the career of Marlene Dietrich in *The Blue Angel* and gone on to become her mentor. He had not worked in years and he threw himself into the job.

Happily, Oleg was hired to design the costumes, including my wardrobe. I relished the compliments his work received. Again, I was on loan to United Artists, a system helpful in promoting one's career. The studio rented your services for more money than they were paying in salary, which tended to enhance their judgment of you.

Von Sternberg was a taskmaster who came to work attired in riding clothes with high leather boots. He carried a riding crop and he brandished it whenever he got excited, which was a good deal of the time. But he had a reputation for making women look spectacular, dating back to his earliest success with Dietrich. He was a genius with camera angles.

The Shanghai Gesture had been a huge success on Broadway, starring Florence Reed and Mary Duncan (soon afterward the wife of the polo player Stephen Sanford). I had the Mary Duncan part as the illegitimate daughter of Mother Gin-Sling, played by Ona Munson. Walter Huston appeared as my father and Victor Mature was Omar the Arab.

Near the end of the picture we played a scene seated at a long dinner table. A carved figurine of each character was placed in front of our plates. After the scene, I asked if I could have the set as a memento of the film. Von Sternberg gave them to me. They were no more than three inches high, very delicate in their detail.

I had already started my next film when *The Shanghai Gesture* was released to devastating reviews. What had seemed dramatic and crisp to us, at the time, struck the critics as hollow and absurd. Singled out for special mention was one of my unforgettable lines. Just before she shot me, I hissed at Mother Gin-Sling: "You're no more my mother than a toad."

Years later, in France, strangers would ask me about *The Shanghai Gesture* as though it had been a work of art. I was to hear many times that the picture was well received abroad.

Movie failures are like the common cold. You can stay in bed and take aspirin for six days and recover. Or you can walk around and ignore it for six days and recover. When I came home from work the night of the first bad reviews, my figurines were missing from the shelf. I asked Oleg what had happened to them.

"Ah, you want to see them, do you?" he asked; his accent seemed more noticeable when he was agitated. "Come, let me show you. I have blown them to bits."

I didn't believe him. But he led me to the backyard and there, on the ground, was the shattered evidence. He had lined up the miniatures on top of the fence, loaded a hunting rifle, and fired a pot shot at each one.

I picked up a few splintered fragments and then threw them to the winds. "Oleg," I wailed, "how could you do this? You know I wanted to save those."

Smugly, he said, "Well, now you cannot. I have blown off their heads. I have executed them. Now you won't be reminded of that dreadful movie."

The next morning, a Sunday, his anger had cooled. Oleg's moods were as mercurial as mine. He jumped out of bed and said, "I'm going to telephone Von Sternberg." It was a kind thought, and the old director, stunned by the reviews, invited Oleg to pay him a visit.

This was one of those times when the company of a woman was not required. But when Oleg returned, raving about Von Sternberg's mansion, I was sorry I hadn't gone along. "That is the damnedest haunted house I have ever seen," he said. The place was built like a medieval castle, surrounded by a moat. In the center of one room was a throne. In another you could press a button and a circle of light rain fell, indoors.

The house was incredible, but then so was Von Sternberg. He was of the old school of Hollywood, when the directors and their stars indulged their whims. Von Sternberg's secret desire had been to live in a castle. So he built one.

Oleg and I lived modestly, in contrast to Von Sternberg and just about anyone else in the movie colony. We had bought a small split-level house once owned by Robert Stack's grandfather. It was close to country living, always the style I preferred. We had a tiny guest bungalow and a chicken coop with white leghorns, the best laying hens in the world.

We drove inexpensive cars and put on a show for no one. A friend of mine said to me one day, "Gene, your house is too small and your car is tacky. No movie star can live like that very long. It just isn't good for you, prestige-wise."

I laughed and said, "Watch me."

It was during the making of *Son of Fury* that I had my first, up-close exposure to mental illness—someone else's. Frances Farmer fell ill. I heard the crew buzzing and gossiping about her. She had thrown a brush at one of the hairdressers, had a tantrum on the set, and literally snarled at people. I was puzzled by her behavior and by the crew's lack of sympathy for her. I did not know how to react. I never dreamed, of course, that I would someday share her status—the role of casualty.

In the 1930s, no actress was considered more lovely than Frances Farmer, with her golden hair and clear, strong features. She had a big talent but felt that acting in movies cheapened it. Her heart was with the stage. She had worked with the Group Theater on Broadway and had starred in *Golden Boy* in 1937. The Group was dedicated to the theories of Stanislavski, known as the Method, or the torn undershirt school of acting.

They were a creative bunch, willing to experiment on or off the stage. Frances had a painful love affair with Clifford Odets, the playwright, and came out of the Group a more vulnerable person.

As her mental condition worsened, she simply would not let people be kind to her. It reached a point where, if a man offered her a drink at lunch, she would snap, "I know. You want me to have a martini so I'll get loaded and you can take me to bed."

She spent a total of eight years in state asylums for the insane, and at one point, so I heard, was reduced literally to making mud pies. Finally, she seemed to be headed for a recovery, and turned up as a hotel clerk in San Francisco. She had offers to appear on the stage and in films, and she took them.

By 1960, Frances had her own television show in Indianapolis and had returned to summer stock. She was also fighting a drinking problem. During that time, having fought a battle of my own with depression, I noticed a photograph of her in a New York newspaper. I found myself pulling for her. But my mother only shook her head. "You can tell from the picture," she said, "that Frances isn't well." I could see it, too. Something was there, in her eyes.

There followed a series of lost jobs and public disturbances. But she did make it. I heard that she quit drinking and became a Catholic and, at last, found a peace that helped her meet her death from cancer in August, 1970.

Frances never left our picture. By the end of it, no one seemed to realize, or care, that she was seriously ill. Two years would pass before her mother had her committed. We had no scenes together and our paths rarely crossed. If someone said she had been acting crazy, I took it to mean difficult and abrasive. My ideas about insanity, up to then, came right out of the movie *Jane Eyre*. What I learned of Frances Farmer's story saddened and, for a time, frightened me. A very gifted actress had been crying out for help, and no one was listening.

After the final scenes were shot for *Son of Fury*, I was delighted when Tyrone Power, who had the male lead, invited Oleg and me to his home for dinner. Ours was still a marriage that few approved, and we had been ignored by what was thought of as Hollywood society. I thought this invitation might be a breakthrough and I hurried home to tell my husband.

I understood it would be just an intimate evening. I had visions of putting on my best gown, dressed to kill, and sitting across from Ty's beautiful French wife, Annabella, at dinner.

When we arrived at their home it turned out to be a party for the cast and crew and assorted friends. The place was jammed and I felt overdressed. I disliked myself for feeling let down. But I was quiet on the drive home. We still had not made the grade with our circle of actors and actresses. I felt like a child with my nose pressed against the candy store window.

Those were the days when I worked all the time, without a layoff, or a rest, finishing one picture and reporting for another—sometimes on the same day. I was up at five o'clock and did my shopping at the market on my lunch hour. Oleg was growing bored and tense and uneasy with the fact that he had a wife whose work paid most of the bills, and who came home to him exhausted most nights.

All through the year of 1941 I wrestled with the psychic cost of the lawsuit my father had filed against me, and his divorce from my mother. Keeping busy was good for me, a kind of novocaine for the mind. But there was no relief for Oleg, who found jobs scarce.

On the weekends, when I could relax and look forward to quiet hours at home, Oleg wanted to be off playing tennis. We began to quarrel. He accused me of trying to Americanize him. I wasn't certain what he meant. I only knew that we said things we regretted. In time the tension turned to anger, and the words to something corrosive.

At one point, when jobs were still not open to him, I blurted out: "You know, Oleg, you will never really amount to anything because you were born a gentleman. You cannot survive in this world of competition."

His voice was low and hard. "Gene, don't forget you said that."

Oleg thought, and we argued about it, that I was attracted by the idea of the poor ex-nobleman, incapable of facing the facts of modern life. But I understood a very modern fact. The Hollywood structure was monopolistic, run by four or five big studios. And in the first year of our marriage, at least, the word had gone out not to hire my husband.

In *Rings on Her Fingers*, I was reunited with Henry Fonda, who detested the script and suffered throughout the film. That was the beginning of his unrest with Hollywood. "This huge money they pay you," he said to me one day, "it just isn't worth it."

I could see him churning, wanting to go back to Broadway. The moment the picture ended he did, and began to do brilliant things, including *Mr. Roberts*. Henry was kind to me, then as always. But I would remind him that if he had not done those awful pictures with me he might never have returned to his beloved Broadway.

Of all the actors I knew, Fonda and Gary Cooper had the best sense of timing, without which no actor can be said to be great. I had heard John Barrymore, in the middle of his play, depart from the script and spit one word: "STOP!" There was absolute silence in the theater. Then, bowing slightly, he said to the cast, as well as the audience, "Now, my dear children, you know the value of a pause." What he meant, of course, was timing.

Rings on Her Fingers was my first comedy part. But it was not a good time for comedy, the time being the final weeks of 1941. On Sunday, December 7, we were filming on Catalina Island; we had just set up our cameras when an assistant came racing down the beach. "The Japanese have bombed Pearl Harbor," he yelled. "We're gonna be at war. We've got to clear out for the mainland right away."

We wrapped up at once and were soon sailing toward San Pedro. The radio reports of the Japanese attack were shrill and disconnected, and led to wild speculation aboard our boat. Some of the cast thought that they might hit the California coast next. For all anyone knew, the waters we were now churning through might have been mined.

I would not want to overstate or embroider what we felt that day. But I remember the sun was setting and as it did the whole western sky turned to shades of red, an ominous sign of the blood that was to be shed.

CHAPTER
10

Our War

I remember the 1940s as a time when we were united in a way known only to that generation. At home we worked hard, believed in what we were doing, and felt we belonged to a common cause.

In one way or another, everyone went to war. Hollywood did, cranking out movies intended to build morale as much as to entertain. Even the comics went to war. Joe Palooka joined the Army, Daddy Warbucks became a general, and Smilin' Jack flew a fighter plane.

The country had begun to mobilize within hours after Pearl Harbor. Women organized teams to sew, bake cookies, collect scrap and wastepaper. Men rejected by the draft drilled as air-raid wardens. Actresses were in demand to appear at the Hollywood Canteen or tour the country selling war bonds. We also said good-bye to our men. Oleg joined the Coast Guard, then transferred to the cavalry, where his riding experience helped him win a commission.

The war news was mixed in 1942, but on the silver screen we were winning nearly every battle. I was cast in *Thunder Birds* and *China Girl*.

With Oleg gone, I lived alone in the house we had built in the mountains overlooking Franklin Canyon, near the Beverly Hills reservoir. After my mother's divorce was final, she and Pat came to visit, staying in the guest cottage. They helped me pick the avocados that ripened in the trees that surrounded the house. We had so many that I shipped baskets of them to friends and relatives all over the country. If they liked avocados, none of our friends or relatives figured to go hungry during the war.

The branches of an apricot tree spread across the roof of the house. One day, on the set of *China Girl*, I asked George Montgomery what I could do to keep the fruit from rotting. George laughed and said, "The best way I know is to eat them." He said he would drop by sometime and collect a few.

One Sunday morning I was sound asleep when a noise on the roof woke me. I thought, what the devil is going on here? I slipped into a housecoat and went to the window. There was George, on a ladder, picking apricots.

"Hi, there," he said brightly. "This is great. Not everybody has fruit in their own backyard." George was not yet married to Dinah Shore. He said he was going to take his harvest to his mother and have her turn it into homemade jam.

When I wasn't working, or trotting off to be with my husband, I did as so many actors and actresses did—I took part in bond drives. I toured all through the Midwest and the South, talking at factories, in auditoriums, and at large outdoor rallies.

While I had always been comfortable in front of a camera, or on a stage, I found it painfully hard just to be myself in front of a crowd. My public shyness was heightened by the shock of hearing my voice amplified for the first time over a loudspeaker.

Once, in St. Paul, I was standing by a curtain, waiting to cross a stage constructed especially for the rally. I was nervous to begin with, and uncertain what I should say, when I heard Chester Morris, our actor-host, call out: ". . . And now we proudly present, Miss Gene Tierney."

I had taken possibly two steps when my left heel caught between the planks and I took a spill, rolling down the rest of the way to the podium. I was dimly aware that the band had given me a fanfare. I looked back and saw my heel still wedged in the floor where I had fallen. I got to my feet, hobbling, held up the other shoe and said over the microphone, "All right, we might as well auction off this shoe. I have no use for it now." I was shaken but unhurt and the crowd, relieved, laughed with me. I then went into my bond-selling speech.

Most of the time I suffered from a fear I couldn't explain or control. I felt assured and composed whenever I slipped into the role of someone else. But appearing before a crowd, as myself, tested me. Once I appeared at a navy base, opened my mouth to speak, and nothing came out. Finally, I forced myself to cough and the words began to come.

I never really got over this kind of "stage fright." I was born shy and still am. I find it unsettling to meet strangers, much less make a speech to them. Acting is fun. You have the protection of a script and the other actors. My problem had less to do with feeling unreal than feeling alone.

Barnstorming the country, selling bonds, "pitching in" —a favorite phrase of that era—should have been an exciting and colorful experience. For many I suppose it was. But for me it was a learning time: about myself, my own insecurities, and a kind of show business I had never known.

At the crack of dawn one morning we stepped off the train in some little backwater town. I was right behind Chester Morris, a wry, plain-spoken fellow who appeared in a lot of fighter-pilot movies, in which someone always seemed to be saying, "Are you going to send that kid up in a crate like that?"

We noticed a group of men, the town dignitaries, lined up along the tracks to meet us. As we walked down this receiving line, I heard Chester say politely to one, "How do you do? I'm Chester Morris."

And the man said, "I'm stiff."

"God, I wish I was," said Chester. But the man's name actually turned out to be Stiff. It was a funny, unintentional bit for an actor, better than some of the material we used at the rallies. This Mr. Stiff was one of those people with a nervous laugh. Later in the day, Chester caught his hand in a car door, and as he swore with pain, Mr. Stiff stood there giggling. They were quite a pair.

Along with the bond tours, many popular radio shows were broadcast from military camps around the country. Once I was a guest of Groucho Marx on his Pabst Blue Ribbon Beer show in San Francisco, where we were to entertain the sailors and marines. During the rehearsal Groucho turned to me and said, "Now, Gene, I think it would be nice if you came out and did a bump."

"A bump?"

"Yes, you know, like a bump and grind."

I said, "I don't think I'm the type."

"You can do it," Groucho assured me. "At least, give it a try."

Well, anything for the boys. I went out and gave a bump and there was absolute, dead silence. No laugh, no reaction, nothing. The audience was as surprised as I was. A Marilyn Monroe could have done a bump and looked adorable. But not me. A bad judgment. I asked Groucho the next day if he wanted the bump again. "No, no," he said, "leave it out." He had decided I was no threat to Gypsy Rose Lee.

Most comics are insecure about their work. I once did a radio show with Milton Berle, and he must have reminded me half a dozen times, "Remember, if there's a laugh, don't step on my laugh."

Finally, I said, "Mr. Berle, I have been in the theater long enough to know about comedy."

He said, "Yeah, but you'll forget." Milton was always in a quandary about his jokes. To Milton, waiting for a laugh to end was like waiting for the final note of "Taps" before breaking ranks. And I did not forget.

In January of 1943 I had a chance to do a costume comedy under the direction of Ernst Lubitsch, called *Heaven Can Wait*, and I gladly accepted. Lubitsch was a little fellow, with straight dark hair combed to one side and a cigar poking out of the corner of his mouth. He had been one of the great European directors and had cast Greta Garbo in the classic *Ninotchka*. He was regarded as the master of urbane and sophisticated comedy.

But he was a tyrant on the set, the most demanding of directors. After one scene, which took from noon until five to get, I was almost in tears from listening to Lubitsch shout at me. The next day I sought him out, looked him in the eye, and said, "Mr. Lubitsch, I'm willing to do my best but I just can't go on working on this picture if you're going to keep shouting at me."

"I'm paid to shout at you," he bellowed.

"Yes," I said, "and I'm paid to take it—but not enough."

After a tense pause, Lubitsch broke out laughing. From then on we got along famously.

Heaven Can Wait was to be my only picture that year. During the filming I discovered I was expecting my first child. I kept the fact to myself for fear the studio would bring in another actress to replace me. Also, your salary was automatically suspended if it became known you were pregnant.

Oleg had come home on furlough from Fort Riley, in Kansas, with babies on his mind. "My mother says you won't be here after the war," he told me, "if we don't have a child. So we are going to have one." Countess Cassini meant, I think, that our marriage would not withstand the separations of war, given the other pressures on us, if we had no other bond. Our marriage had been through some tempestuous moments.

One night, while Oleg was on furlough, and in uniform, we went to a party at the home of Cobina Wright. We were chatting with Gary Cooper and his wife when Oleg wandered into the kitchen. He walked back into the room just as a well-known photographer, overcome with Scotch and feeling playful, tried to kiss me on the neck.

Oleg was in top shape and in a belligerent frame of mind. He spun the photographer around and with one punch sent him reeling into a wall. Rocky Cooper looked at her husband and sniffed, "Well, Gary, you'd never do that for me."

By then someone else had called the military police, and I had to leave hurriedly to get Oleg back home.

My husband was educated in a tradition that said a man was not a man if he could not please a woman. To Oleg, defending a woman's honor—or chasing one—came as a natural instinct. He always contended that I would never have developed an interest in him if he had not been a challenge.

While Oleg was still in the Coast Guard, he attended a party without me. I had a week of early morning studio calls and had disciplined myself to get to sleep early.

So Oleg went off in his sailor suit, and at the party he

met the wife of a French actor, he admitted later. He returned home in the small hours, stumbling drunk, but retaining that last bit of cunning that people have when liquor puts them in domestic peril. He hid his uniform under a couch, but not very well.

The next morning I woke him and asked if he had a nice time at the party. He had trouble opening his eyes and you could tell he was trying hard not to make any sudden movements with his head. He said, "Oh, yes, yes. Very nice."

I said, "I'm leaving for the studio, but I'd like you to meet me later in the day."

"Of course," he said. "Just tell me where."

"At my attorney's office. Here's the address."

At that Oleg sat bolt upright. "What do you mean?" he stammered. "Why? What has happened?"

Silently, I held up his uniform, which I had seen peeking out from under the couch, smeared with lipstick traces. I sensed he had been unfaithful, and I cried. But Oleg turned on his charm and I let him talk me out of my hurt. He was sweet and penitent the rest of his leave, and I gave him the benefit of the doubt.

That episode did not mark the end, or even the beginning of the end, of our married life. But we were falling into that category of people whose needs for each other contain the seeds of a deep hurt.

I had wanted a baby. And I was happy to be carrying mine, thrilled at the idea of starting a family and joining Oleg at Fort Riley.

In March, a week before I was to leave for Kansas, a friend called and reminded me that I had not appeared at the Hollywood Canteen lately to entertain the GIs. I felt guilty about that, and except for spells of feeling tired, I had no reason not to go. I agreed to be there the next night.

There was no reason for me to remember meeting a young lady marine at the Canteen, among the hundreds of people who wandered in and out during the evening. And I would not have remembered, except for the fact that we would meet again many months later, and I would never forget her the rest of my life.

A few days after I appeared at the Hollywood Canteen, I called my doctor. I was covered with red spots on my face. The doctor diagnosed my problem as German measles, something called rubella, and told me reassuringly it would only last a week. He suggested that I postpone my trip for a few days, but otherwise he showed no real concern. Nor did I feel anything except a minor annoyance at the delay in joining my husband. Little was known then about the connection between German measles in early pregnancy and the damage to an unborn child's nervous system.

Soon the spots were gone, and I was at Fort Riley, an army wife, pregnant, joining in the spirit of the people around me. I have often marveled at how the country pulled together during the war. Certainly this was true in an army camp. The women came in droves, often with their children, to put up with discomforts of all kinds. Families accustomed to country club living squeezed into miserable apartments to be near their men.

I met several who were cooking and keeping house who had never before boiled an egg or washed a dish. Everyone seemed to help one another and shared their joys and heartaches. Those of us who had traveled from different parts of the country were treated with kindness by the local Kansans, and marriages were secure in a way that hadn't been possible in civilian life. All of the women I knew went to the same doctor, an aging Irish country medic named O'Donnell, whether it was for their unborn child or a nosebleed.

I had visited Fort Riley once before and knew only too well what the accommodations would be. A small Kansas town had expanded overnight, with hundreds of wives looking for places to live. My first room was in the post guest house, where the walls were made of beaverboard and you could hear everything that went on in the rooms on either side.

In the hall at night, where the only telephone on the floor was located, you could hear the boys calling home. I couldn't help but overhear, and some of their conversations brought tears to my eyes. Some of them were getting ready to ship out for overseas. They knew they might not be talking to their wives or mothers or girl friends again for months or years, or ever.

The voice of a young husband would crack as he asked, "Say hello to the kids for me." And I would have to get up and run the water in the sink to keep from listening.

The building was poorly heated, and in the winter of my first visit I developed a sore throat and cold. During the day, when Oleg was on duty, I refused to trudge through the freezing snow to the commissary for breakfast or lunch. I lived on a package Oleg's mother had sent him filled with cookies, jams, and figs, until I improved.

You were limited in the length of your stay at the guest house, so great was the demand for rooms. After a week you had to look for other housing. Soon the news spread that a "movie actress" was in camp. On my first day, Oleg had left at the crack of dawn, after making a small, embarrassed request. He asked me to do his laundry. He said he kept losing pieces whenever he sent out a load to the base laundry, and now he was down to a bare minimum of shirts, shorts, and socks. I knew he

had been too tired or too forgetful to make out a list,
which was why so many articles were missing. So I went
about the job cheerfully. I was scrubbing away in the
laundry room when a girl looked up from the next basin
and did a double-take.

"Why, you're Gene Tierney, the actress, aren't you?"
she said.

I admitted I was. From then on, wherever I went, even
to take a bath, I had an audience.

For this move to Kansas—my plans were indefinite
until after the baby was born—I had rented a dumpy little
place that I soon discovered was inhabited by mice. I did
not stay there long. I got in the habit of buying my gaso-
line at a station whose owner turned out to be a fan of
mine. One day he told me about a small bungalow for
rent, and I leased it immediately.

I furnished it with as much ingenuity and secondhand
furniture as I could muster. It was really quite attractive
when the decoration was completed. Oleg had been accepted for officer's training, so he was assured of being
at Fort Riley until the end of my pregnancy.

But we had decided that, if possible, I should have the
baby in Washington. Oleg's parents lived there. By now
my mother was working in the Washington department
store and my sister, Pat, was attending school there.

We had to buy our airline tickets with money we had
raised by selling our furnishings.

I didn't have to rack my brain to figure out where our
savings had gone. We were paying for a new house, now
sitting empty, in California. I had lost the money en-
trusted to my father, and spent more in legal costs. For
months now I had been off salary from the studio, and
Oleg was drawing an enlisted man's pay. Our only way
to raise the plane fare had been to auction off the articles
I had collected.

We raised more than enough to pay our way to Washington. But I winced as I watched a friend buy a pair of chairs I had created myself out of old barrels, painting the kegs white and the iron bands red, and covering the seats in red chintz. I would see them through the years in my friend's guest room in New Jersey, flattered that she still had them, but moved by the memories those chairs brought back.

We made our flight to Washington, where on October 15, 1943, our daughter, Daria, was born prematurely. She weighed two and a half pounds. My sister, Pat, had to give her eleven blood transfusions. But she was fair and blond, a beautiful child, I thought, and I was sure she would fill our lives.

CHAPTER

II

Daria

By the time my daughter was a year old, I knew there were troubling signs, but I was uncertain of their seriousness or permanence. Then I read a newspaper article reporting that an epidemic of German measles in Australia had, a year later, produced a generation of defective babies.

I felt a chill as I read on. The story called the epidemic, and its aftermath, "the first hard evidence" of such a link. The virus was believed to be one of the few that the bloodstream will carry to the fetus. The story said that the first month was the most dangerous. I had been exposed in the first month.

I made an appointment with my pediatrician and took the article with me. I had underlined a sentence that said in such cases a loss of hearing would result the first time the baby had a virus or cold. Daria had not seemed to hear well since her first cold.

"Daria has lost her hearing," I said to the doctor. "I'm sure of it. What I need to know is whether this article applies to her condition."

What I really wanted to be told was that she would get well, recover and be a normal child.

Daria had been born with a cataract in the corner of her left eye that could not be removed surgically. She lacked fluid in the inner ear. I told myself these things could be corrected later.

She had, still has, slightly blurred vision in her right eye. Even as a baby, she would hold up her hands, struggling to see them. She had such pretty hands.

The doctor did not encourage me that day. But he tried to be kind, saying her condition in some ways might change. New research was being done. I would not, could not, accept the idea that Daria was retarded or had brain damage. I went through a period of convincing myself that she only had a hearing problem.

One day Howard Hughes called. He had heard that our child was deaf, and he asked if he could bring in his own doctor to examine her. There was not much that went on in Hollywood that Howard did not know, one way or another. Several years had passed since we had dated. I was touched by his gesture, aware that the subject was a sensitive one for a man troubled by his own loss of hearing.

Howard's doctor flew in a specialist from the East, one of the country's top men in the field of children's diseases. My own physician later told me that the man's bill, for one day, came to $15,000, which Hughes quietly paid. But there was nothing those or any other doctors could do. We were advised to place Daria in an institution.

I am not sure that anyone who has never faced such a problem can comprehend the heartache that goes with such a decision.

I resisted giving up Daria. Oleg and I had looked everywhere for help and for any kind of encouragement. We found almost none. Once, I took the child with me to visit Pearl Buck, who had won the Nobel Prize and whose book *The Good Earth* was later a motion picture. Miss Buck—the mother of a retarded daughter—then in her forties, could only offer her sympathy. She said I must come to terms with what had happened; I would find no comfort in self-deception. "These children," she said, "often live to old age. The less of a mind, the less stress one feels, the less sleep they need, the more likely they are to live on."

For years I could not voice the reality of Daria's condition. It was a subject little discussed in those days, and written about not at all. It was another social taboo. In some places, mentally retarded children were still hidden in attics. I often asked God why this had happened to me.

Eventually, I knew I would have to confront these feelings and give up my hope of her recovery. Every doctor Oleg and I consulted, and there were a dozen, gave us the same verdict: Daria was hopelessly retarded. She would need professional care on a permanent basis. She would, they told us, grow to a normal height, but her mind would remain that of a speechless little girl forever.

By the time she was four, I knew we could do nothing else for her. Oleg and I had struggled with her care and loved her so; we had clung as best we could to a sinking marriage. Now we decided to seek a divorce. The added strain of coping with Daria's plight and our own helplessness had exhausted us. The marriage had been weakened by our two jealous natures, and Oleg's frustration at being seen by others, unfairly, as the consort of a movie actress. We both suffered for it.

We sold our house in California, and I returned to the East with my mother, to find a new home for Daria. We settled on the Langhorn School in Pennsylvania. Nothing in my life had so wrenched my heart as did the drive up to the white front doors of the school the day Daria was admitted. The emptiness inside me was like a cave.

She was a sweet little girl, with her golden curls and

soft skin. Physically, she looked like any other little girl turning four.

A few weeks later, my sister and I went back to visit her. Later we drove idly around, enjoying the rolling green countryside, until we realized where we were. My father lived with his second wife in a town nearby, not many miles from Daria's school. We stopped at a store, looked up his address, and decided to drive past.

I don't recall which of us made the suggestion, or why. But sometimes daughters are hopelessly curious about a gone-away father and his new life. We found the house, drove past slowly, but didn't stop. In a large picture window we could see two children, a boy and a girl, both fair-haired, who in a way looked so much like my Daria with those golden curls.

Pat and I drove along in silence. But I thought to myself how cruel it all seemed that someone who left our mother, who had hurt us so, should have healthy children, while mine was retarded.

We had no intention of dropping in on them. I could not have done so, even if we had been expected. The pain was too deep, and now it was all stirred up again.

My father spent the rest of his life as a gentleman farmer on that Pennsylvania estate owned by his second wife. He had four children by her, the oldest a month younger than my brother's oldest child.

Many years later, Butch went to a reunion at Hotchkiss, and a friend mentioned having just met his brother, somewhere in the crowd. Butch was amused. "I have no brother," he said. The fellow stared and said, "Well, he went to school here. Said he was the brother of Howard Tierney."

Then it dawned on Butch. He *did* have a brother,

through his father's *second* family. He had never met the boy, talked to him, or thought about him. By then, Father was already dead and the malice was gone. But Butch was stunned. Can you imagine having a brother and not realizing it, not even in the back of your mind?

As the doctors had warned me, Daria never improved. She has never talked or seen clearly, and has heard few sounds. We have never known the casual joy of sharing a letter or a mother-daughter phone call. But on my visits she is always aware of my presence. She sniffs at my neck and hugs me.

For many years I felt cheated, but I kept it to myself. I had a daughter, and yet I did not. In those days, my friends kept telling me how brave I was. I held my head up and never wept. They were paying me a compliment, they thought, and I thought.

But when my breakdown came, when my illness stripped me of my reserve, I cried all the time. I cried for Daria, and for me, and I cried for hours, until I often didn't know where the tears came from, or what had started them. When I gave up Daria, I was outwardly very strong about what had happened. But, of course, the wound went unattended.

I found myself looking for solace. One day, I happened to be watching a television commercial for a product called White Rain shampoo, which showed a darling little girl with curly blond hair walking under an umbrella. All at once I thought, *That is Daria as she was meant to be.* I realized that there were countless little girls like the one in the television spot, not damaged before birth.

And I made up my mind then not to suffer again over our loss. Ever since, whenever I see a golden-haired moppet of a girl, I say to myself, "Thank God, that child is happy and healthy."

Daria has spent most of her life in three different homes, the latest near Philadelphia, where one of her companions is the retarded daughter of Pearl Buck, now in her fifties. Daria has turned thirty-five. She has the mind of a nineteen-month-old child.

The memory comes back to me now of the day the doctor came for her in the admitting office at the Langhorn School. She looked precious. From the time she was out of the crib, I had dressed her in French clothes, little frocks with initials on them.

I had begun to waver at the last moment. The doctor shook his head and said gently, "Mrs. Cassini, you can't keep this child. You may have another. Why don't you think about that? There is no chance this child will get well."

"Couldn't I keep her around," I asked, "and just love her?"

"No," he said. "That would be unhealthy for you, and hopeless for her."

And so Daria was gone. In the months ahead I became increasingly baby hungry. No one can know how badly I wanted another child. In 1948, Oleg and I reconciled, and a year later Christina, our second daughter, was born fine and healthy.

I don't believe I ever really accepted the finality of Daria's condition until my grandchildren were born. They are adorable, and Tina proved to be such a good little mother that, at last, I was able to tell myself, and to *know*, that life does go on.

Daria's birth had been the beginning of a darkening time for me. I wondered why God had punished me by afflicting my child. I felt guilt I could not explain, and self-pity that I could not throw off. A mental illness may be set in motion by a series of factors, one or all of which awaken the sleeping flaw. This setback was the breeding ground, I now believe, of the emotional problems soon to come. I had been battered by the exposure of my father's weaknesses, but I faced them. Daria's disability exacted a greater cost, the more so when I learned what a vagary of fate had brought it about.

A year after Daria was born, I attended a tennis party on a quiet Sunday afternoon in Los Angeles—at whose home, I no longer remember. A young woman approached me, smiled, and asked if I recognized her. She said she was in the women's branch of the marines and had met me at the Hollywood Canteen.

I shook my head.

Then she said, "Did you happen to catch the German measles after that night?"

I looked at her, too stunned to speak.

"You know," she went on, "I probably shouldn't tell you this. But almost the whole camp was down with German measles. I broke quarantine to come to the Canteen to meet the stars. Everyone told me I shouldn't, but I just had to go." She beamed, then added, "And you were my favorite."

I stood there for a very long minute. There was no point in telling her of the tragedy that had occurred. I turned and walked away very quickly. After that, I didn't care if I was ever again anyone's favorite actress.

I have long since stopped blaming the lady marine, myself, God, or Hitler for what happened to us. But Daria was, of course, a war baby, born in 1943. I suppose it has always been true that, in wartime, the most innocent suffer, too.

Daria was my war effort.

CHAPTER
12

Over There

In the months leading up to World War Two, there was a tendency among many Americans to talk absently about "the trouble in Europe." Nothing that happened an ocean away seemed very threatening. The distant guns were killing strangers.

I could never share those sentiments. I had traveled across Europe at nine, and returned at fifteen to spend two years at a Swiss boarding school. My classmates were from England, Spain, France, Italy, Germany, Egypt, and India; the well-to-do daughters of the world. Most of them and their families, on one side or the other, would find their lives caught like tangled fishing lines in the coming war.

Those years, and those young girls, were special to me, a bar of the music that shaped the woman.

I have always told friends, and believed it myself, that my father sent me to school abroad because he wanted to give me the best possible education. But he also saw it as a means of getting me away from the telephone or, more correctly, away from the boys who kept the telephone

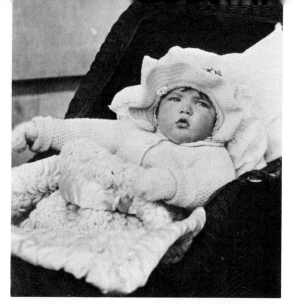

Gene Tierney wasn't the most beautiful baby.

Prettier and daintier at the age of five.

In 1930, at the age of nine.

At age eleven, with sister Pat, age four.

Gene (center) growing up in Fairfield, Connecticut, horse country.

The future star at thirteen.

In costume for an afternoon
tea pageant at age fourteen.

At Brilliantmont School, in
Switzerland, 1937. (Gene is at
left front.)

Gene with mother Belle, sister Pat, and dog Argus.

Gene's father, Howard Tierney,
Sr., as a World War I aviator.

Gene's mother, Belle, in her teens. (This
was mother's favorite photo.)

Gene's brother, Howard, Jr., known as "Butch."

Gene with her daughter Daria, born retarded.

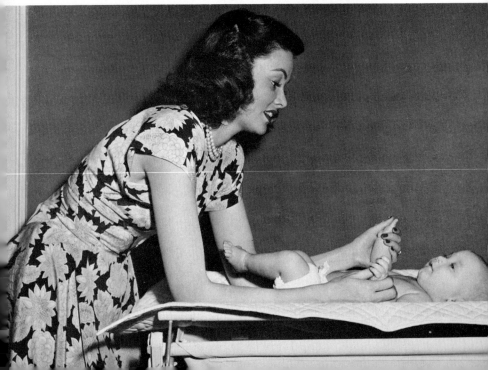

With daughter Tina, age two, at their Beverly Hills home.

With Tina and mother in London.

With husband Oleg Cassini at a Hollywood premiere, 1941.

Howard Hughes, one of Gene's less conventional dates.

With Prince Aly Khan at the races in Epsom Downs.

With W. Howard Lee on their wedding day.

W. Howard Lee.

Gene Tierney today.

Here is Gene in her most celebrated role as Laura, in the film of the same name, with Clifton Webb (as Waldo Lydecker), produced by Otto Preminger for Twentieth Century Fox, 1944.

In the prebikini days of *Leave Her to Heaven*, 1945.

Gene receives a medal for selling war bonds in World War II.

With Rita Hayworth, Stephen Crane (at right), and husband Oleg Cassini.

At lunch with Gary Cooper.

With Henry Fonda in 1962.

With Clark Gable in *Never Let Me Go*, 1953.

With Tyrone Power in *Son of Fury*, 1942.

With Ward Bond in *Tobacco Road*, 1941.

With Humphrey Bogart in *The Left Hand of God*, 1955.

With John Sutton in *Hudson's Bay*, 1941.

With Dana Andrews in *Belle Star*, 1941.

ringing. I was not allowed to date at fifteen, and this re-
striction led to sometimes tearful protests on my part.

Mother was torn between her sympathy for me and
loyalty to my father. One day she mentioned the dispute to
a friend, who was French, with younger children of her
own. The woman threw up her hands. "When my children get to be that age," she said, "I will shoo them right
back to my mother in France, so they cannot be like American children, allowed to run around as they please at
fourteen."

That night my mother repeated the conversation to my
father. "Why, that's a marvelous idea for Gene," he said,
his eyes lighting up. He found a list of European private
schools recommended by *Vogue* magazine, and wrote for
catalogues. He was impressed with one called Brillanmont, in Lausanne, Switzerland. When he had all the
data he needed, we held a family council.

"All right, Gene," he said, "I can afford to send you
over there, but only on these conditions: you have to stay
for two years. You can't come home on holidays, and I
don't know if your mother and I will be able to visit you.
Would you be willing to go on that basis?"

I was being asked to give up my home and family for
two years, not a slight sacrifice for a girl at a sensitive
age. But I answered quickly, without thought: yes, of
course, I would do anything to go. That idea had a special
glamour in the 1930s; to study abroad, to discover another culture and other languages. It was like being appointed, at fifteen, to the diplomatic corps.

That is the way I remember it now. I must have been
homesick, but not enough to take the edge off my first
taste of independence. I learned to trust myself. It was an
unworried, uncomplicated time for me, and my health
was fine.

But the two years, I learned later, were troubling ones

for my parents. By the time I returned, we had lost our home to the bank, and the tension between them was deeper. If I felt any guilt then, I can no longer identify it. Did I feel guilty for not knowing of their distress, or for being away from them and enjoying it? Parents sometimes shield their young from the wrong truths, for the wrong reasons.

I sailed for Europe in the early fall of 1936. My mother had made every arrangement she could think of for my security. She asked a friend, a Mrs. Chumleigh Jones, to keep an eye on me until the boat docked at Le Havre. There I was to be met by a teacher from my school. We would change trains in Paris for Lausanne.

Meanwhile, my Aunt Lelia's husband, Paul Davis, had heard that an actor he knew was to be a passenger. He sent word that his niece would be on board. I was sitting in a deck chair, a day or two out of New York, when the gentleman introduced himself and invited me to tea. Few words were said, and almost none by me, but I enjoyed the stares as I swept into the salon on the arm of the elegant Mr. Douglas Fairbanks, Sr. He was sailing for London to marry Lady Sylvia Ashley. He told me I was very pretty, and I do not think he looked at me as a girl of fifteen.

When the boat docked, the teacher was nowhere to be seen. She had overslept, as it turned out. Mr. Fairbanks offered to share his train compartment with me, as did a Milwaukee dentist and his wife.

All things considered, and as innocent as I thought Mr. Fairbanks's intentions were, I decided I would be better off with the couple from Milwaukee. I had a vision of my parents passing out, if a picture appeared in the papers of their daughter stepping off a boat in the company of Douglas Fairbanks. I don't imagine his fiancée, Lady Ashley, would have been thrilled, either.

Dear Mrs. Jones, my mother's friend, had the ship's radio operator send a wire to our home: "TEACHER NOT HERE. GENE TO EMBASSY WITH COUPLE FROM MILWAUKEE." Mother was more puzzled than panicky, wondering what her child was doing, floating around France with strangers, unable to speak a word of French. The dentist delivered me to the embassy in Paris at about the same time the sleepy teacher appeared to report a missing American girl.

At Brillanmont, I made friendships that were to last a lifetime. Sadly, some of those lifetimes were all too short. The time of Hitler and Mussolini had come. At night we would sit on the floor in our rooms and wage what we thought were grown-up political arguments. Liana Balbo, the niece of a famous Italian aviator, was often at the center of them. Italy had invaded Ethiopia, and some of us seemed to hold her responsible. "We need the land," she shouted back at us, "can't you see?" We tried to form our own opinions and express them, but girls of fifteen or sixteen don't take political upheaval very seriously. We usually ended up laughing.

We would learn soon enough that war flips lives around like soggy laundry in a washing machine. Years later, after the armistice, I began getting letters from my former classmates. Few of the movies that Hollywood made about that period had the drama of the stories their letters told so simply.

Joan Stephens had endured the London blitz, served with the International Red Cross, and after the war was assigned to finding homes for displaced children. Through Joan, I first learned in a personal way of the horrors perpetrated by the Nazis. She wrote of finding children with numbers, like cattle. "Gene," she said, "you can hear all sorts of stories, but this I saw with my own eyes." While traveling with the Red Cross, Joan searched for news of Liana Balbo. Her uncle had died in a plane crash, one possibly arranged, we heard, by Mussolini, who was jealous of General Balbo's popularity and feared him as a potential replacement.

Everywhere Joan inquired in Italy about Liana, she met with silence and evasions. She began to realize that people were shrinking from her, until one day in the office of a lawyer she learned the truth. "I hate to tell you the nightmarish things that happened in my country during the war," he said. "But Liana was murdered by the partisans." She had been at a dinner party when the partisans broke in, rounded up all the guests, dragged them into the street, and shot them in cold blood. A lot of the killing that went on in the late stages of the war was not very selective.

My roommate at Brillanmont had been Sylvia Muir, whose parents were one of England's beautiful couples. Her mother was a stunning blond, her father a partner in Lever Brothers, the makers of Lux toilet soap. I saw him once dressed in a tall gray hat, striped gray trousers and a coat that looked like a cutaway. It is called a morning suit and I was impressed to learn that English gentlemen wore them to their offices.

Sylvia spent the war years at home in London. At the height of the German blitzkrieg a bomb fell so close she was literally knocked out of bed. "It was very inconvenient, really," she said. The British have a way of treating bravery as a necessary but minor chore, such as beating the carpets.

Every time I returned to England through the years, to make a picture, Sylvia was kind and helpful. She rented homes for me, and once hired a governess for my daughter, Tina. I had known Sylvia as a lovely, gay, wistful girl whose attitude toward school was one of indifference. When my own Tina showed no early enthusiasm for schooling, I consoled myself with Sylvia's example. As we struggled over French lessons, Sylvia would often toss her textbook aside and say, "I'm not going to learn this silly language. I'll never use it. I'm going to make my debut and go home and marry the most eligible man in London." And she did. He was wounded in Italy but fortunately recovered.

Sylvia would speak to me in English and I would answer her in French. At Brillanmont, we were on the honor system. One had to do extra assignments if one did not speak French, the required language. Sylvia was willing to do the extra work and I was not. She always admitted her infractions and I admired her honesty. But she had the darnedest workload of homework of anyone in school.

She became a typical English lady, tending her garden, like Mrs. Miniver, living in a lovely home filled with flowers. She died of a stroke in 1975. I will never think of England without her.

Cut off from my own family, holidays, rather than being a lonely and brooding time, gave me a chance to see more of Europe and enlarge the friendships I had begun.

I spent Christmas of 1936 with the family of Dagny Paust in Oslo, Norway. Dagny was a gifted skier, spirited, with a generous nature. She gladly introduced me to a young man she described as "last year's boyfriend." Arne was tall and dark-haired. He spoke only a few words of English and none of French. We practically had to use sign language, but we seemed to understand each other.

Arne, at twenty-four, was still in college. He was very open about his affections, in the Scandinavian way. I was shocked one night when Dagny's boyfriend parked his car and they began kissing in the front seat. Inspired by their example, Arne tried to kiss me. I pushed him away and said, "No, I don't do that." All three of them turned and stared at me.

Arne did not discourage easily. "I save my pennies and come to America," he promised me. The day I left to return to school, he appeared at the railroad depot with an armful of red roses and a book. Haltingly, he said, "I vent to a bookstore and ask for book not for a child." That was his way of saying I was a woman. The book was *After Many a Summer Dies the Swan* by Aldous Huxley, and I was quite flattered. The book was about mistresses and love, written in English. I doubt that he knew what was in it.

As we waited to board the train, Dagny's parents asked, "Gene, aren't you going to let Arne kiss you good-bye?" Another surprise. I could not imagine my mother and father suggesting such a thing. But Arne walked me down to the end of the station and I let him kiss me good-bye.

I hoped he would write, but then came the war, and I never heard from him again.

But Mrs. Paust wrote, telling how the Nazis had invaded Norway. Her husband was thrown in prison, her home commandeered for a German officer. She and Dagny and her son lived in one small room. The Norwegians are a resourceful people. She had learned, through the underground, that the Nazis were taking her husband to have dental work outside the prison. She dressed herself in white, like a nurse, and arranged to be in the dentist's office. When her husband settled into the chair, she leaned over his face and smiled.

In time, Mrs. Paust would win for herself a footnote in the history books. She had a hand in bringing to justice Quisling, the prime minister of Norway, whose name would become synonymous with the word "traitor." On the day Quisling handed over the government to the Nazis, she filmed the entire ceremony, including the scene of Quisling shaking hands and laughing with the Nazis. She hid the reel in a can and buried it in her garden before their home was occupied. At the war-crimes trials, her film was introduced as evidence and helped convict Quisling of collaborating with the enemy.

Dagny's younger brother, Dagfin, was imprisoned by the Gestapo on suspicion of working for the underground to aid the British Royal Air Force. His mother heard they were going to hang him. A trial was held, but the evidence was unclear, and, one way or another, Dagfin won his release, shortly to disappear. In the final weeks of the war, a young boy delivered a message to Mrs. Paust, scribbled on toilet paper. It was from Dagfin. The note said to meet him at the railway station on a certain day. He was coming home to Oslo. She had thought him dead.

By then the Allies had landed in Norway. On the appointed day, Dagfin greeted his family—wearing the uniform of the R.A.F. Mrs. Paust turned pale. Her son had been a spy, after all.

From another of our class, a Danish girl named Mary Louise Bramsen, came yet one more story of escape and exile. She wrote me of the day the Nazis marched into Denmark, when King Gustav defiantly wore a black armband imprinted with the Star of David, as all Danish Jews had been ordered to wear. "If the invaders persecute the Jews," he declared, "they persecute me."

Blond and slender, Mary Louise was the daughter of a Gentile mother and a Jewish father, a banker who had lived in China in his youth and helped bring electricity to that country. Fearful of what might happen if they remained in Denmark, they fled one night to Sweden, the entire family squeezed into a small sailboat for the rough and chilling voyage to safety. I still remember the words of her letter: "You can do anything if you are terrified enough."

One can rarely be certain at what point a young girl

becomes a woman. It was hard for me to imagine my friends facing such trials.

I wrote naive and breathless letters home, marveling at life-styles that were unknown to me. "Mother, dear," the letters always began, and after the usual recital of schoolwork and well-being, the latest gossip would be dropped: "Maria mentioned last night that her mother is dating the Duke of York. They are both married. Isn't it awful?"

Maria was Maria Sieber. Her mother was Marlene Dietrich.

Another letter described the excitement at school over the engagement of one of my classmates to the Maharajah of Jaipur. "Ayesha is waiting for her fiancé to arrive," I reported. "She will be his second wife. He has another at home, but Ayesha says it will be all right because he will love her better than the old one."

At the end of my second school year, in the summer of 1937, I joined my brother and two of his Yale classmates in Paris. They planned to motor across the Continent in a new Ford, with a homemade trailer attached to haul our luggage. On our way to the Italian border we encountered hills so steep we often had to get out and push the car. We visited eight countries, staying at inexpensive pensiones and ferreting out the quaint inns where the food was filling and cheap. Between June and mid-September, I don't believe we missed a museum, cathedral, palace, or battlefield in all of Europe. Including the passage home, our expenses—Butch's and mine— came to eight dollars and forty cents a day.

In Germany we hired a guide named Hugo Naumann, who introduced us to the work of Rubens; he looked like a Rubens painting himself. As young and athletic kids, we were not especially interested in looking at paintings of fat people. But Hugo adored Rubens' art, even located the old master's home and showed it to us. We toured Dresden with him and sat in the church where Bach had played the organ.

Hugo Naumann was an educated man, a professor in the winter months who supported his family as a guide in the summer. He took us to his home in Dresden to meet his wife, and over glasses of beer we talked a little politics. "They are going too far with the Jewish issue," he said. "I like Hitler, he has done good things for the country. But we cannot persecute any race of people."

When we said good-bye, and prepared to leave Dresden, Hugo asked us to write him on our return to America. We did exchange letters with him, up until the day that one came back to me marked "address unknown." Many years later, I picked up an issue of the *Reader's Digest* and found a story with that title—"Address Unknown." And my mind raced back to Dresden, and I wondered if that mild, portly professor was alive or dead.

After the war, I learned from my friends of their experiences, and I ached for what they had lost and suffered and for the wreckage of what had been. Faced with pain, with hate, with despair, little wonder that so often we yearn for the simple pleasures and memories of childhood.

What a different world it was when I first sailed for Europe in 1930 with my mother, sister, and brother to spend six months abroad. The steward on the boat arranged activities for the younger folk. One day he suggested it might be fun to pitch an old champagne bottle overboard with a note inside and see if anyone recovered it.

I was chosen by the group to write the note. Nervous and excited, I simply scrawled: "If found, please return to the Unquowa School, Bridgeport, Conn."

The steward corked the bottle, and one of my friends,

a boy of about eleven named Teddy, tossed it over the side. The message was then forgotten for nearly a year.

Then one day at school during assembly, the principal announced, "We have a letter from France, from a fisherman who says he picked up a bottle at the Bay of Bisque *plage*." The principal cleared his throat. "The fisherman says he picked it up thinking someone had been lost at sea. Would the person to whom this note belongs please step forward?"

I did not budge from my seat. There was a long pause before my brother stood and said, "I'll take care of that, Mr. Churchill." At which point I leaped from my chair, gulped down my shyness, and said, "It's mine. It's me the letter belongs to." So saying, I walked to the stage and fetched the note and the Frenchman's letter. To this day they are framed and hanging in my mother's home.

I suppose life is a little like that, isn't it, a message in a bottle pitched out to sea, to be carried by the winds and the tides, washing up on the beaches we could never imagine.

We cannot calculate the numbers of people who left, fled, or were fished out of Europe just ahead of the Holocaust, people who enriched our science, art, and society. Some of them found their way to Hollywood. One was Otto Preminger, born in Vienna, the son of a man who was once the chief legal counsel to Emperor Franz Josef. Otto was a fine actor in Europe, who went on to become more renowned as a director. He would direct me in the movie that was to be my best-remembered. It was called *Laura*.

CHAPTER
13

Laura

. . . Laura is the face in the misty light,
footsteps that you hear down the hall;
The laugh that floats on a summer night
that you can never quite recall,
And you see Laura on the train
that is passing through.

Those eyes, how familiar they seem.
She gave her very first kiss to you.
That was Laura . . . but she's only a dream.

© *Johnny Mercer**

When you have spent an important part of your life
playing Let's Pretend, it is often easy to see symbolism
where none exists.

The role most often identified with my career was that
of the title character in *Laura.* The part was unusual in

that Laura dominated the story as a presence, felt but unseen, for half the movie. She was the victim of events she had not created and could not control. Laura was a woman of mystery and glamour, unattainable, the kind of woman I admired in the pages of *Vogue* as a young girl.

I have never been easy with explaining things—why this works or that does not. Rehearsals and screening rooms are often unreliable because they can't provide the chemistry, the currents between an audience and what appears on the stage or screen. A great work may stand on its own. But if the chemistry is there, an ordinary story becomes something better. To analyze it further is like trying to explain air.

Laura had the chemistry. I am not being modest when I say that people remember me less for my acting job than as the girl in the portrait, which was the movie's key prop. Then there was the haunting title song by Johnny Mercer, and a tricky plot: Laura, believed to be the victim of a murder, reappears to become a suspect.

Whatever the reasons, through the years the movie became a cult favorite. No salute to Fox is complete without a film clip from it—usually the scene where the detective, Dana Andrews, dozes in a chair and suddenly the girl in the picture appears before him, Laura come to life. I have had people tell me that they set their clocks to get up after midnight in order to catch *Laura* on the late, late show.

I liked the script, but after one reading was unenthused about my role. The time on camera was less than one would like. And who wants to play a painting? The treatment of the story seemed unorthodox. The first half was narrated by the Clifton Webb character, the writer Waldo Lydecker, who is secretly in love with Laura but finally tries to do her in. The second half was told from the viewpoint of the young detective, who falls in love with her portrait. Would the device work? In truth, only Otto Preminger had absolute faith in the project.

I had heard that Jennifer Jones turned down the part before Fox offered it to me. It is possible that I did not mind the part so much as the idea of being second choice. "If Jennifer Jones doesn't want it," I asked Darryl Zanuck, "why should I?"

"The role is right for you, Gene," Zanuck assured me. "You'll be good in it. And, you'll see, this one will help your career."

I had a hunch he might be right, and I always tried to play my hunches. Really, I was in no position to be picky. I had not made a picture in over a year. My husband was still in the army. The extent of our baby daughter's problems was not yet known. I needed to get back to work.

The word "actress" has always seemed less a job description to me than a title. I did not feel I had earned mine yet. *Laura* was to be my first suspense film. Whatever my reservations, I had the title role, a chance to establish myself as a leading lady.

Throughout my career, I was to be cast as a frontier girl, an aristocrat, an Arabian, a Eurasian, a Polynesian, and a Chinese. Producers kept trying to type me as an exotic, slinky creature, the kind who are always leaning against pillars. That wasn't me. Of all the people I have known, I am probably the least mysterious. I had no trouble playing any kind of role. My problems began when I had to be myself.

Starting with the casting of *Laura*, nearly every decision became a contest, but somehow it all worked. The head of the studio, Zanuck, openly disliked his producer, Otto Preminger. In turn, Preminger fired his director, Rouben Mamoulian, and took over the film himself.

Nor was Otto satisfied with the portrait of me done

by Rouben's wife, Azadia, then a popular Hollywood artist. It is one of the curious facts of movie-making that paintings seldom transfer well to film. Otto felt that mine lacked the mystic quality he insisted on having. He sent me instead to pose for Frank Polony, the studio photographer whose pictures of me as a starlet had appeared in so many magazines. Otto had this one enlarged and lightly brushed with paint to create the effect he wanted. So the "portrait" of Laura was, in truth, a blow-up of a photograph.

In a sense, even the title song was a compromise. Preminger had wanted to use Duke Ellington's "Sophisticated Lady" as the theme music. David Raksin, the musical director, had another idea. He came up with the haunting melody that Johnny Mercer blessed with a lyric, and "Laura" became a classic. The song may have been the only part of the movie that did not have the Preminger touch.

Otto had gotten his way with Zanuck in casting two of the major roles: Dana Andrews and Clifton Webb. Both were regarded as gambles. Andrews was unproven as a leading man. Webb had never made a movie, but had spent his career on Broadway and had an image that was, well, prissy.

Webb had just left Noel Coward's *Blithe Spirit*, in which he had appeared for almost a year, virtually quitting the show one night and arriving the next on the set of *Laura*. It was pleasant to observe at close range the professional respect between Clifton and Preminger. The role of the acid-tongued Waldo Lydecker was the most demanding of all, with long stretches of dialogue.

There was a wonderfully brittle edge to Clifton, his manner, his speech, the way he moved. Part of what came across on the screen, the impression of a man very tightly strung, was true in person. After we finished filming, he suffered a nervous breakdown and checked himself into a sanitarium in New England. He came out of it rested and restored, but the main effect of his analysis was to encourage him to treat his mother rudely.

As we prepared to leave his home one afternoon, his mother asked him to help her with her coat. Clifton drew himself up and sniffed, "Fend for yourself."

I scolded him instantly. "Don't blame whatever has gone wrong on your mother," I said. "It's too late for that." I never understood the theory, once popular among doctors, that blamed mental disorders on too little or too much mother love. My own mother was my darling. If we must build cases, certainly one just as strong can be made for the unsettling effect of a father's love suddenly withdrawn or denied.

Laura paid off for everyone connected with it. Clifton Webb's performance won him an Oscar nomination for best supporting actor. The cameraman Otto chose, Joe LaShelle, who had never worked with a first unit before, won the Academy Award for best photography. Joe was determined to make a success of his big opportunity. He would take ages to light a scene. Every time I heard him say, "No, no, it's not right," I could feel my teeth clench, and I knew there went another hour or two of waiting for the lights to be reset.

I was on the set before the sun came up, and tumbled home at eight or nine in the evening. Once Oleg, furious over the eternal delays, walked onto the set and took me by the arm. "Come on," he roared, "it's not worth it. Nothing is worth it. We're going home." And we did.

Oleg knew better. The effort was worthwhile. *Film Daily* chose *Laura* as one of the year's ten best motion pictures. What a tasty moment it was for Preminger, who drove himself, and us, so hard! He was simply tireless. When the rest of the cast seemed ready to drop from exhaustion, Otto would still muster as much vigor as when the day began.

I never felt my own performance was much more than adequate. I am pleased that audiences still identify me with Laura, as opposed to not being identified at all. Their tributes, I believe, are for the *character*—the dream-like Laura—rather than any gifts I brought to the role. I do not mean to sound modest. I doubt that any of us connected with the movie thought it had a chance of becoming a kind of mystery classic, or enduring beyond its generation.

It defied any of the usual Hollywood success formulas. The picture started out with a "B"—due in part to a feud between Zanuck and Preminger. We were a mixture of second choices—me, Clifton, Dana, the song, the portrait. If it worked, it was because the ingredients turned out to be right. Otto held us together, pushed and lifted what might have been a good movie into one that became something special.

Preminger looked the part of a fencing instructor at a Prussian military academy. With his perfectly bald, egg-shaped dome and basset-hound eyes, he could charm and intimidate you at the same time. I should add that I was never around Otto when he was not a gentleman. Unlike certain other directors of that period, he had no insecurity and did not feel obligated to attempt the seduction of his leading ladies.

I never understood the friction between Otto and Darryl Zanuck, although one can assume that two such hefty egos, out of different cultures, would not coexist sweetly. Zanuck was like most of the studio bosses of his day: tough, creative, charming when he had the time, a crude but polished man. He was always fair, often generous, to me.

The war was going our way in 1945, when I co-starred

with John Hodiak and William Bendix in *A Bell for Adano*, based on John Hersey's prize-winning novel. On occasion a fragment of the real war, not the mock one we were filming, would break through the daily chatter. The director was Henry King, one of the gentlest of people. One day on the set he was unmerciful in his criticism of some of the actors. His rudeness was so out of character that I looked at him in disbelief and, I am sure, in disapproval.

Later he called me aside. "You think I've been a brute, don't you?" he asked.

"No," I said uncomfortably, "but you can't speak to people that way. It isn't civilized."

I noticed now his face was flushed. He dropped his voice and said, "I'm sorry I've been so tough today. But I've just learned that my son is missing in action."

Henry's son, an air force pilot, had failed to return from a combat mission. Eventually he was reported to be a prisoner of war and, thank heaven, returned home after the armistice. For Henry King, the war—like so many Hollywood movies—had a happy ending.

Not many weeks later, I was at a cocktail party one evening in Romanoff's when Zanuck told me he was thinking of giving me the part of Ellen in *Leave Her to Heaven*. I had read the novel by Ben Ames Williams, coveted the part, and knew Fox had bought the film rights. The role was a plum, the kind of character Bette Davis might have played, that of a bitchy woman. I don't think I have such a nature, but few actresses can resist playing bitchy women.

I quickly told Zanuck that he would never regret it if he gave me the part. In a few days he called back and said simply, "You're Ellen."

The director was John Stahl, who had started out in the early days of the silent movies. He was an elderly

gentleman by the time I met him, but he still had a reputation for bringing out the best in an actress. I soon realized why. He showed such confidence in me that I
blossomed under his approval.

He could be a taskmaster, too. One Saturday night,
just before quitting time, he suggested we run through
the scene we were to shoot on Monday morning. He
wanted the cameraman to see how the scene would play
so he could work out the lighting of the set. This was a
crucial moment in the picture—Ellen, an insanely jealous wife, drowns her husband's kid brother rather than
risk sharing her husband's affections.

I was anxious for Stahl to see me play the scene and
find out if my interpretation was on the mark. After I
had finished my lines there was a hush. Then suddenly
Stahl groaned. "That was perfect, just the way it should
be done. But, oh, God, you will never get it again, never
in a million years."

I walked over to his chair and said calmly, "Of course,
I will. I've been rehearsing it that way all along. I can
do it again. I promise you."

Ignoring me, he rose and called out, "Quitting time."
He left the set, mumbling, "You will never get it that
way again. Never!"

The rest of the weekend I was a wreck, worrying about
Monday morning. But to Stahl's surprise, I recreated the
scene exactly the way I had rehearsed it.

Cornel Wilde was my leading man, fresh from his success as Chopin in *A Song to Remember.* One scene took
place in the library, where I was to propose to him. Stahl
instructed me: "Most men seduce the woman. You're going to seduce this man. I want you to be like a serpent."

The scene was difficult for Cornel, who was meant to
be weak and couldn't quite bring it off. At the end of
each take, and there were several, the gaffers on the crew

would whistle at me. Ordinarily I wouldn't find a whistle flattering, but in this case it meant approval.

Impatiently, Stahl waved his hand at the crew and turned to Wilde. "*They* all seem to understand how the scene should be played," he demanded, "why can't you?"

Leave Her to Heaven was not an easy film to make. The really good ones seldom are. We went on location to Arizona and to Bass Lake in northern California, and there were long, anxious drives each morning, along roads that seemed to have a precipice at every corner. At one point I had to swim in an icy mountain lake in November, and was pulled out and given nips of whiskey between shots to keep my circulation going.

On location, I enjoyed the company of a lovely young actress in one of her first roles, Jeanne Crain. She played my younger sister and did a fine job.

John Stahl died in 1950, with a long string of superb films behind him, among them *Only Yesterday*, which introduced Margaret Sullavan to the screen, and *The Keys of the Kingdom*, which made a star of Gregory Peck. I am grateful to John for allowing me to play Ellen as I understood her.

As much as any part I played, Ellen had meaning for me as a woman. She was jealous in a sad and destructive way. Jealousy is, I think, the worst of all faults because it makes a victim of both parties. Although treated subtly in the book, and the movie, Ellen was without a doubt insane. She believed herself to be normal and worked at convincing her friends she was. Most emotionally disturbed people go through such a stage, the equivalent of an alcoholic hiding the bottle.

That performance brought my only nomination for an Academy Award. Oleg was beside me, and also beside himself, as we waited in the audience that night through the endless jokes and introductions and acceptance speeches. "You're going to get it," he kept saying, "you're going to get it." I really didn't think so. And when I heard the audience applaud the film clip of Joan Crawford as Mildred Pierce, I knew. Joan Crawford won the Oscar for the best actress of that year.

My own disappointment was lessened by the conviction, new to me, that I had developed a difficult character and not just a pretty face on the screen. I had been challenged by the role, and to have been nominated for an Oscar was excitement enough. *Leave Her to Heaven* became a box office hit. I cherished a call from the producer, David Selznick, and his wife, Jennifer Jones. After seeing the picture at a private screening, they phoned to say how impressed they were with my portrayal of Ellen. Hollywood compliments are not always worth much, but I admired them both and theirs pleased me.

Yet I suppose the most sincere compliment of all came from a gentle black lady who cooked for friends of mine in Cape Cod. When I went to visit their home, they asked in some embarrassment if I would speak to the cook. "She has seen your new film," the wife said, "and when she heard you were coming she threatened to leave."

I went to the kitchen and said hello. We chatted and, after a few minutes, the cook smiled and said, "Oh, ma'am. You sure were mean in that picture. Now that I've seen you, you are real nice."

All during this period, my career was thriving, but my private life was not.

CHAPTER
14

A Stranger on the Set

I remember the movie *Dragonwyck* for a reason unrelated to anything that appeared on film. We had a visitor to the set one day while I was doing a scene with Walter Huston, who played my father.

In a proper doomsday voice, Walter was reading a passage from the Bible when the director, Joseph Mankiewicz, called out: "Gene! Turn slowly and look into the camera."

I turned and found myself staring into what I thought were the most perfect blue eyes I had ever seen on a man. He was standing near the camera, wearing a navy lieutenant's uniform. He smiled at me. My reaction was right out of a ladies' romance novel. Literally, my heart skipped.

Obviously, I could not return his smile. I had work to do. But when the scene was over, I stepped forward to meet the man whose blue eyes had engaged mine, and whose name turned out to be Jack Kennedy. I no longer remember who introduced us, but he said Jack had just returned from the South Pacific. He was with a friend, Ken O'Donnell, who later married the actress Phyllis

Brooks. A coy thought flashed through my mind: I was
glad I had worn a lavender gown for my scene that day.
Lavender was one of my best colors.

That night I wrote a long letter to my sister. I told Pat
I wanted her to meet this strikingly handsome young man
from Boston. She wrote back and asked, "Who is meant
to fall for him, you or me?"

By the time I received her answer, I had seen Jack
Kennedy again at a party given by Sonja Henie. Although I had a date, Jack came alone, and he kept cutting
in on us. Finally he said, "It's a madhouse in here. Let's
go in the other room and dance. It's quieter."

Dance floors do not lend themselves to earnest conversation. But we talked over the music and around it. At
one point he said, "I could dance like this the rest of my
life." The words did not sound trite at all. I decided right
then it would be very easy to fall in love with him. I was
half annoyed with myself, as little as we knew one another, but the thought stayed.

Jack was tall and still thin from the months he spent
in navy hospitals. He had the kind of bantering, unforced
Irish charm that women so often find fatal. He asked
questions about my work, the kind that revealed how
well he already knew the subject. His father had once invested in the movies, he told me. He did not mention, but
I learned later, that his father had an eye for the actresses
of his time, among them Marion Davies and Gloria
Swanson.

We had dinner together, and then another, and Jack
had to leave. We made plans to see each other again in
the East. I finished *Dragonwyck*, a forgettable picture,
but not for me and not for Joe Mankiewicz. It was his
first credit as a director. When Ernst Lubitsch suffered
a mild heart attack just before the shooting began, he
asked Joe, who had written the screenplay, to replace

him. Lubitsch was later seized with the insecurity most of us feel when faced with the prospect that one's replacement might actually succeed.

Watching on the set one day, he turned to me and said, "What have I done? How could I give our picture to this novice? He knows nothing."

It was true that Joe was then unschooled about camera movements. But he was a willing and brilliant man, not embarrassed to ask the cameramen for advice. They responded to his openness. I told Lubitsch I thought his film was in good hands.

Joe Mankiewicz would go on to direct other, better-known movies, including *A Letter to Three Wives*, *All About Eve*, and *Cleopatra*. A nephew, Frank, became a journalist, got involved in politics, and served as Robert Kennedy's press secretary in the campaign of 1968. On the night Bobby Kennedy died in Los Angeles, Frank Mankiewicz read the last medical bulletin to the reporters, and to the country.

John Kennedy came into my life at a good-bad time in that spring of 1946. I was separated from my husband, and though I had not yet filed for divorce, both believed our marriage to be ended. I was nearing the decision to place Daria, my retarded child, in an institution. Jack understood. He told me about his sister Rosemary, who had been born retarded, and how his family had loved and protected her. The subject was awkward for him. The Kennedys did not survive by dwelling on their imperfections. "Gene," he said, after a silence had passed between us, "in any large family you can always find something wrong with somebody."

A few weeks later we had a date for lunch in New York. Jack was now out of the navy and running for Congress. He flew down from Boston, where he had taken part in a St. Patrick's Day parade. He called for me at my mother's apartment, still flushed with the day's excitement. Of course, we Irish don't really need thousands of people surging behind a big brass band to have a parade. One guitar player and a few people whistling will do the job.

In such a mood, we bounded into the street, and he asked, "What shall we do first?"

"I guess a cocktail is in order," I said.

"An inspired idea," he replied.

I suppose we looked like any other young couple having a reunion celebrating a few months late the end of a war that had gone on too long and cost too much. Jack hailed a taxi and quickly noted the driver's name on his cab license. "So you're a Kelly," he declared. "Would you be kind enough to take a Kennedy and a Tierney to the Monte Carlo Club in New Jersey? I know it's against the rules to drive out of New York, but we're hoping you'll risk it. How's your sense of adventure, Kelly?"

The cabbie laughed and said, "Well, now, I can't resist that."

Jack was wearing a new gray felt hat. He lost it, left it behind in the bar, and I don't believe I ever saw him wearing a hat again, not even in a photograph. Early in his presidency, I remember reading that the hatmakers of America protested that he was setting a poor example for the country.

Jack was partial to French restaurants. One night, at the Versailles, in New York, we listened to Edith Piaf sing the love songs that made her famous. One was called *Longtemps*, a line of which I can still quote from memory: "A long, long time after the poets have disappeared, their songs will live in the streets."

Known as the Sparrow, Edith Piaf was a tiny, delicate woman in a simple black dress, with a dozen violins behind her. She sang her heart out, and yours. She was then the mistress of a boxer named Marcel Cerdan, who a few years later died in a plane crash, flying to America to fight for the championship.

I don't recall how many dates Jack and I had, not many, before I told my family and a few friends that I had met a young man who would be President someday. That was his goal. He talked about it in a way that was unselfconscious, as another might talk about going to work in his father's store.

He told me how, after his return from the Pacific, he had sat for hours on a park bench in San Francisco and thought about his dead brother, Joe. His father wanted him to go into politics, as Joe had been expected to do. Joe had been the Kennedy family choice to become the first Irish-Catholic President. He was killed on a secret bombing mission to Germany.

"It wasn't what I had in mind, what I started out to do," Jack said. "But I had a commitment to Joe. And to my father."

In college, he said, he had visions of being a writer. His Harvard thesis had been published as a book, *Why England Slept*. He later edited one about Joe, to which each family member contributed a reminiscence. And he wrote another, called *Profiles in Courage*, while he recovered from surgery for the back injury he suffered when his PT boat had been rammed and sunk.

He was twenty-nine when he ran for Congress under the slogan "A new generation offers a leader." The 11th district elected him by a margin of 78,000 votes.

I could see the drive he had, the sense of power acquired from being steeped early in Boston Irish politics. On occasion, when we visited my mother at her home in Greens Farms, Jack would have with him one of his ward heelers, hearty, rumpled men who left cigar stubs in her ashtrays. Mother fed Jack milk and cookies in the kitchen, but she could not mask her distaste for his companions and didn't try. Once she asked Pat, "Why can't he get a better class of people around him?" Pat laughed and said, "Mother, he's a politician. He's not on a polo team."

I was tense, uncertain how they would react, the first time I took Jack home to meet my family. Butch had heard rumors we might be getting serious, and he did not receive the news gladly. He had done his graduate work at Harvard when Jack was a student there, knew him slightly, and didn't like him or his politics. We were New England Republicans with a natural suspicion of rich Democrats who take up with the poor.

I got out of the car first and dashed ahead to the house, hoping to disarm any resistance. Patiently, Jack stretched out on the thick grassy lawn, hands clasped behind his head, face turned to the sun. He was perfectly content.

My brother would not even let me in the front door. He did not feel, he made clear, that there was any future in my dating a Catholic (the Tierneys were Episcopalian). "Any girl who is going through a divorce," he lectured me, "and has a retarded child, has no business looking to have her heart broken any more. I don't admire you or him for getting mixed up with each other."

With that he headed for his car to go play golf. As he walked past, Jack—still sprawled on the lawn—raised up on one elbow and said, "Hello, Butch."

"Hello, Jack."

Nothing else was said. I was on the verge of tears. But my mother had been observing John Kennedy from her bedroom window. As Butch drove off, she opened the porch door and, motioning with her arm, called out: "Fsst. Young man. I'll let you into my half of the house." Slowly, smiling, Jack got up and together we walked in through the back door.

Jack was single and eligible and not yet a national

figure. Still, we tried to keep our romance out of the gossip columns, and for the most part we succeeded. I visited him once in Washington and sat quietly in the guest balcony while Congress was in session. A reporter spotted me and asked what I was doing there. Thinking quickly, I said that I was studying the government. "Oh, some kind of movie project?" he asked. I nodded. "Something like that."

At that moment Jack picked me out from the floor of the House, waved, and ruined my story. I just didn't think that dating an actress, at that point, would be very good for his career.

I am not sure I can explain the nature of Jack's charm, but he took life just as it came. He didn't try to hide. He never worried about making an impression. He made you feel very secure. I don't remember seeing him angry. He was good with people in a way that went beyond politics, thoughtful in more than a material way. Gifts and flowers were not his style. He gave you his time, his interest. He knew the strength of the phrase, "What do *you* think?"

A few months after I met Jack, I told Oleg it was time I filed the divorce papers, a step we had kept postponing. I was badly shaken by my parents' divorce and for a long while believed that any compromise was better. But by then, ours was less a marriage than an entanglement.

Oleg knew the Kennedys. He liked Jack and did not distrust his intentions. But he worried about what was ahead of me. "Don't you understand?" he said. "Jack can't marry you. No Catholic is going to marry a divorced woman. His family won't stand for it. Gene, be sure you know what you are doing."

Just as Jack Kennedy was a ladies' man, in the nicer sense of the word, so was Oleg Cassini. Many years later, he would tell an interviewer: "I was guilty of many breaches of our marital vows. Mostly, I believe in retrospect, because she was the big star and I was the nothing guy. I had to get even with the world because I was not recognized. There was a recurring, negative pattern. I would get drunk. I would get into frequent fistfights."

When I began to see more of Jack Kennedy, Oleg immediately found comfort with a blond starlet who was getting the full Hollywood treatment. He began to be seen everywhere with her. Even though I believed we no longer had a life together, I was disturbed by his interest in this young girl.

I have no memory of a party where Oleg says we quarreled over her, and I tried to scratch his face. He caught my hands, held me off, and said: "What is this? Are you kidding me? Listen, you're the one who left. How can you demand an accounting of my nights?"

And I blurted out, according to Oleg, "But she's not right for you!"

Those minutes are among the blank spaces, rubbed out or forced out, I don't know. I do not like to see anger expressed physically, and I like it less when I am the one doing it. Oleg and I once threw a few spoons at each other in a scene that was almost comic. Once, in a mental hospital, I would attempt to hurt one of my doctors, but the impulse frightened me more than her, and I regretted it immediately. I considered it a weakness to show temper, and I always tried to control mine, probably at a cost to myself.

Oleg sometimes accused me of being suspicious, insecure, and jealous. Most women are, at one time or another. Falling in love is a lark. Falling out of love is hard, and letting go is harder.

I have always known that I do not handle confusion well. I was tugged now in many ways; still trying to sort out my feelings about Oleg, drawn to Jack Kennedy and he to me, he said. But we were both unsure of where that road would lead. And, finally, as if another distraction was needed, some of my Hollywood friends thought Tyrone Power would be a nice husband for me.

By late 1946, we were filming *The Razor's Edge*. Ty was divorced from the lovely Annabella, and Oleg and I had gone through our public quarreling stage. Ty and I became great friends. Everyone on the set thought he had a crush on me and was rooting for us. I have no doubt that the studio tried to promote a newspaper romance out of our closeness.

There was something about *The Razor's Edge*, the attractiveness of the people in the cast, that inspired good faith. They were a cast of polished professionals: Clifton Webb, Herbert Marshall, Anne Baxter, John Payne, Elsa Lanchester, as well as Ty Power and me. Oleg designed the costumes. He was as ready for the divorce as I was, and neither of us felt uncomfortable.

The film was a homecoming for Power, his first starring role since his return from the marine air corps. Even my family tried to nudge me into his arms. My father read about us in the papers and wrote to encourage me. "Seems like such a nice boy," he said. I did not answer the letter.

The romance was only happening on the screen. I don't recall a set where there was more cheerfulness, much of it provided by our very British director, Edmund Goulding. When he wanted to describe to you how a particular scene should be played, he would step in front of the camera and say, "May I be you?" Then he would promptly act out the entire scene.

Goulding had a butler, with him for years, who practically lived on the set and was almost his double. He dressed in a navy blazer and gray slacks, the same as Goulding, and imitated his speech, or tried to. Goulding

told hilarious stories about his boyhood, working in his
father's London butcher shop. "But, really," he said, "I
always preferred the 'swells.' " His mother often visited
the set and would overhear him weaving a tale of his im-
poverished youth. "Why, Edmund," she would reproach
him, "how can you say that! Why, you had a French
governess at the time." We never knew which to believe
but had a good time guessing.

Ty had an impish streak of his own. For a nightclub
scene, he persuaded the prop man to fill our glasses with
champagne, instead of the usual plain or colored water
used in such scenes. After a few takes, we felt quite gay
and relaxed. This was the silent sequence, with music
over it, showing us doing the town in Paris. We had little
if any dialogue, while Russian gypsies played enchanting music. The scene had a special glow that came out of
our champagne glasses.

Ty and I lunched together often during the filming.
One day, when I was not in the scene to be shot and not
scheduled to work, Ty sent a note to my home: "There
is no sunshine on the set today."

On November 19,1946, there was a party in New York
to celebrate Clifton Webb's birthday, and mine, which
coincided with the opening at the Roxy Theater of *The
Razor's Edge*. In those days a New York premiere was
as close to heaven as an actor could expect to get, and a
great boost to the pictures selected for such treatment. It
was part of the era of tumult and searchlights and huge
crowds, an era long gone.

This was to be the first great postwar splash of Holly-
wood-made razzle-dazzle. Twentieth Century-Fox put us
up in the largest suites in the Barclay Hotel. Thousands
swarmed outside the theater on Seventh Avenue, near
50th Street, with police ropes holding back the crowds. As
they stirred it was like the undulation of the ocean.

I wore a black tulle evening dress and a white ermine jacket, and Van Cleef and Arpels draped me in loaned diamonds. A necklace I wore was bought the next day by a man who wanted it for his wife. The store thanked me for fostering the sale by sending over a gold and sapphire charm.

The guest list for the premiere included sixty delegates from the United Nations, an array of New York socialites, the Duke and Duchess of Windsor, Clare Boothe Luce, Frank Sinatra, opera's Lily Pons and her husband, the conductor André Kostelanetz. As we scurried out of our studio Cadillacs in front of the Roxy, the crowd broke through the ropes and stampeded to get near their idol, Tyrone Power.

We were all jostled in the commotion and I felt a moment of panic. Then, behind me, I heard a voice ring out. It was my mother. "Now, look here," she said clearly, to no one in particular, "this is ridiculous. I will die for a cause but not for a movie premiere."

Somehow we wedged our way into the theater. When the lights came up after the screening, we knew we had a hit. It was a festive group that gathered in the Terrace Room at the Plaza Hotel to celebrate my and Clifton's birthdays. Ty asked if he could stop by my suite after the party. He said he had a small gift for me.

My mother and sister discreetly ducked into the bedroom when Ty arrived. He did not stay long. After a few minutes, I said, "You know, Ty, I'm going up to the Cape tomorrow to visit a friend of my mother's. While I'm there, I hope to see Jack Kennedy."

There was an awkward silence. I opened my hands, palms up, and said, "That's the gist of it."

He nodded. "Have a nice time," he said. And he left, not angrily but quietly. The gift was a pretty silk scarf with the word "Love" embroidered on it. I was flattered by the thought. I kept the scarf for years but never wore it. I finally gave it to Pat.

Ty was warm and considerate. He had a beautiful face. But I could not fall in love with Ty Power, having met Jack Kennedy.

I did stay with my mother's friends at Cape Cod, Hal Wright and his wife. Jack met me at the station, wearing patched blue jeans. I thought he looked like Tom Sawyer.

It was a good week—swimming and sailing, walks on the beach in the moonlight, the pleasure of each other. I met some of Jack's family and later told Pat I thought they were divine. Their loyalty impressed me. The brothers and sisters were attractive and self-assured. They had goals, and they turned out to be working and contributing members of society. Given their wealth, they could have been dilettantes or beachcombers.

We continued to see each other, though we were often separated by most of the country. It was for Jack that I wore for the first time one of the ankle-length, New Look dresses of 1947, made famous by Dior. By then I had taken an apartment in New York with Pat, planning to live there when I wasn't in California making pictures. When I walked out to the car, Jack stared at the length of my dress and blurted, "Good God, Gene, what is that?"

I laughed and said, "Jack, you better get used to it. It's the New Look. You're going to see a lot of them. This is just one of the first."

He was still making a face as the car swung into traffic. "Do you think," he said, "that if someone told me to wear tails in the daytime because it was fashionable, I would?"

I said, "Maybe not, but women do." He just shook his head. He later married a very stylish lady, but I believe it is fair to say that clothes were not his weakness.

We were having lunch one day in New York. Just before we were joined by some of his friends, he looked at me and said, out of the blue, "You know, Gene, I can never marry you." In the chatter, the exchange of greetings as his friends settled into the other seats, I said nothing.

Then it was time for Jack to catch his flight back to Washington. As he moved away from the table, I sat still, and in a voice just above a whisper I said, "Bye, bye, Jack."

He stopped, walked back across the room, and said, his smile a little off center, "What do you mean? That sounds kind of final."

"It is."

We looked at each other for a long, timeless moment. Then he turned and left to catch his plane.

A few years later, I was having dinner in Paris, at Maxim's, with Michele Morgan and her husband. Jack was there, at another table. He was still a bachelor, preparing to run for the Senate. I had put those years and thousands of miles between us, then looked up to find us twenty feet apart. He asked me to dance. As we did, he said, "Isn't it time we started to see each other again?"

I said, no, not for me. I was too crazy about him to risk renewing something that could only end by hurting us both. Less than six months later, I read of his marriage to Jacqueline Lee Bouvier, a bride I felt sure his parents approved of.

From the beginning I should have known our situation was hopeless. I have never talked with reporters about Jack, and until now had never written about us. Only he knew how serious his feelings were. But, obviously, when a man tells a woman he can't marry her, if he feels compelled to say so, then the subject must have been on his mind.

I saw Jack one other time before he became President. In 1956 I had been through my first breakdown and was between hospital stays. An older man, Doc Holden, a New York society figure, a friend of Serge Obolensky and nearly everyone else, invited me to dinner at El Morocco. We ran into Jack. My excitement must have showed when Jack asked me to dance. When we left, Doc looked at me closely and said, "Gene, you're really on air."

The next day Jack dropped by my mother's apartment to see me. He had heard the stories about my illness and cared enough that he wanted to see for himself how I was. At the time I was doing very well.

Mother walked into the living room and sat herself down as we talked. She whispered into my ear, "Gene, I'm going to stay here. He's a married man."

I said, "You don't have to, Mother. It's all right."

"No, it isn't," she said. "I'm not going to leave you alone with a married man, especially when you're both well known."

Finally, Jack smiled and suggested we go for a walk. Outside, under the street lights, we talked about my illness. I told him I had begun to realize that I was one of those people who cannot handle problems and disappointments by trying to work harder.

I asked him about his family. He said Bobby had six or seven kids (on his way to eleven), and I gasped, "My God, what is he trying to do, populate the world?" Jack laughed. "No, only Massachusetts."

When I returned to the apartment, my mother wanted to know what he said. I said, "He asked me, 'Does your mother always sit in the room when you have a friend call on you?' That was the first thing he said."

"And what did you say?"

"I told him, 'Yes, she's terrible.'" And I gave her a quick kiss on the cheek.

In the 1970s, two magazine articles appeared nationally that were embarrassing to me. One said that Jack Kennedy had fallen in love with me but broke off the relationship at the urging of his father, who felt my being a divorcée would impede his political career. The other story claimed his mother had come between us, and quoted me as referring to her as "Rose." In fact, I had met her only once and had never referred to her, in public or in private, as anything but Mrs. Kennedy. We were introduced at a March of Dimes benefit ball in New York, when I was still the wife of Oleg Cassini. The senior Kennedy remarked that night to Oleg on how graceful he thought I was. He said he wished he could hire me to teach his daughters how to walk.

No one really broke up our relationship, not Jack's father nor his mother nor my family. I did not date him again because I knew the consequences would not be happy ones. In truth, ours was a sweet but short-lived romance. When I met him he was a serious young man with a dream. He was not a womanizer, not as I understand the term.

When I would hear someone repeat a piece of gossip about Jack, or read of some lady's confession in the newspapers, I thought of my Grandfather Taylor. I remember being told that he was a staunch defender of President Harding. "They are persecuting him," he would say to my grandmother, "because he has a mistress. And maybe he's an unhappy man." He would wait for her to agree with him. Whether she did or not, he would add, "I don't believe a man's morals have anything to do with his statesmanship."

In the years after we met, and since his death, I have thought often about the charming navy lieutenant who went on to become our youngest President. I wore my heart on my sleeve for a long time. But what digging I do now in the past is an effort to explain my life, not his.

In 1960, when John F. Kennedy was elected to the White House, I sent him a telegram that said, simply: "CONGRATULATIONS. I KNEW YOU WOULD MAKE IT." On the other hand, I had voted for Richard Nixon, a decision governed not by my heart or by the character of the men, but by the conservative influence of my upbringing.

I was to see Jack once more. In 1962 the movie *Advise and Consent*, in which I had a part, premiered in Washington. My new husband, Howard Lee, and I were invited with Otto Preminger and some of the cast to lunch at the White House. I sat next to the President. There was a softness in his eyes when he asked how I had been.

I said, "I'm a very lucky woman, Jack." I glanced at Howard, sitting opposite us. "I have a husband who loves me even when I'm crazy."

Jack laughed, and I think we both then felt comfortable.

Some women feel the best cure for a broken heart is a new beau. In my case, nothing worked out until I met W. Howard Lee, of Texas. At lunch in the White House, looking across the table at my husband, I felt a surge of love. I knew that after many years, I was finally over my feelings about Jack Kennedy.

When he was assassinated in November of 1963, I grieved for his family, and for the country, and for the might-have-been love in all of us.

CHAPTER 15

Divorce, American Style

Unlike the stage, I never found it helpful to be good in a bad picture. Still, I once heard that a Fox executive had said to Darryl Zanuck, "Gene must be a better actress than some people think. How else could she survive so many awful pictures?"

For years it never occurred to me to question the judgment of those in charge at the studio. I sometimes wanted roles I didn't get, or showed not enough interest in some I might have had. But I only refused one script and was suspended for it, about a week. I turned down *Walls of Jericho* because I just could not fathom the character of the girl I was to play. Anne Baxter replaced me.

The word went out at Fox that I was being considered for the lead in *Forever Amber*, based on the sexiest book of that time. Superstardom and riches were forecast for the actress who won the part. I disliked what I heard of the script and thought the story was trash. Oleg urged me to go after the role. I wouldn't. Linda Darnell played Amber.

Perhaps I should have been less anxious to avoid a fight, and refused more scripts than I did. But I was not cut out to be a rebel. Those instincts that made me vulnerable in private served me well in my work. The studio bosses liked the fact that I was not difficult. The public perceived me, I think, as a nice person and held me blameless.

Even indifferent pictures can be useful. They are the way a screen actor tells time and measures distance. They become a kind of calendar and road map.

The Ghost and Mrs. Muir was the movie I made before I went back to Oleg Cassini, limping slightly on a broken foot.

Near the end of 1947, I found myself at a friend's house, bounding up the stairs two at a time, barefoot, hurrying to see her new baby. The friend was Fran Stark, Fanny Brice's daughter, and she thought I was acting when I pulled myself to the top of the steps, grimacing with pain.

"Oh, get up, Gene," she said. "You're all right."

"I can't walk on it," I protested.

"Don't be a sissy," she said. "Stand up and come see the baby."

On the way home, still hurting, I stopped at my doctor's office. He X-rayed the foot and said it was broken. I felt almost jubilant as I called Fran to tell her I wasn't a sissy, after all.

The mishap caused a slight delay in the filming of *The Ghost and Mrs. Muir*, in which I played opposite Rex Harrison. The cast included the gentle young Natalie Wood, then playing little girl parts. I saw no sign of Rex Harrison's famous temper. He was always studying his lines, concentrating.

I had planned to leave at the end of the picture for New York. The director, Joe Mankiewicz, knew I was anxious to get away. He said I could leave as soon as I was able to shoot my last scene. I went to my doctor and, over his objection, insisted that he remove my cast two weeks early. The foot had not completely mended and kept me in pain. But I did the scene and took off for New York.

There Oleg began to court me again. He had started his own company and was on the rise as a couturier. Success agreed with him. He was a calmer, more mellow person.

We had turned to each other instinctively. It was, I think, an acceptance of life by both of us; an admission that things had not gone well apart.

We had ridden out our marriage on a seesaw. But at the end Oleg had been gallant. When one reporter went fishing for an unflattering remark about me, Oleg replied: "Gene is the greatest girl in the world."

The reporter said, "If she's the greatest girl in the world, why are you getting a divorce?"

"You'll have to ask her," he said. "Maybe I'm not worthy of the greatest girl in the world."

I had received an interlocutory decree, but in California a year had to elapse for a divorce to become final. In February of 1948, my attorney, Charles Millikan, called and said he was preparing the papers and I could pick them up on March 10. I told him to wait a little. He laughed and said that sounded like good news. I said maybe it was.

We thought we could patch up our differences. At bottom, they all came down to the fact that I was a movie actress with a large income and Oleg needed his own identity. Now he had one.

Everything else had been a symptom. His fighting, drinking, wandering. My walking around the house at night, studying my lines. I had lived too much with my work and not enough with my husband.

In some ways I knew I would never change him and I told myself I would no longer try. I didn't want him to change. I would be the organized one. I knew he would never have the key to the front door when we returned home after an evening out, so I would have it. I knew he would never know the address when we started out for a party, so I would call ahead.

So we reconciled. A new beginning. Not an ideal one. Oleg needed to be near his business. I would join him in New York after each picture. My absences had been one of our most basic problems. Now we faced separations of up to six weeks. Commuter marriages are hard on the mind, and everywhere else, but we had to give it a chance to work.

I returned to California to begin shooting on *That Wonderful Urge*, with Tyrone Power again as my costar. When we went on location to Sun Valley, Oleg flew out for a few days. The title must have been catching. Another visitor to the set was Linda Christian. Ty was in love with her, they were crazy about each other, and I was happy for him.

During the picture, I realized I was expecting my second child. As soon as I was free, I rushed back to New York. Oleg was designing the costumes for a new Mike Todd musical, and that summer we were often with Mike and Joan Blondell, his wife at the time.

We lived on the top floor of an old brownstone Oleg and his brother Igor had bought. I am not sure why we had no air conditioning, but possibly the shape of the windows and the age of the wiring discouraged us. As a result, we seldom missed a chance to go out to a restaurant or a nightclub, postponing as late as possible our return to those sweltering rooms. In those years, many clubs had signs on the sidewalk advertising not their food or entertainment but "REFRIGERATED AIR."

Then November rolled around, and on my birthday,

the nineteenth, our daughter Christina was born. I was fascinated by her perfection and alertness. She tossed her head back and forth in her cradle from the minute we brought her home from the hospital. I watched and studied her with joy. I knew at last that we had a healthy child.

Not long after the birth of Tina, the studio notified me I was to play Anna Gouzenko in *The Iron Curtain*, a Cold War story about a Russian defector.

There were bitter currents winding through Hollywood in 1948, many of which, I am sad to say, I did not fully understand until years later. The screenplay for *Whirlpool*, in which I played a kleptomaniac, was written by Ben Hecht, but under another name. He had been blacklisted in the industry purge of those suspected of having Communist sympathies. During that period, producers were able to hire talented screenwriters, working under assumed names, at a fraction of their former fees. Ten years would pass before Otto Preminger defied the major studios and broke the blacklist by giving Dalton Trumbo credit for the screenplay of *Exodus*.

I found myself in a new and puzzling phase of my Hollywood years. Oleg and I were trying very hard to rebuild our marriage. He had missed the press and buyer showings in New York that spring to be with me on the set of *Whirlpool*. When I rejoined him in the East, the movie columnists criticized me for not living in California, as if I were somehow being unpatriotic. One wrote that I was "biting the hand that fed me." When I did not go east, there were rumors and raised eyebrows.

I devoted myself to working as often as I could, saving as much as I was able. I was driven by a desperate need to provide for Daria. My goal was to insure an annuity that would yield enough money to cover the care for Daria as long as she lived.

Ma Joad had a line in *The Grapes of Wrath* that

stayed with me: "In a woman it [life] is all in one flow like a stream." Not mine. My life was like drive traffic, all stop and go. I was working, traveling, and trying to be a wife and mother.

Tina went with me in 1950 to London, where I made *Night and the City*, with Richard Widmark. Oleg flew over and we had a little free time together. We went to Paris for my first visit since the war, and he helped me pick out some lovely creations at Piguet that stayed in style for years.

Tina was then about six months old and her nurse traveled with us. England had not yet recovered from the war and many items were still rationed. My English roommate from boarding school, Sylvia Hambro, came to our rescue, bringing us fresh eggs from her house in the country. And the Widmarks supplied us with cases of canned milk they had brought along from the States.

London is a city of gentle memories for me. Whenever I had an afternoon open I went to a different racecourse— in England horse racing really *is* the sport of kings— usually with the Widmarks. It was in London that I tasted my first martini. Everywhere the cast was invited, the host all but met us at the door with a tray of martinis, under the impression that no one in our country drank anything else. (American movies did that.) Not wanting to appear rude I accepted one and soon learned to enjoy a cocktail before dinner.

Whatever problems I have had, drinking was never one of them. I would not allow it. You have to look good before the camera, and liquor shows in a woman's face. Hollywood has turned out some famous drinkers, but I would guess that there is more drinking per square foot in the social life of Bridgeport, Connecticut, or Houston, Texas.

It was in London that I met Noel Coward, whose plays

I had read, and about whom I first heard years before from my Aunt Lelia. She so admired his wit and brilliance, she said, that he was the only man she ever met who terrified her. I could not imagine one so clever as she was holding anyone else in such awe. You can imagine my apprehension when Clifton Webb invited me to dinner, with Noel Coward and Marlene Dietrich.

At school in Switzerland, Miss Dietrich's daughter, Maria Sieber, had proudly shown us a collection of photographs of her mother. Most of them were in costume as Catherine of Russia. Her father paid a visit to the school one day and took Maria and me to lunch. I thought him rather elegant. I had never seen a man with pointed fingernails before.

For Miss Dietrich, I dressed in my very best. For Noel Coward, I decided that if my Aunt Lelia had been intimidated, my only bet was to say very little. I was excited and nervous when Clifton arrived for me at the Dorchester. The glamorous other couple would be waiting for us at the fashionable restaurant.

I was introduced to Miss Dietrich, who was nearly fifty then and had never looked more stunning. When I turned to meet the formidable Noel Coward, he caught me off guard with one of the most flattering remarks ever addressed to me. "I want to tell you, Miss Tierney, you gave me one of the most memorable evenings I ever had in the theater in your film *Leave Her to Heaven*. When I saw the expression on your face in the sequence in which you drowned the boy, I thought, 'That is acting.'"

The unexpected compliment stunned and pleased me. I could not help thinking, this, from one of England's great playwrights and actors. Aunt Lelia, if you could only see me now. The dinner passed for me in a kind of mellow haze.

I finished *Night and the City*, but not without my usual

argument with the makeup man. I had stopped wearing makeup for my roles five years earlier, starting with *A Bell for Adano*. Ingrid Bergman was the only other actress, at the time, who refused to use any. After my first pictures, my brother said to me, "I don't understand why you look so much better to the eye than you do on the screen." After he saw *A Bell for Adano*, all he said was, "You're looking better." For an actress not to need makeup was unheard of in England, and I had to argue my way out of it.

Oleg made his acting debut in *Where the Sidewalk Ends*, in which I played a Seventh Avenue fashion model. A touch of déjà vu. I had worked for John Powers in my late teens, supporting myself between Broadway jobs. Oleg not only did the clothes, he let Otto Preminger persuade him to appear briefly as a dress designer. When he saw the rushes, Oleg slumped down in his seat and moaned, "As an actor I am a good designer."

In one scene I wore a gown described by a movie magazine as the year's "most risqué." Made of American Beauty red velvet, it was off the shoulder and figure-hugging. Preminger called it a "dangerous" dress. The danger came when I tried to walk in it. I managed about six steps and made it safely through the scene. The gown went back to the wardrobe department. Where would I have worn it?

The picture was my fourth with Dana Andrews, then at the beginning of his own serious personal problem. At five o'clock one morning there was a pounding at our door. Oleg was startled to find Dana standing there, unshaven and weaving. I was just waking up, adjusting my robe, when I heard Oleg say, "Dana what are you doing here? It's time for Gene to be getting up to go to the studio."

"I thought we might have breakfast together," he said, his voice thick.

We invited him to stay. Obviously, Dana had not been to bed. He needed to sober up and had turned to us as friends. He was drinking hard and would need years to give it up. I admire him for doing so, as I admire anyone who rids himself of an addiction.

There were not many storybook careers in Hollywood. But an exception was John Lund, with whom I worked on *The Mating Season*, on loan to Paramount in early 1951. John had been a writer for radio in New York, married to a charming girl who was under contract to RKO. They kept testing her for parts that never materialized. Finally, she went to the head of the studio and said, "Look, you have the wrong member of the family. The one you ought to test is my husband." They did. The studio sent for John, gave him a screen test, and signed him to a contract. His wife happily retired to her sewing machine.

She made all of her own clothes, an economy that I am sure John appreciated. She arrived at a cast party one day in a taxi, explaining, "We're saving our money and John won't let me buy a car." Lund was another who refused to be seduced by the trappings of Hollywood.

John Lund, Richard Widmark, and William Wellman were the three actors and directors I admired the most as men in those years. Wellman, the least known of the three, was a flying ace during World War I and had a metal plate in his head. He was attractive in a quiet, virile way. There were certainly men more colorful than these, but they made me more comfortable than anyone else with whom I worked. All were happily married, and I liked their wives. The pick of the crop is taken very quickly in Hollywood.

My mother also found John Lund's looks appealing. She visited the set one day and shook her head. "It's the darnedest business I've ever seen," she said, when I had finished. "Lie in a handsome man's arms all day and then leave to go to your husband."

The career of Richard Widmark, begun in 1947, is still going strong, but his first picture produced his most famous scene. In *Kiss of Death* he pushed Mildred Natwick, an invalid in a wheelchair, down a flight of stairs, as he laughed fiendishly. The laugh was not in the script.

"I was nervous as hell," Dick would explain. "When I didn't know what to do, I laughed. Just so happens I have a weird laugh."

Oleg and I made plans to vacation in Europe that summer with his brother, Igor, and his second wife, Darrah. It was to be a family trip, with Tina and her nurse coming along. The rest of us went ahead and Oleg was to join us in Paris. It was June, the height of the season, a romantic time to see Paris. After two weeks, Oleg called from New York to say he couldn't get away after all. With his encouragement I stayed on, traveling with Igor and Darrah, a tall, exquisite blonde.

My marriage had begun to fall apart again. Our separations were getting more frequent and less painful.

I came home from Europe to make *On the Riviera*, with Danny Kaye, over Oleg's objection. He could not see me doing that comedy. But I was in one of my team-player moods, and I did not care to get into a contract fight. I always felt expendable. Was that one of my frailties? I only know that I never had so high an opinion of myself that I thought I could not be replaced.

At home, too, I felt expendable. At one point, still clinging to the idea that our marriage would work if I could only find the right formula, I convinced Oleg to move to Connecticut. I was going back to my roots. Oleg would commute to New York on the New Haven Railroad. I really wanted that suburban housewife's dream, but I didn't discover it until years later, long after Oleg was gone from my life.

We moved into a house not far from Pat and her husband, Elliott Reid. The first day I drove Oleg to the train, I swung by Pat's house at eight in the morning, wearing a mink coat over my nightgown. I looked at her and said, "*Now* what do I do?"

Pat laughed and said, "Now you go back and clean your house, do your dishes, and get dinner ready."

An hour later I called her back. "I just looked through the cookbook and found a recipe that takes six hours."

Pat said, "Gene, that doesn't mean you have to sit around for six hours and watch it."

I was looking for tasks that would take up most of the day, a bad sign. The country living experiment did not work out for either of us. We moved back to the city.

I finished two other pictures in 1951. The best thing about *The Secret of Convict Lake* was joining Ethel Barrymore for a cup of tea in the afternoon in her trailer. As she poured the tea into lovely china cups, she confided, "I've never been able to drink anything but mild stimulants."

Unlike her brother John, Miss Barrymore had overcome a bout with the bottle, or so I heard. I never questioned her. It was just very pleasant to sit and drink tea out of those delicate cups with this grand old lady, who had given so much to the theater.

As Midge Sheridan in *Close to My Heart*, I had my best role in half a dozen years, the story of a woman who adopts a baby. The part was one that touched the chords of my own experience. I can understand the hunger to have a baby.

I do not mean to overstate or be cloying about the mother instinct, but it was the one certainty left in my life. My marriage was dissolving for a second, and final, time. The idea of commuting between New York and Hollywood no longer made sense to either of us. Oleg had a business to build. I had a career to pursue. My moods were not helped by photographs of my husband in the company of slinky models.

Oleg had great pride. Being the consort to an actress was never a role that he could enjoy. So he constantly tested himself in many ways, including the wild, sometimes crazy fights. There was one on a New Year's Eve with the rich and spoiled Jimmie Costello, my sister Pat's date. And another at the Enchanted Lilac Ball, in New York, when a stranger tried to dance with me. And a time when two drunks in a jeep kept bumping our car, and Oleg leaped out and flattened them both.

The incident that probably best reflected the have-and-have-not nature of our marriage was his near-fight with Howard Hughes. During one of my separations from Oleg, Howard briefly reentered the picture. His efforts to obtain medical help for Daria had endeared him to me.

Oleg was waiting in the garage one Monday night— he had been to the fights at the Sports Arena—when Howard dropped me off after a dinner date. Oleg popped out of the shadows and ran toward the car, shouting, "What are you doing here, Howard? I'm going to beat the [bleep] out of you."

Hughes ducked back into his Pontiac and slammed the door and sped off. As I stood there, open-mouthed, Oleg ran to his car and roared out of the driveway, tires screaming. They raced through Wilshire Boulevard, running red lights, until Howard reached a townhouse he owned in the middle of Beverly Hills. Oleg tried to follow him into the elevator but the guards stopped him.

A month later, Oleg ran into Howard at a party given by Jack Benny. As Oleg related the story later, he walked up to him and said evenly, "I want to talk to you, Howard. Let's step outside."

"Look, I don't want any problem with you." Howard tried to wave him away.

"It's not a question of your wanting to or not. We're having problems," Oleg said. "But let's put the cards on the table. In deference to Gene, I will tell you this. If you intend to marry her, I will be willing to step aside because I am sure you can offer her more than I, at least in wealth and power. However, I want you to put in writing that you are going to marry her, and that you are going to settle on her the amount of money she should have to live as Mrs. Howard Hughes. In that event, I will contain my desire to break your jaw. I will also be happy for her, if that is what she wants."

"I'm from Texas," Howard said. "My word is good enough."

"I know you," said Oleg. "You are a Texas b————s————er." And he walked away.

I did not date Howard Hughes again, and, to my knowledge, he and Oleg managed to avoid each other.

Oleg wanted to protect me, even when I was not always eager to be protected. In turn I was a little too much of a romantic, he thought, too inclined to take for granted the clichés of society.

CHAPTER
16

The Playboy Prince

Argentina was the place, and *Way of a Gaucho* the movie, when I became aware, dimly, that something had gone wrong inside my head.

My personal life was in disarray. Oleg had been given a plane ticket by the studio to join me in Buenos Aires. He never used it. I was desperately unhappy the entire time the cast was on location, and frequently sick. When I returned to Hollywood I filed again for divorce. The marriage was over.

The picture was the first starring part for a handsome young actor named Rory Calhoun. But for me the days passed in a haze.

Not all of it was mental. I had caught cold and was on the verge of pneumonia when I got there. The movie company had taken over a hotel in the pampas, where the peasants assembled in the summer to work under the Peronista regime. I had to report there immediately, miles from nowhere, the sun a living flame and the wind always blowing. I was too ill to work the first week and had to have shots every few hours from the company doctor.

For the first time in my memory, I was snappish and rude on the set. I was impatient with the hairdresser, critical of the director, annoyed by the chatter of the crew. I kept complaining to anyone who would listen that nobody liked me. At first, they kept insisting that, yes, everyone did. I kept saying, no, I'm very disliked. After a while some of them gave up the effort.

Eccentric behavior is not routinely noticed around a movie set. It was the fashion in my time, still is, to feel that all actors and actresses are neurotic or they would not be actors and actresses. Many who said this actually believed it. Some were, and a few even knew what the term meant.

I only knew that I felt like an emotional misfit, and Argentina was not a good place to get one out of a depression. Juan Perón was at the height of his power. The cast was shown much of what his dictatorship had accomplished in the way of public housing and orphanages during tours arranged by the minister of propaganda. We were also invited, ordered, to be at the government mansion at seven o'clock one morning to be received by the Peróns. Evita was not well enough to see us and the visit was canceled, no disappointment to me. I had not recovered from what had now settled into a bad case of bronchitis and was spending whatever time I could in bed.

When I felt strong enough to attend a few parties, I met people who had been treated to other forms of Perón's hospitality—his prisons. They had been political prisoners jailed for the crime of disagreeing with the regime. They were mostly of the moneyed classes who felt that Perón was exploiting the poor and was a menace to the country's few remaining democratic reforms.

You could find no one who openly criticized Perón, out of fear of being reported to the secret police. The atmosphere was grim and the situation a touchy one for the cast. Twentieth Century-Fox was using up frozen assets of theirs to make the picture, with the consent of the government. We were asked not to be discourteous, whatever our opinions might be.

Wherever we went, people treated us warmly. I had never seen such ardent fans in my life as those in Argentina. My hairdresser arrived at my hotel room between four thirty and five in the morning, and we would raise the shades to let in light. Even at that hour there would be fans outside my windows, trying to look in.

We filmed there for three months, and I had brought Tina and her nurse with me. I left them at the hotel, where they could be comfortable, when the cast traveled out to new locations. We would be on the road for weeks at a time, using the rugged terrain of the Argentina countryside. But by Christmas we were back in Buenos Aires.

I was invited to spend the holiday with Henry Alberti and his wife. I had met them in California when Henry appeared with the Argentine polo team. I found myself at an elegant estate outside Buenos Aires called Tortugas, overlooking a country club. It was summer in Argentina and the Midnight Mass on Christmas Eve was celebrated outdoors in a candlelight service. Although the weather created a slight time warp, I listened to the carols and was moved.

One night the Albertis gave a party, and among the guests were two of the renowned playboys of the world —Porfirio Rubirosa and Prince Aly Khan. I was distinctly unimpressed by either of them, but less with Aly Khan. I was aware of his reputation—he had been married to Rita Hayworth and had a long list of conquests. In my mind I labeled him a man of trivia. Nor was I taken with his looks. He had a soft face and looked, I thought, like a thinner version of Orson Welles.

My moods swung unevenly, a symptom (I know now) of manic depression. When the mental balance is delicate, a cold or virus can tip you over. The reaction is most likely to hit when you are weak or over-tired or the body is undergoing a chemical change. Medicines were not available then to control one's moods. No matter. I wasn't even sure I had something that needed treating.

When my mood was high, I seemed normal, even buoyant. I felt smarter. I had secrets. I saw things no one else could see. I could see evil in a toothbrush. I could see God in a light bulb.

I threw myself into my work, thinking that whatever was happening to me could be cured by keeping busy. Argentina and Aly Khan were soon out of my thoughts as I returned to Hollywood to start my next picture. I was loaned to MGM to appear in *Plymouth Adventure*, as a pilgrim's wife who falls in love with the ship's captain, Spencer Tracy. The movie opened as the Thanksgiving feature at the Radio City Music Hall in 1952.

In one respect acting is like tennis. When you play with someone who is better than you are, your own game is more likely to improve. I would have loved doing a more interesting part with Tracy, the finest film actor of my time.

Part of the movie was shot in London, where we rented an apartment in Grosvenor Square. Above the square was the Connaught Hotel, where Katharine Hepburn stayed and waited for Tracy.

My mother thought he was the most tormented man she had ever met. They had lengthy conversations about religion. She had returned to her Christian Science beliefs and could talk about them in an almost mystical way. Tracy was a Roman Catholic, married but long untrue to his wife, and in love with Miss Hepburn for many years.

A few times he asked me to lunch or dinner. He was relieved that my mother came along. These dates were perfectly respectable, but Tracy kept watching the door in case Katharine Hepburn walked in.

Our director, Clarence Brown, was producing another picture in England, *Never Let Me Go*. I accepted the role of the Russian ballerina, opposite Clark Gable, Tracy's friend and drinking buddy. Gable knew that Tracy was a much superior actor, but he was fond of saying that in all the movies they made together Spencer never once tried to steal a scene from him.

My part was physically demanding. To prepare myself I had to endure six weeks of ballet lessons, two hours a day, just to master enough technique to get on my toes and do the few steps that would be required of me. The Russian ballerina Natalie Leslie doubled for me in the long shots.

I was thirty-two then, not an ideal age to be taking up so strenuous an activity as ballet. I took lessons from one of the great dance masters, Anton Dolin, and became a patron, if not a graduate. To this day I love the ballet.

I had my travel squad along: my mother, Tina, and her nurse. Mother had been working in publicity in the Fox offices in New York, a job I helped arrange but one she did with a natural flair. Tina was now four, old enough to be amused by how I earned a living. Whenever she came to the set, Clarence Brown would lift Tina onto his shoulders and say, "Now let's watch Mommy dance."

My feet were soon badly blistered and ached constantly. Gable was patient and considerate. One weekend he flew to Paris and came back with a salve he assured me would relieve the pain in my feet. The ointment helped.

Gable was lonely and vulnerable, still looking for a replacement for Carole Lombard. One day my mother said to me, "Gene, you can have that man if you set your mind to it." She did not understand that at the time I was unable to set my mind to anything, much less Clark Gable.

He invited me to dinner one night and spent most of the evening telling me how much he still loved and missed Lombard, his third wife, killed in a plane crash during the war. He had gone to the scene of the wreckage and stood there for hours. He remembered how, after a quarrel, she had bribed a bellhop to sneak a pair of doves into his hotel room while he slept. Years later, hundreds of doves, descendants of the first two, filled the pens in Gable's backyard.

For all his he-man, no-undershirt screen image, I saw him as sweet and gentle, a hard crust with a soft center. I thought that quality was what came across on the screen and made him adored by so many. I had no romantic interest in Gable. I considered him an older man, and I may have been put off by my mother's eagerness.

I was still subject to abrupt personality changes. One day as Gable, my mother, and I walked into the hotel dining room for lunch, the band began to play the theme song from *Laura*. Mother whispered, "Gene, smile. Recognize the band. They're playing the song from your picture."

Looking straight ahead, my face cold, I said, "They are only making fun of me."

Gable took up with one of the bit players, and later married Kay Spreckels.

I was offered a part in his next picture, *Mogambo*, but declined, knowing the problems of taking a small child to Africa and unwilling to be away from her for six months. The part made a star out of Grace Kelly, who was then dating my ex-husband, over the opposition of *her* parents.

Losing a part was never a very grave matter to me. I was competitive, but mostly within myself. I didn't worry about others. I only wanted to be better than I had been. I didn't resent the role that could have been mine going to Grace Kelly. I thought Ava Gardner stole the movie. Not because she is more beautiful. She can act.

For tax reasons, I was thinking of extending my stay in Europe. We had rented a house in the country, near London, with the fetching name of "Under the Heavens." As we drove up the driveway for the first time, stacks of freshly mown hay lined either side of it. Then the house came into view, a rambling, white stucco cottage, with a spotted Shetland pony grazing in a fenced enclosure.

If the place seemed too good to be true, it was. A week after we moved in, the sheriff notified us that our landlord was in bankruptcy and we had to vacate immediately. I was at the studio when the officers came and carted off all the contents of the house. My resourceful mother found us a lovely apartment facing Hyde Park, and we quickly regrouped.

After London, we moved on to Paris to join my California friends Fran and Ray Stark. Aly Khan was entertaining them and they had found him enchanting. I smiled when Fran said, "The Prince is dying to meet you."

I told her I had been introduced to him in Argentina and had been getting that same message wherever I went. I could not check into a hotel without finding flowers waiting in my room, with his card.

Finally, I agreed to join them for an evening at the theater. I really accepted as a favor to the Starks. Troubled, unwell, and not knowing why, I thought to myself, "That's all I need, some Oriental super-stud."

My first impressions are easily changed, my prejudices quickly swept away. That night, sitting next to Aly

Khan, I remembered a dinner party in New York when his name came up in the conversation. I repeated my judgment that he looked like "a slimmer Orson Welles. I can't understand why so many people seem to find him fascinating."

Tony Pulitzer, of the publishing family, said indignantly, "Well, Gene, he *is* fascinating, so you might as well make up your mind that it's a fact."

Tony was almost angry with me. I was struck then, and still am, by the tendency among certain men to admire a member of their ranks when they hear he is a great lover. They defend him like a hero who has gone to the moon. They get downright fraternal about it. When I met Aly Khan again, I remembered what Tony had said.

I have a way of seeing only the nicest parts of people, and Aly was very kind. I think he knew I was struggling through a difficult time. He was another of those rare men who do not force themselves on you, who hold back and let you make a judgment.

Aly Khan was trained from birth to be cultured and charming. He was the son of the world's then richest monarch, the Aga Khan, spiritual leader to millions of Moslems. Aly was a playboy with twinges of conscience. He demanded his independence but sought his father's approval. For a time he would become Pakistan's ambassador to the United States.

He received a personal income from his father of around half a million dollars. He owned racing stables in France and Ireland and had investments all over the world. He was physically brave, a skilled horseman, fluent in six languages, with a refined manner and voice. He *was* fascinating.

My sister Pat later thought that Aly was a symptom of the illness soon to come. She meant that he was not the kind of man I would have picked out if I had been well and secure. Pat and her late husband, Elliott Reid, known as Sonny, visited me on a trip to Europe and I introduced them to Aly. He barely came up to Sonny's shoulder, but Sonny told Pat: "I can see how women fall for him." Pat was not persuaded. She felt that Aly Khan saw women as trophies.

Meanwhile, I was still fighting myself. I felt dull and spiritless, and I told my mother I thought I needed to see a psychiatrist. The idea offended her. "Nonsense," she said. "All you need is an attractive beau and some pretty new French dresses."

I took her advice with a passion. Fran Stark and I shopped and giggled our way through expensive afternoons at Balmain, Balenciaga, and Givenchy. The four of us, Ray, Fran, Aly, and I, went everywhere together: to the races at Longchamps, to dance at the Elephant Blanc and Jimmy's, then the most popular nightspots in Paris. We lunched at the best restaurants and went to Maxim's for the gala evenings.

After the Starks left for America, Aly and I continued to see each other and became inseparable. And soon it was time for Tina to return home for her summer visit with Oleg. I discovered that the new Swiss governess I had hired for her had no visa, and only a few days remained to obtain one.

I was scrambling back and forth to the American embassy in Paris when a telegram arrived from Sir Douglas and Lady Fairbanks. I was invited to fly to London to attend a dinner party at their home honoring Elizabeth, the future Queen of England. It grieved me to say no, but I didn't feel I could leave until the papers were in order.

Even so, I don't believe I was as disappointed as my

mother, who bemoaned my lost opportunity. For years, she would tell anyone, "That girl turned down an invitation to have dinner with the Queen of England. Can you believe it?"

The mademoiselle's visa did clear, and Tina sailed for a month on Long Island with her father.

I traveled across Europe that summer with Aly Khan. We swam together, sailed together, danced and laughed together. I was his hostess at receptions. His parties were the beginning of the jet set. It was easy to be dazzled at first by that role, greeting his rich and important and sometimes royal friends. I leased a house in southern France, close by Aly's Château l'Horizon.

The months flew by. I did not make another picture in 1953. The producer Paul Graetz flew to Paris from London to offer me the lead in a film to be called *Monsieur Ripois*. I had no interest. "I'm happy as I am," I told him. He turned to Aly, who shrugged and said, "What Gene does with her movie career is none of my concern."

I was in love, or thought so, which may or may not be the same thing. Anyone who gets divorced, no matter how inevitable it was, goes through a period of wondering if they will ever be able to care so much again—or have that much to give anybody else. Aly Khan, I believed then, was my answer.

The warnings of my friends, even of Oleg, had little effect. He was no longer my husband, but Oleg was still my friend. I called him from Europe, sometimes to talk about Tina, sometimes just to talk. I told him about my feelings for Aly.

He was impatient with me. "Look," he said, "you are going to your doom. You are not going to transform this sybaritic Oriental prince into a good Connecticut Yankee." He was loyal and did not want to see me hurt.

The first to caution me was Elsa Maxwell. When she

learned I was dating Aly Khan, she told me, Cassandra-like: *"Prenez garde, mon enfant.* Don't take him seriously. Only I can afford to love him. I'm seventy and he cannot hurt me."

I listened to Elsa politely. It would hardly have been possible to do otherwise. She was a remarkable woman, a plump and tireless product of Keokuk, Iowa, who became the ring mistress of what was then called café society. No one kept secrets from her. No one refused an invitation to her parties. She was among the first to refer to the "chemistry" of men and women. By that she meant: "I want a woman guest to be beautiful. Second, I want her to be beautifully dressed. Third, I demand animation and vivacity. Brains are always awkward at a gay and festive party. Brains are only a requisite when the party is limited to a handful of persons, say six or eight. And, fifth, I expect obedience. It is ruinous if guests refuse to cooperate with a hostess.

"Above all things, a man should be good-looking. Then he should boast a tailor who is an artist. Third, he must not be overly married. This is a matter of attitude. Fourth, men guests must not only dance well but be willing to dance. Finally, all men should have manners. I'd rather they didn't throw bottles out of the window."

To borrow a Jewish word, Elsa was the last of the great *yentas.* She had a wonderfully original mind. Most of all, she understood people. She worried about me in private, and in public, and in print. No one ever wrote a truer line about me than when she wrote of my romances with Jack Kennedy and Aly Khan: "Gene always leads with her heart."

I did not make another picture until the spring of 1954, when I returned to London to do *Personal Affair* for United Artists. Aly had family business to attend to in India, but he telephoned from New Delhi and wherever his travels led him. He flew to London to be with me when the picture was nearing completion.

My qualms about my mental condition were getting harder to ignore. I had engaged a maid in London named Ruby to help care for Tina, but it was I who needed her attention. Ruby had worked for me on other such visits and loved to help me rehearse my lines. One day I just broke down and looked at her with fear and resignation. I could not remember the words. My mind was a wilderness.

"Ruby," I said, "I can't do it. I have to give up. Something is wrong with me."

No one who has never acted can understand how devastating it is to have the lines elude you. This is the essence of acting, giving power and meaning to the words on the page. I had listened with sympathy to stories of how poor Marilyn Monroe stumbled through a script. But I could not imagine it. I had never had such a problem since the day I first resolved to follow the example of my costar "One-Take Fonda."

People might question the depth of my talent. But I *knew* my lines. The director could depend on it. Now the words wouldn't come. How does one compare the feeling of standing on a stage, or in front of a camera, and your mouth won't work? I suppose it is similar to a concert pianist who can't find the right keys, or a pitcher who stands poised on the mound and can't get the ball to leave his hand.

I sent for a psychiatrist who had treated Vivien Leigh. He was of no comfort whatever. I told him, "I just can't carry on."

He studied me and said, "Tell me what you think the problem is."

"I'm involved with a certain man and I am not happy about it."

He nodded. We talked a few more minutes, just "passing time" talk, and he simply wished me luck and left. He offered no suggestion. He didn't seem to think I had a problem. Had the doctor taken my complaint lightly, or had I deceived him? As an actress, I was trained to show emotions I did not feel, or no emotion at all. My concern must have struck the casual visitor as "temperament." But I sensed that my control was slipping away, and I feared what the future might bring.

I would never have gotten through *Personal Affair* had it not been for the loyalty of my Cockney maid, Ruby. She had that traditional British resistance to admitting defeat, even someone else's. When I told her I could no longer absorb the script and would have to quit, she scolded me. "Never mind, Miz Tierney," she said. "You are going to do it. We will go over these lines until you know them in your sleep."

When the filming started I never missed a cue. Ruby simply would not allow me to fail.

Many years later, a doctor would tell me that had I led a more tranquil life my weakness—his word—would never have surfaced. What one inherits is a tendency, not a disease. The life of an actress is hardly tranquil, certainly not one compounded by the rejection of one's father, a broken marriage, and a retarded child. And what instinct led me to become involved with two men, Jack Kennedy and Aly Khan, whose needs would not meet mine? Some people enjoy making the best of a bad situation. Was I now creating bad situations so I could make the best of them?

The doctor also warned me, "Gene, you will never find the man of your dreams at El Morocco." I thought I had.

When the picture was finished, I returned to France

with Aly. Outwardly I was happy. At one point I kept him out of nightclubs for three months, surely a record for him. I wasn't trying to reform him. I simply grew bored with all the parties, the late hours, the chitchat with people you really didn't want to know. I talked him into staying home, entertaining a few friends, playing bridge. I did not expect to turn him into a Connecticut Yankee. But I did hope he would take life more seriously.

I marveled at Aly's ability to become different people. When he stepped off a plane in Ireland he was completely Irish. With the Islamites he was a Moslem. He was English or French, whatever the occasion and the company required. It was as natural for him to make people feel happy and important as it was to breathe.

Aly was very gentle with simple people. He would get out of his car on a dusty road and talk to a beggar or a peddler. The masses loved him, but he was unable, or unwilling, to give up his way of life for them. His homelands were India and Pakistan, countries of tragic poverty, and Aly did not know what they wanted from him. His life was a circus, but they needed food. My brother, Butch, who had been to India, once told me, "Don't ever go there. It will break your heart." I am sensitive about the poor and the underprivileged, and that was always a barrier to any future I might have had with Aly Khan.

Gossip and controversy swirled around us. I learned from Elsa Maxwell that his father, the Aga Khan, was alarmed by the talk that we might marry. Elsa was my champion. "Your Highness," she said, "Gene is a lady. She's educated, traveled, capable of taking her place anywhere."

The Aga would hear no more. "I have always allowed my children to lead their own lives," he said. "But there is something Aly must know. He cannot marry another movie star. He married one. She gave him a daughter, Yasmin. I cannot even see her, despite the fact that she is the first girl baby to be born in our family for two hundred years. Aly is my heir and must consider my people. If he marries Miss Tierney, I will not receive her."

When Elsa repeated that conversation, he was dour and resentful. "You know," he said, "my father had a pretty extensive love life of his own."

I would realize soon enough that marriage was out of the question for us. Whether I ever did more than daydream, I can no longer judge. Our paths crossed at a convenient and wistful time. Aly was on the rebound from Rita Hayworth. I was getting over a divorce and not completely shed of my feelings for Jack Kennedy. Aly was kind and sweet and cheerful. He lifted my spirits and, at a time when I needed it, he brought gaiety back into my life.

He was a magnet to the rich and famous, geniuses of one world or another. When I was living in the South of France, he took Tina and me to lunch in Saint Paul de Vence, a village in the hills. As we left the inn we passed Pablo Picasso on the street, on his afternoon stroll. Aly introduced us to the artist, who took Tina's little hand and said to me, in French: "The child has the most beautiful eyes I have ever seen."

My mother had stayed home on a kind of one-day strike. The night before, Elsa Maxwell had asked twelve guests to dinner, not including my mother, who would have been the thirteenth. She was miffed at Aly for not insisting that she go. To punish us, she refused to join us for lunch, and missed Picasso. She never forgave herself.

Another day we drove to the suburbs of Paris to meet a friend of Aly's, the painter Utrillo. I dressed for the occasion in my latest Balmain creation, an elephant gray, draped jersey, and touched it off with a red velvet beret from Jacques Griffe. I should not have bothered. Poor Utrillo was a frail old man suffering from certain phobias, the worst being his fear of women. After we had visited with his wife and been shown around their home, we mounted the stairs to the artist's bedroom.

There, among literally hundreds of crucifixes, we saw a pathetic old man in his bathrobe. When his wife introduced me, he cringed. Aly explained to me later that the women dearest to his heart, his mother and now his wife, had exploited him shamelessly. His mother, Suzanne Valadon, a well-known painter in her own right, had pacified him with liquor in his milk bottle from the time he was a child, so that he would sleep soundly and she could go off at night to party. He was an alcoholic by the time he was twelve.

Utrillo's wife had sold every painting he ever produced, some of which he had meant to destroy. When we left, I stopped to admire two large murals on his living room walls. They were scenes of the streets of Paris, done with an enormous amount of white. His wife nodded and said, "Thank God, they were painted on a canvas that can be removed from the walls." I understood why the old man distrusted women. I was only sorry that I made him uncomfortable those few minutes before I left his bedroom and went tearing back down the stairs.

But he was pleased to see Aly. I never saw anyone who was not. Aly Khan's life was a constant escape from responsibility. He did not want to succeed his father as the Aga, the spiritual leader of millions. He was a misfit in that world. He craved excitement, not reality. He avoided the mosque, preferring racetracks and nightclubs. His favorite reading was one of those pocket guides on horse breeding, so-and-so out of so-and-so. He always carried one with him and, in idle moments, would study it.

I wanted to understand him. His was not a new story.

The fastest cars, the oldest wines, the prettiest women. Life measured against a stopwatch. Then there was constant pressure from his father, who wanted Aly to play a larger role in the diplomatic needs of Pakistan. Finally, he agreed to return to Karachi, and I knew it was time for the Tierneys to leave for home.

We had spent an interesting eighteen months in Europe, but all of us were homesick and Tina needed to start school. We had not been exiles entirely by choice. I was trying to qualify for a tax exemption. I was still worrying about providing for Daria, and I calculated that I would need at least $280,000 to guarantee her future care.

Europe was then in the process of being rebuilt, and American companies were doing much of the work. To encourage engineers and others to work abroad, the government passed a law making tax-free the wages earned during a specific eighteen-month period if you lived overseas. Actors rushed to take advantage of the law, too. A few succeeded, including Clark Gable.

I returned to find that the dates had been adjusted in such a way that I didn't qualify. I hadn't saved any money, after all.

We headed straight for Connecticut. Tina, nearly six, having lived as an only child, was thrilled to be with cousins her own age. She spoke only French, however, and I fretted about the difficulties she might encounter in school. I worried needlessly. Children learn languages as quickly as good actors learn their lines.

We enjoyed a white Connecticut Christmas that year, with most of our family around us. Daria and my father were missing. Aly had already given me a present, a six-carat, square-cut diamond ring. I wore it on my right hand. The marriage rumors flew thicker than ever. He called almost nightly from Karachi, and we made plans to meet in Hollywood after I started my next picture.

There was still a question about whether Aly could enter the United States. He was embroiled in a long-distance legal battle with Rita Hayworth over child support for Yasmin and visitation rights. His lawyers were negotiating with hers to allow him to come into the country without being served with papers. Rita was now remarried to the singer Dick Haymes.

I had agreed to report back to work for the filming of *The Black Widow*, a murder mystery that also starred Ginger Rogers and Van Heflin. I was not well, my mind was playing tricks. Again, I had trouble with my lines. I would go blank and not recognize the face of someone I had known for years. I would dream that Daria was back with me, and wake up looking for her. I held together through force of habit.

I had terribly mixed feelings about seeing Aly Khan. I missed him, but I had problems neither of us understood and he couldn't cure.

Aly flew to Mexico while he waited for word from Rita's attorneys, and I joined him there on weekends. I brought my mother with me, knowing the press would be hovering around us like fruit flies. Mother provided a screen of sorts, and she was good at answering their questions.

I had already started filming *The Egyptian*, with Edmund Purdom in the role the studio had planned for Marlon Brando, who turned them down. His legal problems resolved, Aly was soon in Hollywood and a daily visitor to the set. He remarked one day on the authenticity of the props and special effects. Harry Brand, the publicity head at Fox, quickly sent out a press release saying that Aly Khan was serving as our unpaid "technical advisor." He was, in fact, an authority on Egyptian history.

My role did not seem to be hurt by the fact that I was sinking into a deeper depression. My princess was shrewd, disturbed, unstable, and menacing. I can only believe I played her faithfully.

I felt all churned up and jittery and attached to some unseen yo-yo string, pulled by Aly and my mother and the studio, everybody and nobody. Aly refused to believe that anything could be wrong with me. He insisted, to me and to anyone who asked, that I needed nothing more than a few weeks of rest on a farm.

As close as I could get to a farm was the back lot at Twentieth Century-Fox. In the evenings Aly and I night-clubbed. On the weekend we crossed the border into Mexico. We quarreled over such things as whose fault it was that the photographers found out where we were, or whether his mother disliked me, and, finally, if we should continue seeing each other. The newspapers had a field day, one morning's headline contradicted by the next:

"GENE, ALY IN NIGHTCLUB TIFF"

"GENE TIERNEY REUNITED WITH ALY IN MEXICO"

"GENE TO GIVE UP FILM CAREER FOR ALY"

"SHOULD GENE MARRY ALY? TUNE IN NEXT . . ."

Hedda Hopper complained that "the trend these days seems to be for our glamour girls to leave the All-American males, fly to Europe, and snag themselves a dashing European." Hedda added that she was "worried about this epidemic disloyalty to Uncle Sam's boys." I suppose I should have been worried that Hedda was worried.

This was the era of foreign aid in Hollywood. Ginger Rogers had fallen in love with Jacques Bergerac. Olivia de Havilland was seeing the writer Pierre Galante. Shel-

ley Winters wanted to marry Vittorio Gassman and Liz
Taylor was engaged to Michael Wilding. Paulette God-
dard had found Erich Remarque.

Everywhere I turned I received advice I did not want
and criticism I could not handle. In the *American Weekly*,
the headline over a story by my friend Elsa Maxwell
read: "TROUBLE AHEAD FOR GENE AND ALY."

I never doubted that what Elsa wrote came out of
feelings deeply rooted in my favor. Of Aly and me, she
had said, "Such an alliance, I believe, cannot help but
mean eventual disillusionment and despair . . . Gene has
a wealth of real mother-love for two small daughters, and
she needs her movie career as a means of insuring their
future. She must realize that a sizable steady income is
important—not a generous dole from a husband whose
ardor may cool and whose purse strings (and those of his
father) may tighten accordingly."

In private, Elsa cautioned me: "Watch out, my dear.
When his love is over, he is cold as stone. You are not
the first, as you know. You will not be the last, as I know."

Aly postponed twice his return to France to be with
me. Finally, he could delay no longer. He needed to visit
his daughter, Yasmin, and settle his differences with
Rita. Then he flew to New York and on to Europe.

Given conditions that were ideal, the prospects for our
love affair turning into anything permanent were at best
marginal. But nervous and unwell, the chances were nil.
Aly was gone and I knew it.

We stayed in touch. There were phone calls and occasional messages, delivered through friends. Then one
day—three years and a hospital or two later—Aly was in
New York. He telephoned my apartment and asked to
take me to dinner. I told him no, I had met a man, Howard
Lee, whom I was going to marry. He said, "I'm glad for
you," and that was the last time we spoke.

Not to my surprise, Aly Khan died in 1960 in the crash of his Lancia sports car near the Bois de Boulogne. I was often frightened and excited at the same time, driving with Aly, his car whipping around the curves on two wheels. He did not die alone, but his companion, the model Bettina, survived. One way or another, his ladies usually did.

I had heard that, in spite of himself, he felt a strong disappointment that he was bypassed by his father in 1957, and his son by a first marriage, Karim, was made the Aga Khan. After that, Aly tried to lead a more serious and useful life, working hard, I'm told, as a delegate to the UN. But at heart he was like a fighter pilot, restless, always looking to see another dawn.

My mother and I read the newspaper account of Aly Khan's fatal accident together. She had loved to play bridge with Aly and found him brilliant. He was, in truth, an intelligent man who dissipated his powers by being a playboy. She put down the paper and said almost casually, "You're lucky you weren't with him."

CHAPTER
17

The Long Night

By the time I finished *The Left Hand of God*, with Humphrey Bogart, I was so ill, so far gone, that it became an effort every day not to give up. I could deceive myself no longer.

How often I had heard people, even my own mother, say, "I went to work instead of having a nervous breakdown." But there comes a point when one has to admit, "I cannot go on. It is destructive to try."

The picture was the fourth I had made even as I felt my mind begin to unravel. I could not hold thoughts. I had no appetite. I felt scared, for no reason. If I was able to work at all, it was through an illusion. A flame burns brightest just before it goes out.

Mother had stayed in Connecticut to look after Tina. I knew that if I got through the picture I had to get myself to a hospital. I learned later that a sister of Bogart's had been mentally ill. He recognized the signs, went to the studio bosses and warned them I was sick and needed help.

They assured him that I was a trouper, was aware how

much had been invested in the film and would not let them down. They suggested that Bogart be kind and gentle. He was nothing less. His patience and understanding carried me through the film. We did not know then that he was himself terminally ill with cancer.

When I think of that time it is like watching a silent movie. There are no sounds, no words. I told my doctors I could observe myself, as though I were outside my own body, all during the filming of *The Left Hand of God.* Later, two doctors went to a theater to see the movie, wondering if the illness showed in my face. It did not. As long as I was playing someone else, I was fine. When I had to be myself, my problems began. I had known of this twist in my character since my bond selling tour during the war, when I suffered such seizures of stage fright, having to make an unscripted talk to ordinary people.

Now I had struggled too long against an enemy I could not identify, in times and places that were strange to me. I was not to make another movie for seven years.

I do not recall a sense of panic about those days, but they were bad ones. I fled to New York, where my mother and I still kept an apartment. My departure from Hollywood was described as a "walk-out." No one understood that I was cracking up. The studio wanted to put me into another picture, thought I was being prima-donna-ish, and suspended me. I withdrew from a part in a television version of Ibsen's *A Doll's House*, turning down a ten-thousand-dollar fee. I was not running away. I was looking for a safety net into which I could leap. I felt like a person trying to get out of a burning building.

I had fame, a face people seemed to admire, friends I could count on, and an income of six figures a year. Why wasn't I happy? Why was I in such a torpor?

Again I found myself living in a fishbowl. Reporters

hounded my family, my friends, my agent. They were told I had been slow to shake off a bad case of influenza. My mother reveled in her role of protective hen. When one caller wanted to know about Aly Khan, my mother replied, "Well, that has been done to death. I don't think she'd want to say any more about that." And then: "You'll have to excuse me, dear. I have to get to the water boiling on the stove. We're steaming her, you know."

"Steaming her?"

"Yes. For her virus."

A few days later we had the phone disconnected.

Maybe the Scotsman Robert Burns thought it would be grand to see ourselves as others see us, but I was never too crazy about the idea. The New York *Post* reported that I was in "a state of nervous agitation," having decided that the obstacles between myself and Aly Khan could not be surmounted. "Gene is hung up over Aly," another friend was quoted. "She always went for the continental type—she's crazy about hand-kissing. But she's also a very conventional woman—reserved, well behaved, a lady. I think she'd like to settle down: a home, a dependable husband, and maybe an occasional picture when she gets a little bored with the social rounds."

My drifting apart from Aly Khan was not the cause of my breakdown. But it would be foolish to say it did not have an effect on me. The things that make us unhappy bloom in strange places. They are seeds crossing in the wind.

The days and nights in the apartment are now reduced to pages in a scrapbook. I have no other recollections of them. To study the pages now is like reading about a stranger.

A friend is quoted as saying: "Gene is a composed, stable girl who is as balanced as it is possible to be in an unbalanced industry."

A New York columnist described a nightclub scene, as I fidgeted with my gloves: "It was quite a performance, and probably an unconscious one. She takes them off with great care and deliberation, one finger at a time. Then, just as meticulously, she puts them back on, smoothing each finger before moving on to the next. I tried counting how many times she did it one night, but after a while it made me nervous just to watch."

I would not think it very pleasant to watch someone crack up. It must be the mental equivalent of watching someone drown. I was in no condition to make any decisions. I needed a doctor, but was afraid to call one.

My depressions were coming more often and lasting longer. I would sit for hours in a chair, an unread book in my lap, not stirring. Then I began to sleep, a day, sometimes two at a stretch. I would wake feeling like a zombie, maybe eat or drink something, and go back to bed. I could not stay awake.

We had returned to Connecticut, to the house at Southport, and the family had gathered around me. I overheard my sister talking to my mother. "I think she's faking," said Pat. "You know Gene. She's so dramatic."

My brother disagreed. "No," he said. "I think something is seriously wrong with her." Butch—Howard, that is; he had gotten a little old for nicknames—sent for our family minister. I told him to leave me alone. He was against me. They were all against me. The minister stayed only a few minutes. "I can't help her," he said. "She needs a doctor."

The next day we drove to Cape Cod to see a famous psychiatrist who summered there. Fran Stark, after a long phone conversation with my mother, had recommended him. Before I saw the doctor, we checked into an inn and went to the dining room for lunch. When my steak came I sent it back to the kitchen, complaining that it smelled bad and had spoiled. I walked out, with my mother at my heels, found a drugstore around the corner, and ordered a milkshake.

Mother was frantic. "Gene," she said, "what are you doing? You can't go on like this. You must eat."

"I won't eat that food," I snapped. "They are trying to poison me."

My mother's mind went reeling back into time, and she remembered her sister Claire, who had refused to eat, who suspected her food was poisoned.

The doctor questioned me for what seemed like minutes, but must have been the better part of an afternoon. He wanted to know who I thought was after me and would want to poison me. I wouldn't tell him. I was worried about the Communists. I didn't know if I could trust him. I don't remember the rest of the conversation. I couldn't remember conversations five minutes after I had them.

No one could get through to me. I would pick up a book and would not see what was on the written page. I would read what I imagined was there, an entirely different story. My sight was affected, too. I saw things that were not there. I would look at a friend and think their eyes were crossed or they were making faces at me.

I watched television hoping to see the Geritol ads for "tired blood." They fascinated me. I kept telling my mother that maybe I needed Geritol. If we had only known how much more I really needed.

The doctor at Cape Cod referred us to another in New York, whose office, coincidentally, was on 57th, across the street from where we lived. This doctor had me admitted to a sanitarium in the city, the Harkness Pavilion, and there to my eternal regret I received my first electric shock treatments. I consented after seeking the advice of several family friends, one of them my attorney,

George Spiegelberg, an eminent man who helped General Eisenhower draft the peace treaty that ended World War II.

I knew nothing about electric shock therapy, and I don't think the doctors at the time knew much more. It was then considered a scientific breakthrough, although opinion was divided about the potential for long-term harm.

The actual medical phrase is electroconvulsive therapy. In simple language, a shock is given to the brain to produce a kind of seizure. The treatment was developed in Italy in 1938. Doctors soon began to use it to treat schizophrenia and cases of severe depression.

When it shocked its victims into some measure of sanity, it seemed to do so by inducing a temporary amnesia. It triggered a physical feeling that was comfortable and benign. You can hardly be depressed over something you no longer remember. The results often were so dramatic that helpless people could soon manage everyday things that once seemed intimidating. They could function: mix with other people, follow a recipe, sit through a movie.

I was prepared as though for surgery. No breakfast. I was told to remove false teeth, if I had any, which I did not. I was injected with a muscle relaxant, then a second drug to maintain normal respiration. What happened next I had to find out later: an electrode was attached to each temple and an alternating current of eighty or ninety volts passed between the electrodes for a split fraction of a second.

In the early days of this therapy, the moment of violent seizure often produced fractures and dislocated bones. The use of muscle relaxants solved that problem.

But the brain, for an instant, is so raced that it cannot function. I was unconscious for four or five minutes, then passed into a peaceful sleep.

I had been given no warning about the possible after-effects, or the violence, or anything at all about what to expect. I was wheeled back to my room on a simple metal hospital cot; no restraints were needed. The consent papers had been signed, I understand, by my mother. She hadn't read them and said later she could not recall signing them. She felt guilty about it for years.

I woke up as if out of a bad dream, the kind that has no shape or detail but you *know* it was bad. I was confused, weak, and disoriented. I recognized no one. The immediate things that had happened, six months to a year before, were peeled from my mind. I had to learn from the doctor and nurses where I was, how long I had been there, what had happened, who the people in my room were.

The next day my family told me I looked better and sounded brighter. I had an appetite again. I was grateful in a way for that first electric shock. Even though I had lost my memory temporarily, I felt improved, no longer depressed. In time I would meet people who actually begged for them. In a sense, they chased the snakes from your mind. They chased everything from your mind.

I was puzzled by the people who popped in and out of my room. They turned out to be my doctors and nurses. I didn't know them and can't describe them now, their names, or whether they were short or tall, young or old. If it was a high price to pay, I had no temper or nerves or complaints.

As she left the sanitarium that day, my mother said to my brother, "I don't understand how Gene got better so quickly. It was like the twinkling of an eye."

Howard said, "Those shock treatments scramble up the brain, so that the thing that's causing the trouble is blocked out. But it doesn't last."

He was right. I had agreed to the shocks not knowing what would happen, and not caring. I had a series of eight. A week after the last one, the fears and the depression came back.

When one is as unhappy as I was, and you can't work it out for yourself, you tend to give up. Mental hospitals are filled with chronically unhappy and lonely people. I had a right to be unhappy. Much in my life had gone wrong. But I could not get my feelings into the open, where I could deal with them.

And so began a new round of seeking help. This doctor. That drug. The newest cure from Vienna. The confusion of not knowing where or to whom one can turn. One doctor suggested I stay home and hire a nurse, as my family had done years before to heal my Aunt Claire. Could I have found the strength? Could they? A sickness of the mind is not a fever, to be watched for a night, hoping it will break.

Most of the doctors we consulted agreed that I needed to be in a sanitarium. I wasn't sure. I was tired of having doctors tell me there were no easy answers, that I had to help myself. I had been introduced to psychotherapy, in which the doctors let you talk, talk, talk, until you find the source of your problem or find another doctor.

Mother was reluctant to have me "put away," as the quaint old phrase went. After her divorce, she had returned with much fervor to her Christian Science faith. She thought kindness and prayer might cure me.

So Howard and Pat were the ones who drove me to the Institute for Living at Hartford, Connecticut, also known as the Hartford Retreat. I changed my mind every few miles. When we walked into the office of the chief psychiatrist, I said sharply, "I'm not going to stay. I'm not going to stay."

The doctor was about fifty, looked and dressed younger, and had a cheerfulness that seemed out of place. He had been briefed by my family and had seen my medical file.

He spoke to me in simple, soothing sentences. He asked how I spent my time.

"Cleaning the kitchen floor," I told him. It was true. When I fell into one of my spells, I would sometimes get an attack of house cleaning. It was something I could do without thinking. I would get on my hands and knees and scrub. Our floors never suffered from waxy buildup.

He said, "You know, Miss Tierney, that you need our help. You have to stay so we can help you."

"You can't force me," I said. My family had already agreed that I would not be admitted against my will.

"No one wants to force you," he said. "But we think it would be good for you. Your mother is tired. It would give her a rest while you relaxed with us. We can work on your problem, and you might even have fun."

I was silent for a moment. Pat and Howard were sitting near me, but neither spoke. At last, I asked, "Do you have any floors I can scrub?"

He handed me a pen and I signed myself in.

Within minutes after my brother and sister left, my mind cleared enough to know that I desperately wanted out of there. I spent a hellish first night—pleading, conniving, trying to reach a telephone to call Howard and ask him to come back and free me. The doctors refused to let me use the phone. The nurses ignored me. For nearly two hours I sat on the steps of the old two-story building where I was to be confined, refusing to budge. I wept. I begged—someone, anyone, help me. Finally, I was yanked to my feet and led to a room. My cell.

I do not believe I had ever heard a sound so penetrating, so defeating, as the sound of the key turning in the lock of that door. What was I doing there, in this so-called mental hospital, this house for nut cases? Wasn't I Gene Tierney, one-time society girl, actress, mother, successful, admired? I felt like a criminal. Most people would, if they were not completely unhinged. You are giving up your personal life, your freedom, your dignity. It was the most degrading moment of my life.

All the next day I huddled by a window and just *inched* out what air I could. Literally. It was winter. The windows were barred and I could raise them only enough to get my fingertips underneath. The retreat had been converted from an old New England home and was heated by steam radiators. The heat was so thick I felt myself choking. I knelt on the floor, sucking in the air that curled in through the bottom of the window, trying to breathe.

Never in my life had I shown any sign of claustrophobia. But I learned then what it was. I was a prisoner of that small room, and of my own mind. Ten, even fifteen years later, my husband, Howard Lee, would have to lead me back to bed in the middle of the night. I would walk in my sleep and open a door to let in the air.

The hardest feeling to deal with is guilt. What have I done? To myself. To my family. One feels trapped, buried alive. During the next few weeks, when I could not get near the phone, I was given a series of five more electric shock treatments. The psychotherapy wasn't working. Mother was told that I had been difficult, angry, and stubborn, would not answer their questions or do what they asked. And I mocked the doctors. I imitated their voices and how they walked and gestured. For me, such behavior was clearly irrational but not all that hard to explain. I had gone through life saying yes, being nice, doing as others pleased. Now, when I no longer had full control of my mind, I was subconsciously indulging a desire to resist and say no.

The shock treatments left my days a gray blur. Doors were opening and closing. I was in and out of a dream. One day, when I was recovering from the last of that series, an attendant led me for a walk around the grounds. When she stopped to talk to another nurse, I looked up and saw that a gate fifty yards away had been left open. I was wearing a heavy fur coat over a light cotton dress. It was winter in Connecticut and a bed of snow covered the grass. Without hesitation, I threw off the coat and made a mad dash for the gate. It was not really an expensive fur, but if it had been sable I still would have shed it gladly to help me in my flight.

Suddenly I was through the gate and into the street, running wildly, my lungs straining, hearing the voices trailing behind me, knowing the attendants were on my heels.

I do not know how many blocks I ran. But I ducked into the first store I could reach, thinking only to get to a phone and call my brother, *please*, to come and save me. I had a mania about the telephone. But the nurse soon appeared in the doorway, a large woman, shoulders heaving as she caught her breath. Five or six others from the asylum staff piled in behind her. They started toward me slowly, fanning out, until I was backed into a corner.

I was completely unaware of what else was happening around me. There must have been, surely, salespeople and customers in the store. I suppose they were as wild-eyed as I was. Finally, the attendants surrounded me like a caged animal. When I spoke, my voice was surprisingly calm. The few moments of freedom had somehow restored a little of my dignity. "I'll go with you," I said, "but don't touch me. Don't try to put a straitjacket on me. Don't put a hand on me."

They did as I asked. Someone handed me my fur coat. There were still traces of snow on it. "Here," she said softly. "Put this on. You're shivering."

The incident of my "escape" made me a more celebrated figure around the hospital. I had been there three weeks. I thought I was better and ached to go home. I could think of little else. Now I was watched constantly.

I was no lunatic. I was normal half the time, not enough to allow for my release but enough to confound the doctors. After I settled down, had been there six weeks, the doctors decided my family could visit me. The news thrilled me. Having been confined, cut off, seeing no one, talking to no one that I loved, hating and dreading the loneliness, the idea of seeing my family again was like salvation.

They organized their visits to bring me back into the family circle. One week my brother and his wife, Jane, would visit. The next, my sister and her four children would come. They would take me to lunch, give me an airing. And all the while I was begging the doctors to release me.

Twice a week I would tell the doctor assigned to me the story of my life, interspersed with pleas to go home. No encouragement was offered. He would nod and say, "Please continue," or respond with a sentence that usually began, "What I hear you saying is . . ."

My moods ranged from pangs of great compassion for others to utter revulsion at what I witnessed and was now a part of—this human zoo. I befriended an old woman who could only eat milk and bread because she would choke if she tried to chew. The mixture would become mush and dribble from the corners of her mouth and down her chin. I cried for her but, after a while, could not bear to look at her.

I really could not identify myself with those other sick people. To be half well is a treacherous way to be. It is not unlike being able to see half the time, and never knowing when or for how long your sight will fail.

Over the next eight months I underwent nineteen more electric shock treatments, a grand total, I think, of thirty-two. Pieces of my life just disappeared. A mental patient once said it must have been what Eve felt, having been created full grown out of somebody's rib, born without a history. That is exactly how I felt.

Little by little, my world became the hospital and the people in it. After a time the shock treatments left me physically ill, nauseated, and I came to dread and fear them. The doctors assured me that the shocks would control my depression, the side effects were temporary and, eventually, I would recover my memory. In most cases, the pattern is the same: the distant past, the past of childhood and adolescence, is the first to reappear. The middle past returns more gradually. The weeks preceding the treatment are gone, and irretrievable.

The horror of that experience I cannot fully recapture. One feels, yes, like a lab rat. Once, after I had awakened from the anesthesia, the nurse who had put me under was standing over my cot. Through some instinct deep inside me, I recognized her face, knew what had happened, and shouted, "How dare you let them do that to me!" And with that I lashed out with my fist and slugged her in the eye.

Up to then I had accepted everything, if not always in a friendly spirit, at least passively, not doing anything naughty or violent. But that day I had suffered all the shock treatments I could endure, and I took it out on the first face that was familiar to me.

The nurse was furious, of course. She yanked me by the arm and snapped, "You're coming with me." She locked me in a ward where all the idiot cases were. I was so sick, I thought they were all Stanislavski method actors. I stood there applauding, repeating myself—"Aren't they wonderful? Aren't they good actors?" They were dreadful-looking people, their heads bobbing, their mouths hanging open, drooling down the front of their hospital gowns. Some of the women had hair on their faces.

That was only part of my punishment. A few hours later, the same nurse came for me and said, "Now I have something else for you." She shoved me into a room that was nothing but a box. It had no toilet, no running water, no window. After some time, I had no way of telling how long, I started to sob. I needed to go to the bathroom. I leaned my head against the door and pleaded to be let out. Finally, they came and led me back to my own section.

Patience is a commodity for which the demand always exceeds the human supply. I had a doctor at that hospital —I won't name him—I detested. He went out of his way, I thought, to be unkind. I realize curtness may be a part of a doctor's technique, but it is not one to which I respond very well. Another patient wore her hair in a boyish bob, a sort of Irene Dunne look, and I cut mine in the same way. I thought it would be becoming to me, as it was to her. When the doctor saw what I had done, he snapped, "Why are you copying that girl's hairdo? That is a silly thing to do."

Fashion and styles had been my passions. That doctor had a way of hitting you where it hurt. Another time I reported to his office wearing sandals, with the toe and heel out. He took one look and said, "What are those things, bedroom slippers? I don't want to see you wearing them again." They were, in fact, beach sandals, the latest rage on the French Riviera.

You do not realize how ill you are until tiny episodes become the major events in your day. I felt the doctor was trampling on my love of life.

Not until I left the sanitarium and reflected on some of the things I had experienced did I understand how susceptible I had become to picking up other people's habits. I had the tendency before. It was part of my equipment as an actress. But my illness, and my confinement, seemed to accentuate it. One girl kept tapping her foot as she talked, her leg shaking with the constant motion. I found myself doing the same thing. The habit meant, for me as it did for her, getting away. She was to return home soon. It represented freedom.

The shock treatments achieved a sort of plateau in my behavior and I was released to my mother's custody. I should have been elated the day I walked out the front door and stepped into her car. I felt only relief. I was calm, mechanical, vague. The apartment seemed familiar, yet strange. I couldn't recall what foods I liked. I didn't know where anything was. It was like beginning life all over again.

Mother was sure that everything would be all right. Tina was attending school, and the three of us were together. I began, not very successfully, to pick up the threads of my world.

C H A P T E R

18

Windmills
of the Mind

I had known Cole Porter in Hollywood and New York, spent many a warm hour in his home, and met the talented and original people who were drawn to him.

It was at Cole's, in 1946, that I told Somerset Maugham I was up for a role in the movie version of his book *The Razor's Edge*. He smiled and said, "You have my vote." A few days later, Fox gave me the part. A coincidence—maybe not.

Cole Porter liked to entertain a dozen or so of his friends with lavish dinners, followed by long, mellow evenings in the living room, everyone arranged around the piano, hearing for the first time the songs that in six months would sweep the country; songs like "I Love Paris" and "All of You" and "From This Moment On."

Through Cole I met Katharine Hepburn and Joan Fontaine and David Wayne and George Cukor. Once Cukor, who had directed Greta Garbo in *Camille*, arrived for dinner carrying a lunch pail. It was no joke. George had to watch his weight. When the rest of us sat down to the gourmet dishes Cole laid out with great pride, George took out his fresh fruit and organic foods. Cole had a fit, and so did his French chef.

Cole was one of those who kept in touch when the hospital released me. One of the traumas of being an ex-mental patient is getting used to seeing people again, mixing and being around them. You tend to shrink into a shell, afraid of contact with the world outside your door. The question that plagues you is not, will I know when I am well, but will my friends know?

Cole Porter invited me to lunch that spring of 1958 in New York. We had troubles to share. He told me he faced surgery soon and was going to lose his leg. I nearly cried. I knew he had been in constant pain, had undergone several operations since a horse threw him years before. He was quiet and uncharacteristically gloomy.

I touched his hand and said, "Cole, losing a leg is terrible, but nothing is worse than losing your mind. You have the most beautiful mind and the most creative talent, and you will never lose that."

I was fine when it came to cheering up others, not so fine with myself. The weeks turtled past and, suddenly, I was in a new depression. What caused it, and why, I can't recall. For a long time not much was needed to set me off. A picture. A word. A scene on television.

One day—not then, but another time—I was in the checkout line at a supermarket. On the cover of one of those weekly scare tabloids was the photograph of a man murdered in a bathtub. I immediately had a vision of my daughter, Tina, in a bathtub, dead. I was hysterical when I got home. People who are sensitive to shock create their own worlds. And that is fairly shocking, to see a picture of a man bleeding in a bathtub.

I had fallen into my pattern of sleeping around the

clock. Mother tried to be tolerant and handle the problem lightly. We sought more solitude at the house in Connecticut, and when she needed to be away she hired a woman to stay with me. One day she left early in the morning and returned late in the evening, and I had slept the entire time. Mother tried to wake me when she came in. "You know, Gene," she sighed, "it really doesn't pay to hire someone to watch you."

A few weeks later we moved back to New York, and then came the episode on the window ledge. I remember the police arriving, the pain on my mother's face, a doctor dabbing at my arm with alcohol before the needle stung the vein. When I woke up, I was on my way to Topeka, Kansas.

My first days at the Menninger Clinic were filled with feelings of hopelessness, of resignation. I would never leave. Never recover. In that state of mind you don't think much. You just function. I marked the time between three meals and a tranquilizer at night to help me sleep. A blessed moment. I looked forward to that pill and the sleep it brought. There went eight hours with no effort.

Actually, I was comfortable. The room was little different from what you would have found in most college dormitories. It contained a single bed, a tiny bathroom, a desk, a bureau, and a window that didn't open. The walls were cream-colored and bare except for one mirror.

My brother had my power of attorney, was handling my money, and came to the sanitarium to make the arrangements. He had taken over my accounts when the bills came in for two mink coats, one for me and one for my mother. I had bought them during one of my "highs."

When Howard learned that my care would run $25,-000 a year, he went to Dr. Karl Menninger and asked if he could suggest any way to reduce the cost. My illness had devoured a large chunk of my savings. "The only thing I can recommend," said Dr. Karl, "is putting her in a public institution."

He was not being unsympathetic. The hard truth is that repairing a broken mind is expensive, more so today. The treatment at many state hospitals was often crude and insensitive and worse. I was fortunate. I could afford Menninger's, considered by many the best psychiatric facility in the world. The sanitarium had been established in 1925 in a converted farmhouse on the western edge of Tokepa. Some of the patients mortgaged their homes to stay there.

After a week or two, I was assigned to a program of light therapy—arts and crafts and regular counseling. It was hoped that rest and seclusion would produce some improvement. Thankfully, an early decision was made not to subject me to additional shock treatments. My record showed they had not been helpful. There were still oceans of blankness in my memory from the previous ones.

I faced a slow, unsteady recovery. My brother remembers sitting on the lawn with me on a visiting day at Menninger's, when I smiled and said teasingly, "I've got a secret."

"You can tell me."

I pointed to the sky and said, "See the sun up there? Well, the Russians are going to blow up the sun tomorrow and we're all going to be killed. But don't tell anybody."

Butch was frightened for me. He was talking to a person who believed what she was saying.

Two doctors were assigned to me, a psychiatrist, Dr. Philip Holtzman, who prescribed my medication, and a psychologist, Dr. Anne Wilkens, who worked the floor, making the rounds.

I had asked for a woman to take my case. My mother had told me I had a choice, and I decided, "I'm tired of talking to men. I think I would like a woman, a woman who can be my friend." Dr. Wilkens was petite, blond, and cute with very high-heeled shoes. I learned to listen for the clickety-clack that told me she was coming down the hall.

She was not a mother figure. There was another woman doctor on the staff who was quite stout, an earth mother sort, who became a comforting maternal image to many of the patients. In turn they became little, mealy-mouthed, submissive stepdaughters. That relationship would have been terrible for me.

My breakdown had been the result of a gradual series of hammer taps. My recovery was to be an attempt to climb a greased pole. I had periods of temper, of delusions, of religion. I sometimes prayed twenty times a day and temporarily, at least, felt better for it.

At Menninger's, I met a young priest whose parish had been in a Chicago ghetto. What he had seen there, and his inability to change things, had broken his mind. When he was ill he would get the look of the devil in his eyes. But he would be lucid from time to time and regard the inmates as his flock. He told me once, "You know, you could do a lot of good in here. The people here look up to you. Why don't you try?"

After that conversation, I quit praying for myself and prayed for the children who were there. I talked to them and offered to help with their projects. One, a teenage girl, had threatened to kill herself. She was often violent and given to breaking chairs. When she felt herself losing control, she asked for a treatment known as "the cold pack." I thought her very brave.

To me the cold pack was the worst indignity of my confinement. It was not meant to be cruel or inhuman or to punish you. The cold pack was simply one of the ways of rearranging your mind, of shocking you back into sanity, or so the doctors hoped. When my time came, I felt only that I had been dehumanized.

I was wrapped from the neck down in icy wet bedsheets, my arms strapped to my sides. It was like being buried in a snowbank. Tears poured down my cheeks as the minutes ticked away. I couldn't move. I lost the feeling in my hands and feet. My mind was in a panic. For perhaps the first time in my life I actually thought, "Thank God, I'm a pretty woman. Maybe the floor doctor will see me crying and feel sorry for me, *a pretty woman crying*, and he will make them unbind me." It became my only hope. I was meant to be in the cold pack for an hour. I don't think my heart could have survived that long.

The doctor did release me after thirty minutes. Even in that shortened exposure, I was so shocked, so affected mentally by being enshrouded like a mummy in those chilly, clammy sheets, I walked for days with my arms out from my sides, bent at the elbow, like wings. It was an unconscious reaction to being unconfined. My arms would not dangle or relax against my body.

There is a certain amount of innocence connected with mental illness that is terribly sad. Many patients are treated as though they are dangerous, and some are. Dr. Karl Menninger, who with his father and brother founded the clinic, conducted a Bible class and I joined it on those days when I was well enough. Once a scripture about love and hope and the mercy of God was being discussed, and I rose and said bitterly, "Try to explain that to the patients on South Ward Two."

Dr. Karl motioned for me to sit down. Such outbursts were not uncommon, and several people were talking at once, each ignoring the other.

South Ward Two contained the patients thought to be dangerous or hopeless or both. They were let out of their rooms only under strict supervision, or under restraint. I spent a month in the ward myself, locked in a room not much bigger than a walk-in closet, with a window that faced a brick wall. Once a day we were brought into a common room for observation. Half a dozen guards were on duty in case the patients attacked each other. The rest of the time I had no contact with anyone except the attendant who brought my food. I was in solitary confinement, and incredibly I had volunteered to be placed there.

My room was directly under South Ward Two. I had come to believe that the children up there were making noises like animals. I could actually hear them. I fixed it in my mind that it was my duty to get up there and convince them to behave in a more dignified way. So I asked, I actually implored, Dr. Wilkens to transfer me.

When she asked why, I said, "I need to be there."

My conversation was vague and guarded, as it often was. But I realized later that my use of the word "need" persuaded her. I felt I needed to help the children. She took it to mean that I was at a point where I might lose control, become suicidal, and needed to be in a maximum security ward. My request was granted.

I no longer heard the animal noises and I was puzzled. When I was let out of my room briefly each day, I moved among the patients, asking questions. Some of them would just as easily have choked me as answer.

By the end of the month I was frantic to return to my old room. I had spent too many hours alone with nothing but a pencil and paper to occupy my time. I drew sketches that were thrown away, started letters that were never finished. I grew more afraid of the other patients.

I was meek and passive when I was released, and Dr. Wilkens sent for me. She asked me if I thought I had been helped. I told her I didn't know, but that the animal noises had stopped. She seemed startled, then began to question me.

Finally, she said, "My God, Gene, no. You *did* hear animal sounds, but not upstairs. There are real animals across the street, on the other side of the brick wall that faces your room. It's a zoo."

I just stared at her. And I realized, with a sinking feeling, that I had put myself in a dangerous and miserable place for no reason at all.

Even the best mental hospitals are, in a sense, and I don't mean this in a flippant way, a menagerie. I sometimes mix up the patients in my mind, which one had which problem, but it seemed to me that there were no two alike. One girl had murdered her mother and father, and showed no guilt whatsoever. When a nurse asked if she didn't need a bathrobe, she replied, "Yes. My mother had one. Why don't you send for it?"

Then there was a girl who claimed the Mafia was after her. And another who insisted her whole family was crazy and she was waiting at the clinic until they all got well. I met a lawyer who wanted to be a psychiatrist. And a doctor who *had been* a psychiatrist, a distinguished one, who spent his days in the workshop where we all did arts and crafts. One day he stood up and, with the swipe of an arm, cleared the table in front of him. Blocks and woodcuts and paints went flying. "I designed these programs," he shouted. "I'll be damned if I'll come in here and perform them." I learned later that he had, indeed, developed many new therapies.

Patients constantly tried to outwit their doctors. Even a sick mind can connive. One businessman talked to his doctor as though he were trying to put over a deal, a used-car salesman trying to close a sale. The doctor had this poor man, Vern, tearing newspapers into strips. It was a mindless task, meant to calm the nerves, but I could not imagine anything more frustrating than to turn newspapers into confetti.

When the doctor came to check on him, Vern would put his arm around the doctor's shoulder in a very cozy way and tell him: "Now, I feel that you and I have finally come to an understanding. I'm so much better. I really think I'm ready to go home." He was so eager to get out, and I wondered if the delays and turndowns would ever discourage him. Eventually, he improved enough to warrant his release. A few days before the big moment, he died of a heart attack.

Some people get very sentimental when they are ill. Maybe they had been very tough characters, even hoodlums, but now they became children again. One such man took up the violin and the rest of us had to suffer through his endless practice sessions. No one wanted to offend him, but he just wasn't quite getting there, and his music did not evoke moonlight and roses.

One woman always read a book after her electric shock treatments. We all reacted differently. I could no more have read a book, or retained anything, than I could have played pro football. The man with the violin always sat next to the woman with the book. She was an older woman, very bright, ill off and on since the age of sixteen. Once she remarked to me, "You know, under ordinary circumstances, if I was in this state on a visit I would be staying at the governor's mansion." What she said was probably true. Her father, at one time, had been the president of a Latin American country.

In one of my own periods of delusion, I imagined her to be a nun . . . so quiet, and serene, sitting there reading her books.

In a curious way, I knew I was getting well when I could read books again. I have always been a good reader. Even between scenes of a motion picture, I liked to pick up Voltaire and just turn to any page. But when my mind malfunctions I can't read. I can't concentrate. The words that I see are not the ones the author wrote. My doctors have been fascinated by this turn, but no one has explained it.

During the first months of my stay at Menninger's, I imagined that the Communists had changed all the books as part of a conspiracy to take over the country. I believe this notion took root from a movie I had seen about Hitler's order to burn the books in Nazi Germany. But I was never a political activist and why Communism so disturbed my private mind I do not know.

But I had given up going to the Menninger library when, one day, I noticed an attendant reading a play by George Bernard Shaw, *Man and Superman.* On an impulse I grabbed it out of his hands. To my surprise I could read what was actually written there. "Bernard Shaw," I said. "Where did you get this wonderful stuff? Where did you find a book by Bernard Shaw?"

"In the library," he said, bewildered.

"I must get it," I said.

My sessions with Dr. Wilkens were going well. Our conversations usually began with her asking me what I had been doing. I was always at work on one project or another. I made bowls out of enamel and copper. I designed two tables out of tiles and black wrought iron that were really quite nice. I gave one to my brother and one to my sister. I wanted to make more and sell them, but there was no procedure for doing so.

I have always believed that having an outlet for their products would do wonders for the self-worth of the inmates. I know I would have felt very fulfilled, like an artist, if I had sold any of my work. I was never embarrassed or self-conscious over the idea of a movie star, so-called, knitting sweaters or making ashtrays or tables.

I was beginning to respond, to open up, to examine the disappointments in my life: my father, my marriage, the helplessness I felt when I had to give up Daria. I had learned from the weeks I spent on South Ward Two that not even a doctor can read what is locked in one's mind.

At some point a funny little memory came back to me. An English teacher in high school had scolded me gently for overusing the word "nice." She said, "Gene, you write pleasant stories, but 'nice' is not the only word in the English language."

Did that habit suggest a clue to my later problems? Perhaps. I wanted everything to be nice—people, places, times. But the world isn't always a nice place.

Early in August of 1958, I was told to appear before members of the medical staff for an interview. If I passed, I would be released to my family. I was dressed neatly and quietly, without jewelry, in my own clothes. I felt pale and edgy, like a young girl applying for her first job. I was applying for my freedom.

I sat behind a two-way glass. The doctors could see me, but I could not see them. I found it disconcerting, hearing these disembodied voices. My nerves were so keyed up that I remember nothing of their questions or my answers.

One moment I was inside the booth, the next I was out, and Dr. Wilkens was standing in front of me, smiling. She told me I had passed. I was going home. She tried to relax me by saying that the next time she saw me, she hoped it would be on a movie screen. Then it hit me. What would I do now? Could I go back to my career? Yes, I thought, that would be nice. There was that word again. Nice.

CHAPTER
19

A New Season

Within days after my release from Menninger's, I was vacationing with my mother and daughter in Aspen, Colorado. There I met the tall Texan who would become my second husband. It was not exactly a meeting of unfettered spirits.

Howard Lee was in the process of divorcing Hedy Lamarr. Long before the tourists were to take over the town, he had built a lodge called the Villa of Aspen (formerly the Villa Lamarr). Given his circumstances, and mine, the odds hardly favored our meeting, much less falling in love.

In Aspen at the time were mutual friends of ours, a Houston oilman named Johnny Mitchell, and his wife, Allyne. They had in mind a little match-making, although Howard was not what one would call a willing buyer. When he heard my name, he sputtered, "No way! I have had my fill of movie actresses."

But Johnny Mitchell is very persistent. A short, jolly, Pillsbury doughboy sort of man, Johnny made his fortune in oil, but many of his friends are in sports and show business. For years he owned the famed Balinese Room in Galveston.

He tracked down Howard one day in a pizza parlor in Aspen and insisted that he join us that night for dinner. Reluctantly, Howard agreed. Johnny promised him he would "meet a girl entirely different from what he expected."

If he expected, or feared, a "Hollywood" type, I no longer fit that description—if I ever did. Through the early part of the evening, I kept calling him "Mr. Lee." After a while he said, "Gene, why don't you call me Howard? I get kinda tired of that Mr. Lee stuff."

I said, "You didn't ask me."

"Well, hell, I didn't ask if I could call you Gene."

Howard Lee had grown up in the oil business, had worked in the fields as a boy. His grandparents had been Virginia farmers, distantly related to Robert E. Lee. He had a strong jaw, blue eyes, a face so handsome his college chums had called him "The Sheik."

Howard was staying on in Aspen, but I planned to visit Hollywood and then return to Connecticut. After dinner, over drinks, he told me he had seen me once before, in the audience of a Broadway play. I was with my mother, he said, and Hedy had pointed us out.

He knew I had been in a mental hospital but did not seem uneasy or even very curious about it. We were together two of my last three nights in Aspen. When we said good-bye he mentioned he might come east at the end of September to watch the World Series, if the New York Yankees were playing. I invited him to stop off in Connecticut.

My return to Hollywood was not a triumphant one. I had not made a picture in nearly four years. I would soon turn thirty-eight. But I made no attempt to avoid people, or to conceal the fact of where I had been and what had

happened to me. Everyone seemed genuinely glad to
see me. When I toured the lot at Twentieth Century-Fox,
I was mobbed by old friends. Executives, directors, actors,
and carpenters came forward to shake my hand or give
me a hug.

Life magazine carried a picture story under the headline: "Welcome for a Troubled Beauty." I tried to describe how I felt by quoting Shakespeare's sonnet:
"When, in disgrace with fortune and men's eyes,/I all
alone beweep my outcast state,/ and trouble deaf heaven
with my bootless cries,/ and look upon myself and curse
my fate . . ."

I wanted to make the point that I was fortunate. My
illness was a curable one, not cancer or something worse.
I was responsible for it, not anyone else. Now I wanted
to go back to work. Under my old contract with Fox, I
was due $100,000, and I owed the studio one more pic-
ture. I agreed to return in December to begin filming.

A story in *Time* magazine was captioned, "Reborn
Star." That, as matters turned out, was a bit premature

Howard Lee did come east, but he missed the World
Series, even though the Yankees were meeting the Milwaukee Braves. He spent the week in Greens Farms and
watched the games on television. Tina and the rest of the
family took to him as quickly as I did.

He was that contradiction in terms, a quiet Texan. But
he proved so understanding and gentle that any qualms I
may have felt about being a burden to anyone began to
fade. I don't know if someone who has led an undisturbed
life can fathom that kind of self-inflicted pain: the worry
of being a responsibility to someone else, perhaps destroy-
ing another innocent human being.

But Howard made it clear he wanted to continue seeing
me. Tina, who was then going on ten, was the first to
decide that his intentions were serious. One night, while

we were getting our coats to leave the house, she whispered, "Mama, he's in love with you."

I laughed. "How can you tell?"

She said, "I just saw him take off his wedding band."

With his divorce from Hedy not yet final, Howard, in the way of some Texas gentlemen, wore his wedding ring out of honesty. And, possibly, as a reminder to himself of recent missteps.

He went home to Houston to attend to his business, then flew back to spend Thanksgiving with us. He had seen no hint of my mental problems, but in the back of my mind I was nagged by the thought that he didn't understand what a minefield it could be. Three months after we met, we were talking about getting married. Howard insisted that our happiness would free my mind forever.

Of course, we could make no plans until his divorce was final. As it turned out, the details would take two years to settle.

In mid-December I began preparing for my trip to California and my movie comeback. My mother and I decided to spend Christmas Eve in New York and fly to the coast the next day. But that night something inside me came uncaged. I felt an anxiety so deep it was like a blade twisting inside me.

I learned later that I telephoned Howard at his home in Houston. He said there was a quality in my voice he didn't recognize. I was rambling and not very coherent. Mother came on the line and said that we had changed our minds about flying to Hollywood. I had decided to go to Menninger's instead so the doctors could check me over before I went to work.

In the past my behavior had changed gradually, with a symptom or two waving like flags. But now I had a desperate, almost physical need to return to the sanitarium. No matter how painful part of that experience had been, I wanted to be there. I have asked myself many times what possessed me. I still don't know. Was I like a soldier who needs to revisit the scene of his combat and, in that way, relive his courage? Or was I afraid to go back to the movies, afraid of what pressures I might find there? My doctors theorized that subconsciously, I was trying to avoid whatever Hollywood had come to mean to me.

Dr. Holtzman was there to receive me when I arrived at Menninger's. He was visibly distressed. "Why are you here, Gene?" he asked. "You don't need to be here."

"I think I do," I said. "I want you to examine me. I'm scared and I don't know why."

The longer we talked, the wilder the look in my eyes became. I told Dr. Holtzman I felt as though I were inside the wrong skin. Finally, he said, "If we admit you, Gene, I want you to give us one year. I don't think it helps you to be in and out of here after six or eight months. Will you promise me to stay a year?"

I hadn't thought in terms of time. A year. I hated to accept that condition, but I said I would. I was weary of fighting myself.

I felt as though I was watching someone drown. Even now I ache to think of the anguish those around me must have felt. I signed myself back into Menninger's on Christmas Day, 1958. Mother was heartbroken. After I was settled into my room, she sighed and said, "I think I'll go downtown to the Salvation Army and have Christmas with them."

I said, "Mother, you have two other children. Go home. Fly back to Connecticut and spend the holiday with them. Forget about me for a while. I'll be all right."

But she went into town and had dinner at the Salvation Army. She just felt it was a Christian thing to do, sharing time with those who maybe were lonelier than she and I.

I talked to Howard Lee the first three nights I was back in the sanitarium. Then I had to tell him that I couldn't talk to him, or anyone, for a while, but I could receive mail. He promised to write.

Two weeks after I arrived, Dr. Holtzman knew that I really did need to be there. I had sensed my own downfall. I was sicker than I had ever been. I felt lost, without hope, less than childlike. I could not perform any task more complicated than having to feed myself. We were starting over. Whatever I had gone through in the past, the therapy, the shocks, the discoveries, none of it counted now.

I went through a week or two of just vegetating. Medication helped. Then Dr. Wilkens brought me art supplies and encouraged me to paint. Out of a sick mind it is amazing what beauty will come. I painted pictures I could never duplicate when I was well.

And I began to write. During that fuzzy gray time, I wrote down everything I could remember about world history. When Dr. Holtzman stopped by, I began to give him a history lesson. When he displayed some impatience, I said, with a sigh, "If you don't sit still and be quiet, how can I teach you about history?"

Dr. Holtzman was not a very good-looking man. But he was quiet, strong, neat, and gentle. He had helped Dr. Karl Menninger write his book, *The Human Mind*, a textbook classic on mental illness. When I was creating a fantasy of one kind or another, Dr. Holtzman didn't pressure or crowd me. He let me play them out.

Long before my mind returned, I was able to occupy my hands. I took up needlework. Once involved, I couldn't stop. Over the next several months I turned out two large rugs, five pillows, forty sweaters, three full-length knit dresses. In a dim way, I was able to assess my situation, and found it bearable, even acceptable. Once beyond the point of any danger to oneself, of the need for restraints or harsh physical measures, the institutional life is itself narcotic. The actual time one spends with a doctor, or receiving therapy or medicine, is quite small; I would guess an average of less than an hour a day. Rest and make-work fill your time, allowing the mind, hopefully, to unwrinkle and renew. It is not much different, I imagine, from being in a home for the aged.

An interesting process began to take place. I stopped worrying about whether I would ever get out, or even if I was crazy. I assumed I was or I wouldn't be there. From that point on, without realizing it, I had begun the journey back to becoming a whole person. I had cleared a big hurdle. I had accepted my sickness and quit fighting my confinement. But you do walk a fine line. The danger is in getting too secure, too comfortable. In time the doctors would have to prod me to get me out.

By March, when I was able to receive visitors again, Howard Lee flew up from Houston every other weekend to visit me. Few people would have been capable of such devotion and understanding. I realized my good fortune and drew strength from it.

My moods were still unpredictable—I would lose my temper in a flash—but most of the time I was reserved and methodical. I felt obligated to treat the other patients kindly and understand their problems. Perhaps I was motivated not so much by their needs as mine, a desire to be accepted for myself. No one fussed over the fact that I was Gene Tierney, the actress. There are no celebrities, you see, in a mental asylum.

In April my mother came for one of her regular visits. We played bridge with two other patients in a lounge furnished with card tables and television sets. The game was going along pleasantly when, without a word, one of the ladies put down her cards, got up from the table, and left.

Mother stared after her. Then she looked at me, dumbfounded. "Gene," she said, "what is the matter with that woman?"

Dear Mother. A breach of etiquette had been committed and, worse, a bridge game possibly ruined.

I said sternly, "Mother, you are in a sanitarium where people have mental trouble. Don't ever ask what is wrong with someone. Just pay no attention. We'll get someone else."

The incident was quickly forgotten. Later, we had dinner and then I excused myself. "Mother, dear," I said, "you'll have to go home. We're having a party and I have to help decorate the gymnasium tonight."

She said, feeling a little slighted, I think, "You act as if you were in a school."

"Uh-huh," I said, nodding. "It's sort of like a school."

Of course, overadjusting is one of the dangers of being institutionalized. One loses the capacity to make decisions, to think, to care. Being told what to do, and when, over too long a time, becomes deadly to the spirit.

I had always been a brute for work. I had plunged myself into the mindless things that passed my time. I sewed and knitted and crocheted until I was virtually a one-woman factory. Whenever the lady at the knit shop saw me coming, her jaw dropped. "Oh, no," she would say, "you can't have finished the last yarn I sold you?" I annoyed the other patients at times with my quiet intensity, just sitting there, knitting. And so the days passed to the rhythm of my clicking needles.

In June, my brother Howard came to see me. He asked how I spent my time. I told him I sewed and played bridge and went to the clubhouse and drank Cokes.

"Gene," he said firmly, "don't you think you ought to

have a job? It would be good for you to work. Let me
speak to the doctor about it."

Dr. Holtzman believed that the quickest path to recovery was to be positive with me and not allow me to
wallow in my illness. He welcomed the suggestion of my
going to work. He asked me what kind of job I thought
I would like.

I said, "Well, I love clothes and fashions. I'd love to
work in a dress shop if one will have me."

I don't know how many calls were made, or how many
merchants refused. A tolerant and independent woman
named Billie Talmadge offered me a job as a salesclerk
in her Topeka dress shop. I was to be an out-patient. I
was terrified at the thought of working at a real nine-
to-five, the sets-don't-get-torn-down job, of waiting on
customers, of maybe being rejected by the other clerks.
Terrified and excited. Wanting and not wanting.

Dr. Wilkens, bless her, encouraged me. "You remind
me of the fighter Ingemar Johansson," she said. I thought
the comparison strange. I didn't read the sports pages and
was only vaguely aware that a big boxing match had
taken place that month. Dr. Wilkens explained that she
had followed the story of the Swedish fighter who, as a
young Olympian, had lost his nerve in the ring and ran
from an opponent. But he had come back, in June of
1959, to knock out Floyd Patterson to win the heavy-
weight championship. "Gene," she said, "you are going
to come out of this a champion." It was lofty talk, but
it helped. I needed encouragement, not sympathy.

An arrangement was made for me to live in the home of
a sweet old lady, the widow of a doctor, and report two
days a week to the hospital. My landlady, Marguerite
Craig, was in her late sixties. She was cheerful and uncomplicated and created a wonderful atmosphere for me.
I came to love her very much. I warned her I could not

cook. Left to my own devices, I would have to survive on baloney sandwiches. But I told her I would do all the dishes and keep the house clean, if she would do the cooking. That was our bargain, one of the best I ever struck.

Howard Lee visited me often in her home, and Marguerite was smitten with him. She kept carrying on about how handsome he was. In the coy way of young sweethearts, I apologized for the fact that he did not talk much. She laughed and said, "Tell you what. During the pauses you can just enjoy a good look at him."

Working in the dress shop was a tonic for me. I sometimes think I could have been very contented with a career as a saleswoman. Of course, I was the object of some curiosity. One day I overheard two customers whispering about my age. One of them said, "Well, she has to be close to fifty because I was in high school when I saw her movies and I'm such-and-such now." At the time I was not yet thirty-nine.

Billie Talmadge paid me forty dollars a week and I always owed her more money than I made, because I was always buying dresses. In my heart, I believe that I eventually got well because of the kindness of my doctors and co-workers and the love of Howard Lee. All the girls in the store knew I was engaged to him. A young army officer used to stop by the shop regularly, and one night I went with him and another couple to a party. The next day, one of the salesgirls said, "That officer called while you were at lunch and wanted your phone number. No one would give it to him." Then she smiled and said, "We all like Mr. Lee."

I could not begin to know what pressures Howard faced, from whatever sources, to love me or leave me. But he handled them with ease and humor. My brother once said to him, "Do you have any idea what you are getting into? You could be taking on a tremendous responsibility."

Howard Lee said, "Yes, and I know I can cope with it."

Curious. The Howards in my life have been plentiful and interesting and important to me. My father, brother, my second husband, an uncle (Howard Beatty), and the elusive Mr. Hughes.

In a sad-comic way, my engagement to Howard Lee once put me in a threatening position. I had befriended at Menninger's a girl named Maggie, a pretty hairdresser with a violent streak. She had been abandoned by a boy-friend who paid her bills but had stepped on her heart. She often seemed envious of me when Howard visited.

One day she was allowed to leave the grounds, and my mother invited her to go into town with us. We stopped at a pastry shop for a snack and, idly, my mother asked Maggie if her mother was living. She became enraged, began to scream, stormed out of the shop and into the street. I had to use all my persuasion to get her back into the car and soothe her feelings.

After a while, Maggie said something to the effect that I must like my life, having been a movie star, and en-gaged, and able to come and go from the hospital.

Knowing how volatile she was, I did not answer very quickly. I could not guess what her reaction would be—envy, anger, tears. Finally, I said, "Well, nothing is per-fect, Maggie. My life isn't so hot." Then I added, "But it is a good idea to get married if someone you love asks you."

Years later I ran into her in another city, purely by accident. She was well, or seemed to be. And she had got-ten married.

Meanwhile, I had developed another bond with Dr. Anne Wilkens. She, too, was in love and hoping to marry. She was dating another doctor on the Menninger's staff. The patients would see them having lunch together and whisper with glee. It was like rooting for two of your high school teachers to fall in love.

When she announced her engagement, going on forty,

she told me, "You know, my grandmother always predicted that I would marry late." She laughted and said, "Well, I'm getting married and my granny sure called her shot."

In a sense she became my friend and counselor as well as my doctor. But I had my bad times, my days of temper, though they were getting rarer, and we had our disagreements. Once she refused to allow me to see Howard Lee, who had flown up from Houston and was waiting in the visitors' lounge. She felt I was in no condition to see him —I had turned snappish and unstable—and she did not want me to risk losing him.

I got furious. As we argued, I suddenly leaned across her desk and started to muss her hair. She drew her head back and, her voice cool and soothing, said, "Gene, you don't want to do that."

Instantly, I caught myself and slumped back in my chair. I was contrite and embarrassed. Now I apologized: "No, no, of course not. I'm so sorry. Can I do anything? May I fix your hair?"

It was completely out of character for me to try to hurt anyone, much less a friend. I did so in a moment of blind anger because I wanted what I could not have. After a while I whispered, "But I've *got* to win sometime."

Her eyes searched mine and she said, "It looks to me as if you're winning now, Gene." She meant the fact that Howard Lee loved me, and I was beginning to understand the forces in my life that overloaded my mind, and I was able to show my temper instead of stifling it.

Little by little, I was learning discipline and patience. I did not undergo analysis as such. It was psychotherapy and counseling that I needed. The quiet in a sanitarium slows you down, and you begin to understand the things that puzzled you.

The press rediscovered me in the fall of 1959, while I

was working in the dress shop in Topeka. I was not embarrassed to be found there, doing an honest day's work among warm and decent people. Nor was I ashamed to talk about my illness. It was the result, I said, of "my lack of understanding what I could cope with and what I could not. I learned that carrying on while you're broken is not the answer. I tried to work harder and harder, thinking that work would cure everything. All it did was make things worse."

What I said, I meant. I did not blame any doctor or any hospital or any other person for what I went through. I do remind myself that for a long time not enough was known about the fragile balance of the mind. They know more now.

They are not so quick today to subject a person to electric shocks, a barbaric practice I would never wish upon anyone else and would not again endure myself. Nor do they automatically assume that every disturbed mind is the product of a mother or father who was cruel or warped or didn't care. Most parents do the best they can. Some of us are inadequate, but we try. It pleases me to remember the lady in the gift shop at Menninger's, who sold greeting cards. She said to me once, "I like you the best of all the patients here. You're not always complaining about your mother and father."

When I accepted my handicap, my doctors told me, "Now you are going to get well, because you know you have a weakness." But it took me four years to face the truth. Up to then, I committed myself to treatment because I thought my family felt I should, and I told myself I was pleasing them.

The years of mental illness, the hopeless days behind locked doors, are still a nightmare time to me. It was as if a curtain had been drawn over my mind. A cliché, I suppose, but true. I cannot forget the cost in time and love and the common hurt of others in raising that curtain again.

The kindness of others made my return to society possible. Richard Widmark wrote a gentle, teasing note from Hollywood: "Hurry back, or there will be nothing left for us to play but Ma and Pa Kettle pictures."

A dear friend from school days at Miss Porter's invited me to her home for weekends when a lot of people were afraid or embarrassed to have a mental patient around. Each morning she would send her little daughter up to my room with a breakfast tray, with a rosebud in a vase. I heard her tell the child not to ask me questions. "Gracie, come here a moment," she said quietly. "Remember, the first requisite of a lady is to be kind."

Children have a curiosity that is irresistible. Once, one of my nieces asked how I could stand being locked up. I said, "Mikie, in a factory where the china is turned out according to a certain pattern, week after week, month after month, every now and then there is a damaged piece.

"It is called a reject and it is sold more cheaply than the good china. I can stand being locked up because I know I can be repaired. I must get myself into a condition where I am whole. It is all right to see yourself for a time as a reject. But you mustn't mess up your life with behavior that isn't your true self. Just don't let yourself be sold as an imperfect piece of workmanship. You may have a weakness, but you needn't accept second-rate behavior or a second-rate life. Then you make your decisions with the help of those who love you."

It was a fairly long speech, for me. I said it patiently and with forbearance. I don't know if Mikie understood, but it made me feel better. All I meant was that we can be born with a flaw, or develop one. We can be rejected —by a parent, a lover, or friends. But people are not pieces of china. We can help ourselves and seek help from others. We can fight back and become whole again. The pity is not in failing. It is in not trying.

I had gone through all of the stages known to a mentally sick person. I had given up, fought back, shrunk from people, reached out, been overwhelmed by petty things, looked into a bottomless pit and found hope.

If it is possible to make a general statement about the people one finds in a mental ward, it would be that all of them have this in common: they feel unloved, alone, and unwanted. Loneliness devours them. Even when they have no privacy.

Rebuilding my own strength was a slow and fragile task. But one weekend I went with my family to a friend's home in Connecticut for a few hours of tennis and leisure. By Monday morning I would be back in my room at the hospital. I looked at my daughter, Tina, and I thought, "What future is there for her if I don't get well? How can she exist with a mother who is in and out of hospitals?"

Then I noticed she was holding the hand of my brother. I wasn't alone. My family would protect Tina if anything happened to me. I watched her small hand clinging to the larger one of her uncle, almost lost in it, and I realized, *there is love here*, and it will bring me out of my depths.

I gave Dr. Holtzman his year, the one I promised to stay, and he kept his word. In November of 1959, I was summoned to the office of Dr. Karl Menninger, the founder of the clinic, the man the patients referred to, usually with affection, as "the Great White Father."

Although I liked and respected Dr. Karl, my contacts with him had been infrequent, and my favorite was his younger brother, Dr. Will. I would see Dr. Will now and then in the cafeteria, and he would greet me with, "You're looking very pretty today, Gene." It wasn't his flattery that appealed to me. He was the one who went around raising funds for research, scouting the country for business support. In a place where people lived their dreams and illusions, and the doctors sometimes talked only to each other, I liked the fact that Dr. Will was part of the real world. I was then on a realism kick. The harder I looked at life, the sooner I thought I would get well. Money was real. Dr. Will raised money. I liked him.

But Dr. Karl was kind and charming when I went to see him. He said he had read the reports on me. He thought I had been helped by working in town. He said I might continue to have my ups and downs, but I could learn to live with them. Finally, he said, "We are going to give you your release. You know right from wrong. There is no reason you can't have a happy life."

He stood up then, and smiled, and in a manner so formal it was almost as though he were making a wedding toast, he said, "I wish you good luck."

As I left the sanitarium for the second time, I felt eager and confident for the first time in many years. I had learned that the mind is the most beautiful part of the body, and I was grateful to God and the Menningers that I had mine back.

CHAPTER
20

Epilogue:
My Favorite Role

A relationship often needs a nudge, a bit of stage direction, if it is to grow into a union. In the natural course of events, men drift and women act.

I was being "coached" in my romance with Howard Lee by my sister-in-law, the former Jane Hewitt, of Cambridge, whose father, Erastus Hewitt, had been a neighbor and close friend of the poet Robert Frost. Jane has a poetic soul and a clever mind, a nice blend, and I found her advice fun even when I could not use it.

Years ago she and my brother struck the kind of bargain that is the key to many marriages. No matter how they prospered, he said, or what he gave her, minks and lovely things, he wanted her to cook his dinner every night. As long as I have known them, she has—such dishes as fish baked in a cream sauce, with peeled grapes floating, and the correct wine from their cellar.

Jane is one of those blessed people, equal to any situation. I left my dog with her once and the newness of the surroundings undid his good manners. Jane assured me that keeping the floors clean would be no problem if she could locate her "super duper pooper scooper."

During the year I was at Menninger's, her father came to visit me. He knew I was fearful of what my absence was doing to Tina. His eyes held mine and he said, "Don't you worry about this little girl of yours. My daughter can manage any situation."

For months Jane looked after Tina, until Oleg came for her and took her back to New York. It was good that she could be with her cousins, and then with her father. When a child is apart from her mother, the rest of the family needs to tighten the circle.

By the time I was released from the Menninger Clinic, my engagement to Howard Lee had moved into its second year. He did not seem to think that was very long to wait. Men don't. But Jane encouraged me to date other men, if only to make Howard jealous. "Gene," she said, "what you have to remember is, life is just once around the track."

Emergency measures were really not needed. On July 11, 1960, W. Howard Lee and I were married in Aspen, where we met. In New York that day, a reporter ran into Oleg Cassini and found him preoccupied. She said he paused and told her, "My wife got married today." I was touched by what those words implied. I know that if it had been up to Oleg, we might never have divorced. He was a product of the European culture, one that opposed divorce through thick and thin, that held a man did not discard his wife for some girl of the moment. Oleg has never remarried.

We are in some ways closer today than when we eloped, and we are bonded by the fact of our two daughters. From the time of my illness, Oleg has borne the expense of Daria's care and has assisted Tina when she needed it. Fortunate is the woman who has a loving husband, and an ex-husband who remains her friend.

I had been offered different lives by men who were colorful and original. But all the time, perhaps without knowing it, what I wanted and needed was the solid citizen. I remembered the warning of the doctor who, referring to Aly Khan, had said I would "never meet the man of my dreams in El Morocco." I know now, and knew soon enough, that he was right. Howard Lee took over my life sweetly, gently, and forever.

He is secure, even-tempered, and relaxed. He is a proud man with a gentle side, who is as much at ease in a garden or in the kitchen as he once was around an oil derrick. The walls of his office are adorned with photographs of the fields and rigs once worked by his family, including Spindletop, the Beaumont, Texas, discovery that ushered in the new industrial age.

Howard came along in the heyday of the oil wildcatter, men who built fortunes on borrowed equipment and lost them on the turn of a card. His sister married Glenn McCarthy, who built the Shamrock Hotel in Houston and became the model for the character of Jett Rink in Edna Ferber's novel *Giant*.

Ours had to be one of the strangest courtships on record, covering two years, half of it while I was on furlough from a mental hospital. By choice, most of our dates were quiet ones, dinners for two and pleasant drives.

But once we attended a party given by Ray and Fran Stark in New York, and Howard met Oleg Cassini, his brother, Igor, and Aly Khan. He was very comfortable with them, so sure of himself that I suspect some of the guests felt cheated. Not I. Howard was so quiet compared to the other men I had known, but his was the quiet of the forest. The Starks, who had been among the first couples to accept Oleg and me, were as quick to embrace Howard. They liked his lack of pretense. He was so natural, so without guile; he made an ideal straight man for Ray, an incurable punster.

Howard asked Ray why a movie he had just seen and enjoyed, *The Birdman of Alcatraz*, did not have a bigger success. "I guess," quipped Ray, "because it was a fowl picture."

During that same time, we joined Joseph Cotten and his first wife, Lenore, for an evening in New York, where Joe was appearing on Broadway. That night Howard and I left the hotel and could not get a taxi to the theater. Finally, I grabbed his hand and said, "Listen, you're with an old New York working girl and there are other ways to get to the theater besides a cab. Follow me." I led the way to the Fifty-ninth Street subway and we got out on Broadway, one block from the theater. Howard had expressed some misgivings, having read for years about New York's famous muggings. I told him I used to ride the subway all the time when I was a young girl starting out as an actress. He laughed and said he would like to have a picture of that.

After the play, we rode to "21" in a glistening new Rolls-Royce Silver Cloud that Joe had given Lenore on their anniversary. I don't know if one should look for symbolism or not. But we started out the evening on the subway and came home in a Rolls-Royce. Sometimes life is like that, and sometimes the other way around.

The night was a special one for me in another way. The Cottens had been a part of my Hollywood good times, the Sunday tennis parties with a group that had reached out to Oleg and me—Jennifer Jones and David Selznick, Lilli Palmer and Rex Harrison, the Sam Goldwyns and the David Nivens.

On our way to her car, Lenore had said to me, "Gene, I'm not sure, but your Howard Lee may be the handsomest man I ever saw." Hearing women talk about how men look can be silly or boring or both. But show business is partly a flesh market, and the subject of beauty, male or female, preoccupies us. For the record, of the three best-looking men I have ever known, none were actors: my husband, Howard Lee, Jack Kennedy, and Dr. Denton Cooley, the Houston heart surgeon.

A reporter once asked me who I thought was the most attractive man in the world. After a long, blank silence, I blurted out, "Anthony Eden." It seemed a frivolous thing to say about a man of such distinction, and for years I was embarrassed, thinking that the former British prime minister might have read that remark.

A few months after that night in New York, Lenore Cotten died while Joe was on location in Italy. He eventually married another lovely girl, an actress named Pat Green, and we catch up with them from time to time when they appear on the dinner theater circuit.

I was thirty-nine when I married Howard Lee and settled quietly in Houston. I had not made a film in five years and was no longer in demand. I did not find it traumatic to face the fact that my brightest hours were gone, some of them having slipped away without my even knowing it. I felt safe, protected. But a small, nagging part of me would not turn loose of whatever cord still held me to my craft.

In 1961, I was signed for the role of Constance Mac-Kenzie in *Return to Peyton Place*, to be directed by Jose Ferrer, one of my earlier leading men. I had to withdraw from the role when I became pregnant, a happy discovery that would have offset any professional loss easily had I not miscarried and lost the baby at four and a half months. Eleanor Parker replaced me in the mother's part.

When no one else in Hollywood would offer me an opportunity, Otto Preminger did. A friend, genuine and unafraid, Otto signed me in 1962 for the all-star cast he was assembling for *Advise and Consent*. I was to play Dolly Harrison, the Washington hostess who has an affair with the Senate majority leader (Walter Pidgeon). It was my first film since *The Left Hand of God*, and I immediately ran into a problem unrelated to my ability to act. I was considered uninsurable because of my mental history. Otto told the insurance company flatly that, if they rejected me, he would cancel his coverage with them for this and any future productions. They caved in. That was quite a risk for Preminger to take. I could have fallen ill again. Thankfully, I didn't.

I had not worked since 1955 and no effort ever came to me any harder. But in my background had always been a determination to see a job through. Preminger's act of heart and firmness spurred me on even more.

My part was less than major, but it had glamour. I was dressed by Bill Blass in black and white, as Oleg had often costumed me. I enjoyed playing a mature woman in a film that dealt with mature subjects. In my youth, my taste had always run to what I called cut crystal and champagne pictures; deep rugs, chandeliers, and gay weekends. Swimming to the side of a pool and stretching out a hand for a glass of champagne. Pictures that made life seem secure, when everything else in the world is insecure. But times change and good films capture those changes.

Howard joined me during the shooting. His daughter, Donna Lee, worked in the office of John Tower, the Texas senator. Soon she was being escorted around town by a member of the cast, Lew Ayres, which made Howard a little nervous. He kept saying, "But the man is my age. He's old enough to be her father." Lew later married an airline hostess, younger than Donna.

Those weeks in Washington were like being a part of one continuing diplomatic reception. There was our cast luncheon at the White House, where I saw Jack Kennedy again. We sailed on the presidential yacht, the *Honey*

Fitz, as the guests of Bob and Ethel Kennedy. We attended a dinner party at the home of Jean Kennedy Smith, and another at the French embassy. I reminisced with Jean about the first time I had met her family at the Kennedy compound at Cape Cod. She reminded me that Teddy, the youngest brother, then about thirteen, kept asking me to dance. I nodded and remarked that Ted was interested in girls even then.

She winked and said, "Yes, and he still is."

After *Advise and Consent*, a year passed before another part would come along. I had no intention of returning to films as a career, but I did want to keep a foot in the door. On a visit to California, I ran into the director George Roy Hill at a party. He was casting *Toys in the Attic*, Lillian Hellman's play about a neurotic southern family, and I told him I wanted to go back to work.

Hill said politely, "Gene, the only part I haven't cast yet calls for an older woman."

I said, "We can always dye my hair gray."

I played the mother-in-law of Dean Martin, who was my own age. But I had added a few pounds, and we salted my hair with flecks of gray.

Three years had passed since my remarriage, and all during that time Howard had been pressing me to let him meet my father. Steeped in the Texas and southwestern traditions, Howard was anxious to assure him that his daughter was in good hands. I had seen my father once in sixteen years. Although I had told him the stories often, Howard did not understand my coldness, the resentment I still felt because he had abandoned my mother, and had sued me for fifty thousand dollars, making me feel less a daughter than an investment.

Father had written at one point, saying he hoped to meet my new husband, but I had not written back. I had avoided the subject whenever I could, but in late 1963

Howard brought it up again during a vacation in Aspen. We were planning to be in New York in a few weeks, and I agreed, with mixed emotions, to invite my father to meet us there. I didn't even have his phone number in Pennsylvania and called an aunt to get it.

When I told her why I was calling, she broke into sobs over the phone. "Gene, I didn't phone you," she said, "for fear of upsetting you. But your father is dead." He had died of cancer a few days before. I felt no pain, no shock, nothing. I felt I had lost my father all those years ago. But when I looked at Howard, his eyes were wet, and I knew he had been hoping to bring us together.

A door to my past had closed.

In 1964, Fox still owed me a picture from my last contract, which called for ten films in seven years. To finish out the contract, I was given a very small part, almost a cameo, as Brian Keith's wife in *The Pleasure Seekers*. In the leading roles of romantically active playgirls were Ann-Margret, Yvette Mimieux, and Carol Lynley, part of a new generation of Hollywood beauties.

The picture was a melancholy time for me. I had not made it for the money, or for pride, or even a final taste of glory. I had wanted to make the picture to finish the cycle and close the book, and recapture for one last time the fun that making movies had been for me—candy for the soul. But the Hollywood I knew was gone. The star system that created me and the other so-called Fox girls no longer existed.

I had to be honest with myself. I had not played a major role in ten years. Any studio that offered me one would be gambling on my health. I would be remembered, according to *Newsweek* magazine, as one of Hollywood's five most poignant beauties. The others were Louise Brooks, a star of the 1920s, Frances Farmer, Ilona Massey, and Joan Collins. But Hollywood always had a truer measure of worth than beauty or even talent. What was your last box office?

I was forty-four, too young to retire to Sunset Boulevard, too old to start over. My part in *The Pleasure Seekers* was so undemanding it caused me no difficulty, but not much pleasure.

Another door had closed.

In March of 1969, I appeared in an episode of *The FBI* on television. In December of that year I played the crippled wife of Ray Milland—my costar of eighteen years before—in a made-for-TV movie, *Daughter of the Mind*, produced by Twentieth Century-Fox.

That appearance was to be my last before the cameras, not entirely by choice, but certainly without complaint. I had a fulfilling career: thirty-three feature films and three Broadway plays. My leading men included Gable, Tracy, Fonda, Ty Power, Bogart. I was fortunate to have been nominated for an Academy Award (*Leave Her to Heaven*) and to have played a part, Laura, that a song and a portrait helped make mine forever.

Houston is a far piece from Old Hollywood, but I have a role now that I think becomes me. I am a grandmother, and I can play that game with the best of them. My Delphina and Jasmina were born on the same day, two years apart, and now I have a year-old grandson, Alexander. They are the children of Tina, who made her debut in Houston, went to Rome to study, and found an Italian husband, Giuliano Granata. I suspected she would.

My life in Houston is settled and relaxed. I do my own marketing, keep house, play bridge, shop, and do what charity work I can. I have made friends and they guard my privacy. I am recognized by some, and the name often brings a startled second look. But no one fusses and I am grateful.

I hole up now and then and do nothing for days but

read, sometimes losing myself in Voltaire or Tolstoy. I still see a doctor once a month, sometimes more often. I appreciate my life, and my health, in a way that I never could when I was very young and very sure.

In a Houston department store one day, I burst into tears unexpectedly when a salesgirl asked, "May I help you?" I know she was stunned and bewildered, but how could I explain? How could I tell her what thoughts and memories that perfectly innocent question unleashed? Of all the people, and all the ways, I had been helped—in my career, and through the long, slow, uneven recovery from mental sickness.

It is difficult to write or talk about any form of mental disease, especially your own, without sounding as though you were examining a bug under glass. I had an undying curiosity about what was wrong with me, but I could never bring myself to ask a direct question and no one would tell me in words I could understand.

Once I stole a book from the desk of one of my doctors, stayed awake all the next night reading it, and knew less than when I started. In time I realized, and my doctors confirmed it, that a name or a label is less important than admitting I have a weakness.

There are words used in the practice of psychiatry that have no more meaning to the average ear than certain bird calls. Paranoia. Schizophrenia. Manic depression. Hallucinations.

But try this: once I gained twenty pounds in a matter of weeks on a diet that consisted mainly of bread-and-butter sandwiches and chocolate bars. When I finally snapped out of it, and Howard asked me what had been in my mind, I remembered my fantasy clearly. I imagined that I was pregnant and eating for two. Each night I would give birth, and each morning the Communists would steal my child.

Another time I dreamed that Daria was no longer in an institution, but was in the home of another couple down the street from us. Howard found me in the middle of the night, pounding on their door, demanding that Daria be returned to me. They hardly knew us but were very kind about the scene I had caused.

I can no longer doubt that the main cause of my difficulties stemmed from the tragedy of my daughter's unsound birth and my inability to face my feelings, trying instead to bury them. I regretted too many things: finding out that a father who taught me that honor was everything was not an honorable man. Marrying against my parents' wishes and proving them right. Twice falling in love with men with whom I had no future.

My kind of mental illness is a stress disease. The problem is in the blood, in the chemical balance, but it can be triggered by petty things and minor distractions. Your personality disintegrates, along with your own willpower. You have to accept being led.

One recent Christmas I found myself helpless at the thought of making a turkey dressing. I had a house filled with grandchildren and I was coming down with flu, and the turkey dressing did me in. I went through a depression that lasted for days. Later, a friend said, "Gene, you can buy it at the grocery store." Now why hadn't I thought of that? The grocery store!

I used to worry about going places after I was well, and seeing people I might have been around when I was acting peculiar. But now I accept myself as I am, and so do my friends. I had to know that when a day came, or many of them, when I felt depressed, I wasn't going mad. It was all right to be unhappy.

In many ways I have been fortunate. In one hospital I knew a girl who could never comb her hair. The nurses feared she would use the comb to hurt herself. She heard voices that told her wicked or senseless things. The voices I heard—usually my brother's—gave me pep talks, telling me, "You're going to get well."

I have skated on thin ice as far as responsible behavior is concerned. I have been disagreeable, rude, insulting, and withdrawn. But except for the incident at the neighbor's house, I have remained more or less under control, even during my deepest depressions. I had no compulsion to throw things, or to break all the dishes, or force myself on the delivery man. My eyes might assume a wild expression when I was ill, but I was not wild within. Really, I have been lucky. Some bottomless instinct made me hang on to a thread of respectability.

I was admitted to three different hospitals—sanitariums, if you prefer—over a period of six years. A dozen doctors treated me. I had a total of thirty-two electric shock treatments. During my first confinement, I was taking more medicine than any other patient. So there is hope for everybody.

One thing I did learn: if you are going to be mentally ill it is like anything else, like the best country club or the best hotel. The most expensive places are always the most desirable. I used up every cent I had earned as an actress. I consider myself well now, but I know I have to make an effort to stay that way. I still take medication, and I am subject to periods of odd behavior. As the old saying goes, "The crazy person says, 'Everyone is crazy but thee and me.'" To make any progress at all, you first have to accept the fact that you have an illness. If it takes saying out loud, "I am sick, I am insane, I am a crazy person," one must say it.

I have gone through such a time, and more, and survived.

I traveled in a world that once was—Hollywood of the war and immediate postwar years. And I existed in a world that never is—the prison of the mind. If what I have learned from these experiences can be summed up in one sentence, it would be this: life is not a movie. But I do not make that point in a sad or regretful way. I can only wonder, if my life *had been* a movie, would a director have cast Gene Tierney to play the part? The bitter with the sweet makes for a better part.

Gene Tierney's
Feature Films

THE RETURN OF FRANK JAMES (20th, 1940) 92m.

Producer, Darryl F. Zanuck; director, Fritz Lang; screenplay, Sam Hellman; art directors, Richard Day, Wiard B. Ihnen; music director, David Buttolph; camera, George Barnes, William V. Skall; editor, Walter Thompson.

Henry Fonda (Frank James); Gene Tierney (Eleanor Stone); Jackie Cooper (Clem); Henry Hull (Major); John Carradine (Bob Ford); J. Edward Bromberg (Runyon); Donald Meek (McCoy); Eddie Collins (Station Agent); George Barbier (The Judge); Ernest Whitman (Pinkie); Charles Tannen (Charles Ford); Lloyd Corrigan (Mr. Stone); Russell Hicks (Prosecutor); Victor Kilian (Preacher); Edward McWade (Col. Jackson); George Chandler (Roy); Irving Bacon (Man); Frank Shannon (Sheriff); Barbara Pepper (Nellie); Stymie Beard (Boy); Lee Phelps (Bartender); Adrian Morris (Detective); Milton Kibbee (Reporter).

HUDSON'S BAY (20th, 1940) 95m.

Associate producer, Kenneth Macgowan; director, Irving Pichel; screenplay, Lamar Trotti; art directors, Richard

Day, W. B. Ihnen; music, Alfred Newman; camera, Peverell Marley, George Barnes; editor, Robert Simpson.

Paul Muni (Pierre Esprit Radisson); Gene Tierney (Barbara); Laird Cregar (Gooseberry); John Sutton (Lord Edward Crewe); Virginia Field (Nell Gwyn); Vincent Price (King Charles); Nigel Bruce (Prince Rupert); Morton Lowry (Gerald Hall); Robert Greig (Sir Robert); Chief Thundercloud (Grimha); Frederic Worlock (English Governor); Montagu Love (Governor); Ian Wolfe (Mayor); Chief John Big Tree (Chief); Jody Gilbert (Germaine); Dorothy Dearing (Girl); Reginald Sheffield (Clerk); Keith Hitchcock (Footman); Lilyan Irene (Maid); Jean Del Val (Captain).

TOBACCO ROAD (20th, 1941) 84m.

Producer, Darryl F. Zanuck; associate producers, Jack Kirkland, Harry H. Oshrin; director, John Ford; based on the novel by Erskine Caldwell and the play by Kirkland; screenplay, Nunnally Johnson; art directors, Richard Day, James Basevi; music, David Buttolph; camera, Arthur C. Miller; editor, Barbara McLean.

Charley Grapewin (Jester); Marjorie Rambeau (Sister Bessie); Gene Tierney (Ellie May); William Tracy (Dude Lester); Elizabeth Patterson (Ada Lester); Dana Andrews (Capt. Tim); Slim Summerville (Peabody); Ward Bond (Love); Grant Mitchell (Geo. Payne); Zeffie Tibury (Grandma); Russell Simpson (Chief of Police); Spencer Charters (County Clerk); Irving Bacon (Teller); Harry Tyler (Auto Dealer); Charles Halton (Mayor); George Chandler (Clerk); Marian Free (Clerk); Dorothy Adams (Susie May); Mae Marsh (Woman); Jack Pennick (Policeman).

BELLE STARR (20th, 1941) 87m.

Associate producer, Kenneth Macgowan; director, Irving Cummings; based on the story by Cameron Rogers,

Niven Busch; screenplay, Lamar Trotti; art directors, Richard Day, Nathan Juran; music, Alfred Newman; camera, Ernest Palmer, Ray Rennahan; editor, Robert Simpson.

Randolph Scott (Sam Starr); Gene Tierney (Belle Starr); Dana Andrews (Major Thomas Crail); Shepperd Strudwick (Ed Shirley); Elizabeth Patterson (Sarah); Chill Wills (Blue Duck); Louise Beavers (Mammy Lou); Olin Howland (Jasper Tench); Paul Burns (Sergeant); Joseph Sawyer (John Cole); Joseph Downing (Jim Cole); Charles Trowbridge (Col. Bright); Howard Hickman (Col. Thornton); James Flavin (Sergeant); Charles Middleton (Carpetbagger); Stymie Beard (Young Jaks); Mae Marsh (Preacher's Wife); Kermit Maynard (Union Officer); Franklyn Farnum (Barfly); Cecil Weston (Mother).

SUNDOWN (UA, 1941) 90m.

Producer, Walter Wanger; director, Henry Hathaway; based on the story by Barré Lyndon; adaptation, Charles G. Booth; screenplay, Lyndon; art director, Alexander Golitzen; music, Miklos Rozsa; special camera, Ray O. Binger; camera, Charles Lang; editor, Dorothy Spencer.

Gene Tierney (Zia); Bruce Cabot (Capt. Bill Crawford); George Sanders (Major Coombes); Harry Carey (Dewey); Joseph Calleia (Pallini); Sir Cedric Hardwicke (Bishop Coombes); Carl Esmond (Kuypens); Reginald Gardiner (Lt. Turner); Marc Lawrence (Hammud); Gilbert Emery (Ashburten); Dorothy Dandridge (Kipsang's Bride); Woodrow Strode (Tribal Policeman); Horace Walker (Lecherous Old Man); Emmett Smith (Kipsang); Jeni LaGon (Miriami); Edward Das (Pindi).

THE SHANGHAI GESTURE (UA, 1942) 106m.

Producer, Arnold Pressburger; associate producer, Albert de Courville; director, Josef Von Sternberg; based on the play by John Colton; screenplay, Von Sternberg; assistant directors, Charles Kerr, Fred Pressburger; art directors, Boris

Leven, Howard Bristol; music, Richard Hageman; camera, Paul Ivano; editor, Sam Winston.

Gene Tierney (Poppy Charteris); Walter Huston (Sir Guy Charteris); Victor Mature (Doctor Omar); Ona Munson (Mother Gin-Sling); Phyllis Brooks (Dixie Pomeroy); Albert Bessermann (The Commissioner); Maria Ouspenskaya (The Amah); Eric Blore (The Bookkeeper); Ivan Lebedeff (The Gambler); Mike Mazurki (The Coolie); Clyde Fillmore (The Comprador); Grayce Hampton (The Social Leader); Rex Evans (Brooks); Mikhail Rasumny (The Appraiser); Michael Delmatoff (The Bartender); Marcel Dalio (The Croupier); John Abbott (The Escort).

SON OF FURY (20th, 1942) 102m.

Producer, Darryl F. Zanuck; associate producer, William Perlberg; director, John Cromwell; based on the novel *Benjamin Blake* by Edison Marshall; screenplay, Philip Dunne; music director, Alfred Newman; camera, Arthur Miller; editor, Walter Thompson.

Tyrone Power (Benjamin Blake); Gene Tierney (Eve); George Sanders (Sir Arthur Blake); Frances Farmer (Isabel Blake); Roddy McDowall (Ben—As a Boy); John Carradine (Caleb Greene); Elsa Lanchester (Bristol Isabel); Harry Davenport (Amos Kidder); Kay Johnson (Helena Blake); Dudley Digges (Bartholomew Pratt); Halliwell Hobbes (Purdy); Marten Lamont (Kenneth Hobart); Arthur Hohl (Capt. Greenough); Pedro de Cordoba (Feanou); Dennis Hoey (Lord Tarrant); Robert Greig (Judge); Ray Mala (Marnea); Clifford Severn (Paddy); Heather Thatcher (Maggice Martin); Lester Matthews (Prosecutor); Ethel Griffies (Matron); Mae Marsh (Mrs. Purdy); James Craven (Guard); Olaf Hytten (Court Clerk).

RINGS ON HER FINGERS (20th, 1942) 85m.

Producer, Milton Sperling; director, Rouben Mamoulian; based on the story by Robert Pirosh, Joseph Schrank;

screenplay, Ken Englund; art directors, Richard Day, Albert Hogsett; music, Cyril J. Mockridge; camera, George Barnes; editor, Barbara McLean.

Henry Fonda (John Wheeler); Gene Tierney (Susan Miller/Linda Worthington); Laird Cregar (Warren); Shepperd Strudwick (Tod Penwick); Spring Byington (Mrs. Maybelle Worthington); Frank Orth (Kellogg); Henry Stephenson (The Colonel); Marjorie Gateson (Mrs. Fenwick); George Dessey (Fenwick, Sr.); Iris Adrian (Peggy); Thurston Hall (Capt. Beasley); Clara Blandick (Mrs. Beasley); Billy Benedict (Newsboy); Edgar Norton (Payl); Frank Coghlan, Jr. (Page Boy); Evelyn Mulhall (Miss Alderney); Bob Ryan (Attendant); Herbert Vigran (Cab Driver).

THUNDER BIRDS (20th, 1942) 79m.

Producer, Lamar Trotti; director, William A. Wellman; based on the story by Melville Crossman; screenplay, Trotti; special commentary, John Gunther; camera, Ernest Palmer; editor, Walter Thompson.

Gene Tierney (Kay Saunders); Preston Foster (Steve Britt); John Sutton (Peter Stackhouse); Jack Holt (McDonald); Dame May Whitty (Lady Stackhouse); George Barbier (Grampa); Richard Haydn (George Lockwood); Reginald Denny (Barrett); Ted North (Cadet Hackzell); Janis Carter (Blonde); Montague Shaw (Doctor); Viola Moore (Nurse); Nana Bryant (Mrs. Black); Joyce Compton (Saleswoman); Bess Flowers (Nurse); Peter Lawford (British Cadet); Selmar Jackson (Man); Charles Tannen (Recording); Harry Strang (Forest Ranger); Walter Tetley (Messenger Boy).

CHINA GIRL (20th, 1942) 95m.

Producer, Ben Hecht; director, Henry Hathaway; based on the story by Melville Crossman; screenplay, Hecht; art directors, Richard Day, Wiard B. Ihnen; music, Hugo W.

Friedhofer; camera, Lee Garmes; editor, James B. Clark.

Gene Tierney (Miss Young); George Montgomery (Johnny); Lynn Bari (Capt. Fifi); Victor McLaglen (Major Weed); Alan Baxter (Chinese Boy); Sig Rumann (Jerubi); Myron McCormick (Shorty); Bobby Blake (Chinese Boy); Ann Pennington (The Entertainer); Philip Ahn (Dr. Young); Paul Fung (Governor); Tom Neal (Capt. Raines); Chester Gan (Japanese Officer); Fred Kohler, Jr. (Flyer); Beal Wong (Sergeant); Bruce Wong (Officer); Allen Jung (Japanese Officer).

HEAVEN CAN WAIT (20th, 1943) 113m.

Producer-director, Ernst Lubitsch; based on the play *Birthday* by Lazlo Bus-Fekete; screenplay, Samson Raphaelson; art directors, James Basevi, Leland Fuller; music, Alfred Newman; camera, Edward Cronjager; editor, Dorothy Spencer.

Gene Tierney (Martha); Don Ameche (Henry Van Cleve); Charles Coburn (Hugo Van Cleve); Marjorie Main (Mrs. Strabel); Laird Cregar (His Excellency); Spring Byington (Bertha Van Cleve); Allyn Joslyn (Albert Van Cleve); Eugene Pallette (Mr. Strabel); Signe Hasso (Mademoiselle); Louis Calhern (Randolph Van Cleve); Helena Reynolds (Peggy Nash); Aubrey Mather (James); Tod Andrews (Jack Van Cleve); Leonard Carey (Flogdell); Clarence Muse (Jasper); Dickie Moore (Henry—Age 15); Dickie Jones (Albert—Age 15); Trudy Marshall (Jane); Florence Bates (Mrs. Craig); Clara Blandick (Grandmother); Anita Bolster (Mrs. Cooper-Cooper); Grayce Hampton (Albert's Mother); Alfred Hall (Albert's Father); Nino Pipitone, Jr. (Jack—As a Child); James Flavin (Policeman); Scotty Beckett (Henry—Age 9); Doris Merrick (Nurse).

LAURA (20th, 1944) 88m.

Producer, Otto Preminger; directors, Preminger, Rouben Mamoulian; based on the story by Vera Caspary; screenplay, Jay Dratler, Samuel Hoffenstein, Betty Reinhardt; art directors, Lyle Wheeler, Leland Fuller; music, David Raksin; camera, Joseph LaShelle; editor, Louis Loeffler.

Gene Tierney (Laura); Dana Andrews (Mark McPherson); Clifton Webb (Waldo Lydecker); Vincent Price (Shelby Carpenter); Judith Anderson (Ann Treadwell); Dorothy Adams (Bessie Clary); James Flavin (McAvity); Clyde Fillmore (Bullitt); Ralph Dunn (Fred Callahan); Grant Mitchell (Corey); Kathleen Howard (Louise); Lane Chandler (Detective); Aileen Pringle (Woman); Buster Miles (Office Boy); Jane Nigh (Secretary).

A BELL FOR ADANO (20th, 1945) 103m.

Producers, Louis D. Lighton, Lamar Trotti; director, Henry King; based on the novel by John Hersey; screenplay, Trotti, Norman Reilly Raine; art directors, Lyle Wheeler, Mark-Lee Kirk; music director, Alfred Newman; special effects, Fred Sersen; camera, Joseph LaShelle; editor, Barbara McLean.

Gene Tierney (Tina); John Hodiak (Major Joppolo); William Bendix (Sergeant Borth); Glenn Langan (Lt. Livingstone); Richard Conte (Nicolo); Stanley Prager (Sergeant Trampani); Henry Morgan (Captain Purvis); Montague Banks (Giuseppe); Reed Hadley (Commander Robertson); Roy Roberts (Colonel Middleton); Hugo Haas (Father Pensovecchio); Marcel Dalio (Zito); Fortunio Bonanova (Gargano); Henry Armetta (Errante); Roman Bohnen (Erba); Luis Alberni (Cacopardo); Eduardo Ciannelli (Major Nasta); William Edmunds (Tomasino); Yvonne Vautrot (Francesca); John Russell (Captain Anderson); Minor Watson (General McKay); Grady Sutton (Edward); Minerva Urecal (Italian Woman); Harry Carter (Non Com); Eva Puig (Woman); Earl Easton (Boy Violinist); Frank Lackteen (Photographer); Ed Munday (Emancipated Man); Nino Pipitone, Jr. (Boy).

LEAVE HER TO HEAVEN (20th, 1945) 110m.
Producer, William A. Bacher; director, John M.
Stahl; based on the novel by Ben Ames Williams; screenplay,
Jo Swerling; art directors, Lyle Wheeler, Maurice Ransford;
camera, Leon Shamroy; editor, James B. Clark.

Gene Tierney (Ellen Berent); Cornel Wilde (Rich-
ard Harland); Jeanne Crain (Ruth Berent); Vincent Price
(Russell Quinton); Mary Philips (Mrs. Berent); Ray Collins
(Glen Robie); Gene Lockhart (Dr. Saunders); Reed Hadley
(Dr. Mason); Darryl Hickman (Danny Harland); Chill
Wills (Leick Thorne); Paul Everton (Judge); Olive
Blakeney (Mrs. Robie); Addison Richards (Bedford); Harry
Depp (Catterson); Grant Mitchell (Carlson); Milton Parsons
(Medcraft); Betty Hannon (Tess Robie); Mae Marsh (Fish-
erwoman).

DRAGONWYCK (20th, 1946) 103m.
Producers, Darryl F. Zanuck, Ernst Lubitsch; direc-
tors, Joseph L. Mankiewicz, Lubitsch; based on the novel by
Anya Seton; screenplay, Mankiewicz; art directors, Lyle
Wheeler, J. Russell Spencer, Thomas Little, Paul S. Fox;
music, Alfred Newman; choreography, Arthur Appel; camera,
Arthur Miller; editor, Dorothy Spencer.

Gene Tierney (Miranda); Walter Huston (Ephraim
Wells); Vincent Price (Nicholas Van Ryn); Glenn Langan
(Dr. Jeff Turner); Anne Revere (Abigail); Spring Byington
(Magda); Connie Marshall (Katrine); Henry Morgan
(Bleecker); Vivienne Osborne (Johanna); Jessica Tandy
(Peggy O'Malley); Trudy Marshall (Elizabeth Van Borden);
Reinhold Schunzel (Count De Grenier); Jane Nigh (Ta-
bitha); Ruth Ford (Cornelia Van Borden); Trevor Bardette,
Arthur Aylsworth, Clancy Cooper, Tom Fadden, Addison
Richards (Farmers); Gertrude Astor (Nurse); Douglas
Wood (Mayor); Steve Olsen (Vendor).

THE RAZOR'S EDGE (20th, 1946) 146m.

Producer, Darryl F. Zanuck; director, Edmund Goulding; based on the novel by W. Somerset Maugham; screenplay, Lamar Trotti; music, Alfred Newman; song, Mack Gordon, Goulding; art directors, Richard Day, Nathan Juran; camera, Arthur Miller; editor, J. Watson Webb, Jr.

Tyrone Power (Larry Darrell); Gene Tierney (Isabel Bradley); John Payne (Gray Maturin); Anne Baxter (Sophie); Clifton Webb (Elliott Templeton); Herbert Marshall (Somerset Maugham); Lucille Watson (Mrs. Louise Bradley); Frank Latimore (Bob MacDonald); Elsa Lanchester (Miss Keith); Fritz Kortner (Kosti); John Wengraf (Joseph); Cecil Humphreys (Holy Man); Harry Pilcer (Specialty Dancer); Cobina Wright, Sr. (Princess Novemali); Albert Petit (Albert); Noel Cravat (Russian Singer); Isabelle Lamore (Maid); Andre Charlot (Bishop); Adele St. Maur, Frances Norris, Hermine Sterler (Nurses); Forbes Murray (Mr. Maturin); Joseph Burlando (Cure); Marie Rabasse (Flower Woman); Bess Flowers (Matron); Frances Ray (Trollop); Louis Mercier (Little Frenchman); Bud Wolfe (Corsican); Dr. Gerald Echeverria (Doctor); Eddie Das, Hassan Khayyam (Hindus).

THE GHOST AND MRS. MUIR (20th, 1947) 104m.

Producer, Fred Kohlmar; director, Joseph L. Mankiewicz; based on the novel by R. A. Dick; screenplay, Philip Dunne; assistant director, Johnny Johnson; art directors, Richard Day, George W. Davis, Stuart A. Reiss; costumes, Oleg Cassini, Eleanor Behm; music, Bernard Herrmann; camera, Charles Lang; editor, Dorothy Spencer.

Gene Tierney (Lucy); Rex Harrison (The Ghost of Captain Daniel Gregg); George Sanders (Miles Fairley); Edna Best (Martha); Vanessa Brown (Anna—Grown Up); Anna Lee (Mrs. Miles Fairley); Robert Coote (Coombe);

Natalie Wood (Anna—As a Child); Isobel Elsom (Angelica); Victor Horne (Eva); Whitford Kane (Sproule); Brad Slaven (Enquiries); William Stelling (Bill); Helen Freeman (Author); David Thursby (Sproggins); Heather Wilde (English Maid); Stuart Holmes (Man on Train).

THE IRON CURTAIN (20th, 1948) 87m.

Producer, Sol. C. Siegel; director, William A. Wellman; screenplay, Milton Krims; art directors, Lyle Wheeler, Mark-Lee Kirk; music, Alfred Newman; camera, Charles G. Clarke; editor, Louis Loeffler.

Dana Andrews (Igor Gouzenko); Gene Tierney (Anna Gouzenko); June Havoc (Karanova); Barry Kroeger (Grubb); Stefan Schnabel (Ranov); Edna Best (Mrs. Foster); Nicholas Joy (Dr. Norman); Eduard Franz (Major Kulin); Frederick Tozere (Col. Trigorin); Noel Cravat (Bushkin); Christopher Robin Olsen (Andrei); Peter Whitney (Winikov); Leslie Barrie (Editor); Mauritz Hugo (Leonard Laetz); John Shay (Sergeyev); Victor Wood (Captain Class); Anne Curson (Helen Tweedy); Helena Dare (Mrs. Kulin); Eula Morgan (Mrs. Trigorin); Reed Hadley (Commentator).

THAT WONDERFUL URGE (20th, 1948) 82m.

Producer, Fred Kohlmar; director, Robert B. Sinclair; based on the story by William R. Lipman, Frederick Stephani; screenplay, Jay Dratler; music, Cyril Mockridge; camera, Charles B. Clarke; editor, Louis Loeffler.

Tyrone Power (Thomas Jefferson Tyler); Gene Tierney (Sara Farley); Reginald Gardiner (Count Andre de Guyon); Arleen Whelan (Jessica Woods); Lucille Watson (Aunt Cornelia Farley); Gene Lockhart (The Judge); Lloyd Gough (Duffy); Porter Hall (Attorney Ketchell); Richard Gaines (Mr. Whitson); Taylor Holmes (Attorney Rice); Chill Wills (Justice of the Peace); Hope Emerson (Mrs.

Riley); Frank Ferguson (Findlay); Charles Arnt (Mr. Bissell); Francis Pierlot (Barrett); Forbes Murray (Mr. Vickers); John Davidson (Butler); Charles Tannen, Jack Gargan, Bob McCord (Reporters); Gertrude Michael (Mrs. Whitson); Percy Helton (Drunk); Bess Flowers (Party Guest); Robert B. Williams (Special Policeman); Bill Philips (Waiter); Harry Tyler (Counterman); Eula Guy (Mrs. Beggs); Eddie Parks (Artist); Frank O'Connor (Bailiff).

WHIRLPOOL (20th, 1949) 97m.

Producer-director, Otto Preminger; based on the novel by Guy Endore; screenplay, Ben Hecht, Andrew Salt; art directors, Lyle Wheeler, Leland Fuller; music, Alfred Newman; camera, Arthur Miller; editor, Louis Loeffler.

Gene Tierney (Ann Sutton); Richard Conte (Dr. Bill Sutton); Jose Ferrer (David Korvo); Charles Bickford (Lt. Colton); Barbara O'Neil (Theresa Randolph); Eduard Franz (Martin Avery); Constance Collier (Tina Cosgrove); Fortunio Bonanova (Feruccio); Ian MacDonald (Store Detective); Bruce Hamilton (Lt. Jeffreys); Alex Gerry (Dr. Peter Duval); Ruth Lee (Miss Hall); Larry Keating (Mr. Simms); Mauritz Hugo (Hotel Clerk); Jane Van Duser (Miss Andrews); Helen Westcott (Secretary); Roger Moore (Fingerprint Man); Margaret Brayton (Policewoman); Sue Carlton (Elevator Girl); Ted Jordan (Parking Attendant); Mack Williams (Whorton).

NIGHT AND THE CITY (20th, 1950) 95m.

Producer, Samuel G. Engel; director, Jules Dassin; based on the novel by Gerald Kersh; screenplay, Jo Eisinger; art director, C. P. Norman; camera, Mac Greene; editors, Nick DiMaggio, Sidney Stone.

Richard Widmark (Harry Fabian); Gene Tierney (Mary Bristol); Googie Withers (Helen Nosseross); Hugh Marlowe (Adam Dunn); Francis L. Sullivan (Phil Nos-

seross); Herbert Lom (Eristo); Stanislaus Zbyszko (Ora-
gorius); Mike Mazurki (Strangler); Charles Farrell (Beer);
Ada Reeve (Molly); Ken Richmond (Nikolas); Eliot Make-
ham (Pinkney); Betty Shale (Mrs. Pinkney); Russell Westwood (Yosh); James Haytar (Figler).

WHERE THE SIDEWALK ENDS (20th, 1950) 95m.

Producer-director, Otto Preminger; based on the novel
Night Cry by William L. Stuart; screenplay, Victor Trivas,
Frank P. Rosenberg, Robert E. Kent; art directors, Lyle
Wheeler, J. Russell Spencer; music, Lionel Newman; camera,
Joseph LaShelle; editor, Louis Loeffler.

Dana Andrews (Mark Dixon); Gene Tierney (Mor-
gan Taylor); Gary Merrill (Scalise); Bert Freed (Klein);
Tom Tully (Jiggs Taylor); Karl Malden (Lt. Thomas);
Ruth Donnelly (Martha); Craig Stevens (Ken Paine);
Robert Simon (Inspector Foley); Harry Von Zell (Ted Mor-
rison); Don Appell (Willie); Neville Brand (Steve); Grace
Willis (Mrs. Tribaum); Lou Krugman (Mike Williams);
David McMahon (Harrington); David Wolfe (Sid Kramer);
Steve Roberts (Gilruth); Phil Tully (Ted Benson); Ian
MacDonald (Casey); John Close (Hanson); John McGuire
(Gertessen); Lou Nova (Ernie); Oleg Cassini (Mayer);
Louise Lorimer (Mrs. Jackson); Anthony George, Barry
Brooks (Thugs); Louise Lane (Secretary); Kathleen Hughes
(Secretary); Peggy O'Connor (Model).

THE MATING SEASON (Par., 1951) 101m.

Producer, Charles Brackett; director, Mitchell Leisen;
screenplay, Brackett, Walter Reisch, Richard Breen; art directors, Hal Pereira, Roland Anderson; music, Joseph L. Lilley;
camera, Charles B. Lang, Jr.; editor, Frank Bracht.

Gene Tierney (Maggie Carleton); John Lund (Val
McNulty); Miriam Hopkins (Fran Carleton); Thelma Ritter
(Ellen McNulty); Jan Sterling (Betsy); Larry Keating (Mr.

Kallinger, Sr.); James Lorimer (George C. Kallinger, Jr.); Gladys Hurlbut (Mrs. Conger); Cora Witherspoon (Mrs. Williamson); Malcolm Keen (Mr. Williamson); Ellen Corby (Annie); Billie Bird (Mugsy); Samuel Colt (Col. Conger); Grayce Hampton (Mrs. Fahnstock); Stapleton Kent (Dr. Chorley); Bob Kortman (Janitor); Franklyn Farnum (Director); Jimmy Hunt (Boy); Bess Flowers (Friend at Wedding); John Bryant (Usher at Wedding); Jean Ruth, Laura Elliott (Bridesmaids); Charles Dayton (Best Man at Wedding); Beth Hartman (Receptionist); Mary Young (Spinster); Martin Doric (Maitre D'); Tito Vuolo (Industrialist); Gilda Oliva (Telephone Girl); Baker Sichol (Cashier); Willa Pearl Curtis (Goldie).

ON THE RIVIERA (20th, 1951) 90m.

    Director, Walter Lang; based on the screenplay by Rudolph Lothar and Hans Adler; adaptation, Jessie Ernst; screenplay, Phoebe and Henry Ephrom; songs, Sylvia Fine; music director, Alfred Newman; art directors, Lyle Wheeler, Leland Fuller; choreography, Jack Cole; camera, Leon Shamroy; editor, J. Watson Webb, Jr.

    Danny Kaye (Henri Duran/Jack Martin); Gene Tierney (Lilli); Corinne Calvet (Colette); Marcel Dalio (Philippe Lebrix); Jean Murat (Periton); Henri Letondal (Louis Foral); Clinton Sundberg (Antoine); Sig Rumann (Gepesux); Joyce MacKenzie (Mimi); Monique Chantal (Minette); Marina Koshetz (Mme. Cornat); Ann Codee (Mme. Periton); Mari Blanchard (Eugenie); Eugene Borden (Announcer); Joi Lansing (Marilyn Turner); George Davis (Leon); Franchesca Di Scaffa (Elna Petrovna).

THE SECRET OF CONVICT LAKE (20th, 1951) 83m.

    Producer, Frank P. Rosenberg; director, Michael Gordon; based on the story by Anna Hunger, Jack Pollexfen; adaptation, Victor Trivas; screenplay, Oscar Saul; art directors, Lyle Wheeler, Richard Irvine; music director, Lionel Newman; camera, Lee Tover; editor, James B. Clark.

Glenn Ford (Canfield); Gene Tierney (Marcia Stoddard); Ethel Barrymore (Granny); Zachary Scott (Greer); Ann Dvorak (Rachel); Barbara Bates (Barbara Purcell); Cyril Cusack (Limey); Richard Hylton (Clyde Maxwell); Helen Westcott (Susan Haggerty); Jeanette Nolan (Harriet); Ruth Donnelly (Mary); Harry Carter (Rudy); Jack Lambert (Matt Anderson); Mary Carroll (Millie Gower).

CLOSE TO MY HEART (WB, 1951) 90m.

Producer, William Jacobs; director, William Keighley; based on the novel *A Baby for Midge* by James R. Webb; screenplay, Keighley; music, Steiner; art director, Leo K. Kuter; camera, Robert Burks; editor, Clarence Kolster.

Ray Milland (Brad Sheridan); Gene Tierney (Midge Sheridan); Fay Bainter (Mrs. Morrow); Howard St. John (I. O. Frost); Mary Beth Hughes (Arlene); Ann Morrison (Mrs. Barker); James Seay (Heilner); Baby John Winslow (Himself); Elizabeth Flournoy (Receptionist); Ralph Byrd (Charlie); Gertrude Hoffman (Mrs. Madison); Fred Graham (Guard); Lee Prather (Farmer); Lois Hall (Young Mother).

WAY OF A GAUCHO (20th, 1952) 91m.

Producer, Philip Dunne; associate producer, Joseph C. Behm; director, Jacques Tourneur; based on the novel by Herbert Childs; screenplay, Dunne; art directors, Lyle Wheeler, Mark-Lee Kirk; music, Alfred Newman, Sol Kaplan; camera, Jarry Jackson; editor, Robert Fritch.

Rory Calhoun (Martin); Gene Tierney (Teresa); Richard Boone (Salinas); Hugh Marlowe (Miguel); Everett Sloane (Falcon); Enrique Chaico (Father Fernandez); Roland Dumas (Julio); Lidia Campos (Tia Maria); John Henchley (Gaucho Tracker); Douglas Poole (Pallbearer); Mario Abdah (Horse Dealer); John Paris (Foreman).

PLYMOUTH ADVENTURE (MGM, 1952) 105m.

Producer, Dore Schary; director, Clarence Brown; based on the novel by Ernest Gabler; screenplay, Helen Deutch; assistant director, Ridgeway Callow; art directors, Cedric Gibbons, Urie McCleary; music, Miklos Rozsa; camera, William Daniels; editor, Robert J. Kern.

Spencer Tracy (Capt. Christopher Jones); Gene Tierney (Dorothy Bradford); Van Johnson (John Alden); Leo Genn (William Bradford); Dawn Addams (Priscilla Mullins); Lloyd Bridges (Coppin); Barry Jones (William Brewster); John Dehner (Gilbert Winslow); Tommy Ivo (William Button); Lowell Gilmore (Edward Winslow); Noel Drayton (Miles Standish); Rhys Williams (Mr. Weston); Kathleen Lockhart (Mary Brewster); Murray Matheson (Christopher Martin); John Dierkes (Greene); Paul Cavanagh (John Carver); Noreen Corcoran (Ellen Moore); Dennis Hoey (Head Constable); Hugh Pryne (Samuel Fuller); Matt Moore (William Mullins); William Self (Sailor); Elizabeth Flournoy (Rose Standish); Loren Brown (Sailor).

NEVER LET ME GO (MGM, 1953) 96 m.

Producer, Clarence Brown; director, Delmer Daves; based on the novel *Came the Dawn* by Roger Bax; screenplay, Ronald Millar, George Froeschel; music, Hans May; art director, Alfred Junge; camera, Robert Krasker; editor, Frank Clarke.

Clark Gable (Philip Sutherland); Gene Tierney (Marya Lamarkina); Richard Haydn (Christopher Wellington St. John Denny); Bernard Miles (Joe Brooks); Belita Valentina (Alexandrovna); Kenneth More (Steve Quillan); Karel Stephanek (Commissar); Theodore Bikel (Lieutenant); Anna Valentina (Svetlana Mikhailovna); Frederick Valk (Kuragin); Anton Dolin (Marya's Partner); Peter Illing (N.K.V.D. Man); Robert Henderson (U.S. Ambassador); Stanley Maxted (John Barnes); Meinhart Maur (Lemkov).

PERSONAL AFFAIR (UA, 1954) 82m.

Producer, Anthony Darnborough; director, Anthony Pelissier; based on the play *A Day's Mischief* by Lesley Storm; screenplay, Storm; music, William Alwyn; camera, Reginald Wyer; editor, Frederick Wilson.

Gene Tierney (Kay Barlow); Leo Genn (Stephen Barlow); Glynis Johns (Barbara); Walter Fitzgerald (Henry); Pamela Brown (Evelyn); Megs Jenkins (Vi); Michael Hordern (Headmaster); Thora Hird (Mrs. Usher); Norah Gaussen (Phoebe); Martin Boddley (Police Inspector).

BLACK WIDOW (20th, 1954) 95m.

Producer-director, Nunnally Johnson; based on the story by Patrick Quentin; screenplay, Johnson; art directors, Lyle Wheeler, Maurice Ransford; music, Leigh Harline; camera, Charles G. Clarke; editor, Dorothy Spencer.

Ginger Rogers (Lottie); Van Heflin (Peter); Gene Tierney (Iris); George Raft (Detective Bruce); Peggy Ann Garner (Nanny Ordway); Reginald Gardiner (Brian); Virginia Leith (Claire Amberly); Otto Kruger (Ling); Cathleen Nesbitt (Lucia); Skip Homeier (John); Hilda Simms (Anne); Harry Carter (Welch); Geraldine Wall (Miss Mills); Mabel Albertson (Sylvia); Aaron Spelling (Mr. Oliver); Tony De Mario (Bartender); Virginia Maples (Model); Richard Cutting (Sgt. Owens); James F. Stone (Stage Doorman); Frances Driver (Maid); Michael Vallon (Coal Dealer).

THE EGYPTIAN (20th, 1954) 140m.

Producer, Darryl F. Zanuck; director, Michael Curtiz; based on the novel by Mika Waltari; screenplay, Philip

Dunne, Casey Robinson; art directors, Lyle Wheeler, George
W. Davis; music, Bernard Herrmann, Alfred Newman;
camera, Leon Shamroy; editor, Barbara McLean.

Jean Simmons (Merit); Victor Mature (Horemheb);
Gene Tierney (Baketamon); Michael Wilding (Akhanton);
Bella Darvi (Nefer); Peter Ustinov (Kaptah); Edmund Pur-
dom (Sinuhe); Judith Evelyn (Taia); Henry Daniell (Mi-
kera); John Carradine (Grave Robber); Carl Benton Reid
(Senmut); Tommy Rettig (Thoth); Anitra Stevens (Nefer-
titi); Carmen de Lavallade (Egyptian Dancer); Ian Mac-
Donald (Ship's Captain); Peter Reynolds (Sinuhe—Age 10);
Mike Mazurki (Death House Foreman); Edmund Cobb
(Patient); Michael Ansara (Hittite Commander); Paul Salata
(Egyptian Official); George Chester (Nubian Guard); Donna
Martell (Lady in Waiting); Mimi Gibson (First Princess);
Tyler McDuff (Cadet); Geraldine Bogdonovien (Tavern
Waitress); Angela Clarke (Kipa).

THE LEFT HAND OF GOD (20th, 1955) 87m.
Producer, Buddy Adler; director, Edward Dmytryk;
based on the novel by William E. Barrett; screenplay, Alfred
Hayes; assistant director, Ben Kaddish; art directors, Lyle
Wheeler, Maurice Ransford; music, Victor Young; camera,
Franz Planer; editor, Dorothy Spencer.

Humphrey Bogart (Jim Carmody); Gene Tierney
(Ann Scott); Lee J. Cobb (Mieh Yang); Agnes Moorehead
(Beryl Sigman); E. G. Marshall (Dr. Sigman); Jean Porter
(Mary Yin); Carl Benton Reid (Rev. Cornelius); Leon
Lontok (Pao-Ching); Victor Sen Yung (John Wong); Philip
Ahn (Jan Teng); Benson Fong (Chun Tien); Don Forbes
(Father Keller); Candace Lee (Girl); Sammee Tong (Ser-
vant); Noel Toy (Woman in Sarong).

ADVISE AND CONSENT (Col., 1962) 139m.
Producer-director, Otto Preminger; based on the novel
by Allen Drury; screenplay, Wendell Mayes; assistant direc-

tors, L. C. McCardle, Jr., Don Kranze, Larry Powell, Charles Bohart; art director, Lyle Wheeler; music, Jerry Fielding; camera, Sam Leavitt; editor, Louis Loeffler.

Franchot Tone (The President); Lew Ayres (Vice President); Henry Fonda (Robert Leffingwell); Walter Pidgeon (Senate Majority Leader); Charles Laughton (Senator Cooley); Don Murray (Senator Anderson); Peter Lawford (Senator Smith); Paul Ford (Senator Danta); Gene Tierney (Dolly Harrison); Burgess Meredith (Herbert Gelman); Eddie Hodges (Johnny Leffingwell); George Grizzard (Senator Van Ackerman); Inga Swenson (Ellen Anderson); Paul McGrath (Hardiman Fletcher); Will Geer (Senate Minority Leader); Betty White (Senator Adams); Edward Andrews (Senator Knox); Malcolm Atterbury (Senator August); J. Edward McKindley (Senator Hanson); William Quinn (Senator Hendershot); Tiki Santos (Senator Kanaho); Raoul DeLeon (Senator Velez); Tom Helmore (British Ambassador); Hilary Eaves (Lady Maudulayne); Chet Stratton (Rev. Birch); John Granger (Ray Shaff); Rene Paul (French Ambassador); Janet Jane Carty (Pidge Anderson).

TOYS IN THE ATTIC (UA, 1963) 90m.

Producer, Walter Mirisch; director, George Roy Hill; based on the play by Lillian Hellman; screenplay, James Poe; music, George Duning; camera, Joseph F. Biroc; editor, Stuart Gilmore.

Dean Martin (Julian Berniers); Geraldine Page (Carrie Berniers); Yvette Mimieux (Lily Prine Berniers); Wendy Hiller (Anna Berniers); Gene Tierney (Albertine Prine); Nan Martin (Charlotte Warkins); Larry Gates (Cyrus Warkins); Frank Silvera (Henry); Charles Lampkin (Gus).

THE PLEASURE SEEKERS (20th, 1964) 107m.

Producer, David Weisbart; director, Jean Negulesco; based on the novel by John H. Secondari; screenplay, Edith

Sommer; music, Lionel Newman; assistant director, Joseph Lenzi; camera, Daniel L. Fapp; editor, Louis Loeffler.

Ann-Margret (Frank); Anthony Franciosa (Emilio); Carol Lynley (Maggie); Gardner McKay (Pete); Pamela Tiffin (Susie); Andre Lawrence (Andres); Gene Tierney (Jane Barton); Vito Scotti (Neighborhood Man); Isobel Elsom (Dona Teresa); Marice Marsac (Jose); Shelby Grant (American Girl); Raoul de Leon (Martinez); Brian Keith (Paul Barton); Antonio Gadez (Flamenco Dancer); Emilio Diego (Guitarist); Peter Brocco (Arturo); Ida Romero (Receptionist); Warene Ott (Spanish Girl); Warren Parker (Mr. Morton); Gino Sabetelli (Admiring Young Man); Shirley Parker (French Girl).